MEDIA STUDY FRONTIERS *IN* CHINA

EDITED BY
CUI LIN AND WU MINSU

authorHOUSE®

AuthorHouse™
1663 Liberty Drive
Bloomington, IN 47403
www.authorhouse.com
Phone: 833-262-8899

Published by AuthorHouse 11/22/2022

ISBN: 978-1-6655-7538-6 (sc)
ISBN: 978-1-6655-7537-9 (hc)
ISBN: 978-1-6655-7536-2 (e)

Library of Congress Control Number: 2022920855

Print information available on the last page.

CONTENTS

FREE FROM BARRIERS: AN ANALYSIS OF THE CURRENT SITUATION OF CHINA'S BARRIER-FREE FILM INDUSTRY

Gao Xiaohong and Cai Yu

Abstract: Barrier-free films, as the name implies, are movies that help people with visual or auditory disabilities to remove barriers from watching movies, and enable people with disabilities to understand what the stories mean by "listening" or "watching". It usually translates, decomposes, and transforms the audio-visual language of the film by adding sign language, subtitles, or explanations on the basis of the original film, so as to be appreciated by people with hearing impairment and visual impairment. China's barrier-free film industry began in the beginning of this century. In 2019, after investigating the public welfare project Guangming Cinema of Communication University of China, Jia Zhangke, the vice chairman of the China Film Directors Association, presented the "Proposal on the Development of Barrier-free Film Industry in China", suggested to support the development of barrier-free movies from the aspects of legal policy, theater construction, and social care. This shows China's emphasis on the development of a barrier-free film industry, while also reflecting that the industry is still in the initial stage of development and faces many problems and challenges. This paper aims to sort out and discuss the creation methods, social values, and future challenges of barrier-free movies in China, so as to form a clear and accurate understanding of the past and present life of China's barrier-free movies, and to provide some new ideas and new means for the development of China's barrier-free film industry.

Keywords: Barrier-Free Movies, Visually Impaired People, Accessibility

The Chinese term "无障碍" (no barrier) is translated from "barrier free" or "accessibility", which means that anyone should be able to access and utilize information equally, easily, and without barriers under any circumstances. In the early 1960s, with the influence and promotion of international social groups, the concept of "barrier-free" began to take shape[1]. Its predecessor comes from the "normalization principle" proposed by N.E. Bank-Mikkelsen of Denmark.

Meeting the growing intellectual and cultural needs of the visually impaired, improving their social welfare, and assisting the high-quality development of the social and cultural life of the visually impaired - these are important parts of the country's modernization drive. As we usher in the "new era", in addition to accessible physical facilities such as roads, ramps, handrails, etc., accessibility at the intellectual and cultural level that demonstrates humanistic care and shares cultural achievements demands equal or even more attention.

1. Concepts and Practices of Barrier-free Films

Film, as an important carrier of cultural communication, has gradually entered into the scope of barrier-free communication in communication studies. The first research topic is on the accessibility of audio-visual languages in film and television content. Therefore, the research on barrier-free films starts from the study of how to make accessible films and eliminate the barriers of information reception for visually and hearing-impaired people.

---

[1] Anonymous. The Formation of the Concept of "Barrier-free"[J]. Outlook Weekly, 2002(17):20. 佚名. "无障碍" 概念的形成[J].瞭望新闻周刊,2002(17):20.

(1) Definition of the Concept of Barrier-free Films

Barrier-free films, as the name suggests, are movies that help people with visual and hearing impairments to remove obstacles, so that people with disabilities can "listen" or "see" and understand. It is generally made by adding sign language, subtitles, or commentary on the basis of the original film, and then synthesized by professional technology, which is specially designed for visually impaired and hearing impaired people to use.

According to different audiences they serve, barrier-free movies can be simply divided into three versions: 1) those that are convenient for visually impaired people to "listen", 2) those that are convenient for hearing-impaired people to "see", and 3) those that are convenient for both visually impaired people to "listen" and for hearing-impaired people to "see". Among them, accessible movies that can either be "listened to" and "watched" have their corresponding accessible content translation methods to make up for accessibility. The production of the two-in-one version that can allow the audience to both "listen" and "see" is done with superposition of the first two translation methods - there are subtitles or sign language to compensate for hearing impairments, and video descriptions to compensate for visual impairments.

Humans' acquisition of information mainly depends on the senses. The visual sense dominates the five senses, accounting for almost 80% of the available information. Since vision is the most important source of information for human beings, visually impaired people face a much greater obstacle than hearing impaired people when appreciating film and television works. Therefore, in barrier-free communication studies of films and television, it is particularly important to answer the question of how to translate film and television works to visually impaired people to make up for the lack of visual information, therefore making the works accessible. It is because of this that barrier-free films discussed in this paper are mainly ones that use the video description method and are oriented to visually impaired groups.

(2) Barrier-Free Films for Visually Impaired Groups

Video description is a method of converting visual images into audio descriptions. It is also known as visuals in the oral form. Its modus operandi is explaining and describing the visual components in film and television works without increasing or decreasing the length of the original film and disturbing the original dialogues and sounds. Generally speaking, the visual components that need to be explained and described include: changes in time, changes of space, shifts of scenes, characters' actions and body language, relationships between characters, and key details and foreshadowing that will affect the plot.

Current video description methods can be divided into two types: Live Audio Description and Pre-recorded Description.

Live Audio Description refers to volunteers serving as docents at the film screening site, explaining the film for the visually impaired. This generally occurs in a movie theater or screening place. The working mode is showing the original film while asking a film interpreter to explain it on the spot. The advantages of Live Audio Description are: first, it is highly interactive, has a strong sense of being present, and can shorten the distance between the audience and the volunteer, and build a bridge for intellectual communication between the two parties, creating a good movie-watching atmosphere; second, it relaxes the professional requirements for interpreters, lowers the service threshold for oral video descriptions, and improves the timeliness of the selected movies, so that visually impaired audiences have the opportunity to enjoy the same movies that are being screened in theaters. This description method does not require editing and post-packaging of the film, and there is almost no post-production pressure. On the other hand, there are also some shortcomings: first, Live Audio Description has high requirements for the professional skills of volunteers, who are generally big-hearted people recruited society-wide, who may have more than enough vividness and congeniality when narrating, but insufficient accuracy; secondly, Live Audio Description has high requirements on the status of the volunteers of the day: each barrier-free film explanation service lasts for nearly two hours, and the service quality depends on volunteers' physical conditions, emotional status, and energy level. Even if the manuscripts are prepared in advance and their emotions are mobilized, the effects of narration in different sessions will be different. Third, the demand for Live Audio Description is large and the number of volunteers is limited. There may be conflicts in the time allocation of volunteers, and so it is difficult to guarantee the quality and quantity of screenings of accessible films.

Since the 21st century, "blind movie theaters" have appeared in some cities in China one after another. "Xinmu Cinema", or "Heart Eye Cinema", China's first non-profit cinema for the blind, adopts the model of Live Audio Description, and invites volunteers to serve as narrators to explain the film to visually impaired audiences on the spot. As of April 2021, Xinmu Cinema has carried out a total of 956 movie narrations online and offline, directly benefiting nearly 40,000 visually impaired audiences.

Different from Live Audio Description, the Pre-recorded Description mode is based on digital copy technology. The recording process is usually carried out in a professional recording studio, and each recording session is equipped with dedicated recording engineers and monitor personnel, who oversee the richness, texture and appeal of the narrators' voice, so that the voice can impact hearts and so there is harmony between the narration and the original sounds of the film. After the recording session, the post-production team will denoise and level the vocal track, and then mix and synthesize it with the original sound of the film. They ensure the high fidelity of the sound quality and tone, but also make the sound elements of the film full of artistic beauty and aesthetic interest.

The Guangming Cinema project of Communication University of China adopts the mode of Pre-recorded Description. The project team utilizes its professional advantages to perform a series of procedures such as dubbing, editing, mixing, and packaging of the film. So far, more than 400 copies of barrier-free film works have been produced. Although the creation process is procedurally complex and demands higher requirements for creators, the advantages of image descriptions created in the pre-recorded mode are equally obvious. On the one hand, production results can be standardized. Once the production is completed, it can be mass-produced and widely disseminated, allowing visually impaired people to enjoy accessible films anytime, anywhere, further reducing their threshold to enjoying movies. On the other hand, because it is pre-recorded and screened later, the mode breaks the linear restrictions of Live Audio Description, which facilitates revisions and adjustments of the scripts, leaving room for fine-tuning and continued betterment. During the writing process, teacher and student volunteers not only can accurately describe the content of the pictures, but also deeply explain the connotations and values of the stories behind the pictures, so that visually impaired people can not only understand "what is happening now" when they enjoy the movie, but also the "causes and reasons of the occurrences" and "the intended directions of the plot", so as to richly and wholistically perceive and cognize a movie.

2. The Significance and Value of Barrier-Free Films

The World Health Organization estimates that there are 40 to 45 million visually challenged people worldwide. As equal members of the human family, those with disabilities have the same human rights and dignity as able-bodied people. As an important part of the national public culture service system, the development of the cultural industry for people with disabilities has received more social attention in China.

(1) Cultural Tactile Paving[2]: a New Field of
Barrier-free Environment Building

In August 2012, China's "Regulations on the Building of Barrier-Free Environment" came into effect, which not only provides sufficient conditions for persons with disabilities to participate in social life on an equal basis when it comes to accessible facilities, but also take into the overall consideration barrier-free communication and social services. So far, the construction of China's barrier-free environment has expanded from tactile paving - the material level - to the fields of information exchange and intellectual culture. Different types and forms of barrier-free cultural services have gradually emerged across the country.

---

2 Gao Xiaohong, Chen Xingang. Guangming Cinema: Research and Practice of Barrier-Free Audiovisual Communication. Chinese Editors Journal. 2019(03):4-7+25. 高晓虹, 陈欣钢.光明影院:无障碍视听传播的研究与实践[J].中国编辑,2019(03):4-7+25.

In recent years, the Chinese film industry has continued to flourish. Movies are like a "spiritual bridge". The process of watching movies together and chatting about movies can shorten the distance between people and enhance relationships. Closing cultural gaps and building communication bridges through films and television, movies can help people with disabilities actively integrate into social life and reduce their loneliness aggravated by their disabilities.

Indeed, narrations and productions of barrier-free films for the visually impaired are creating "cultural tactile paving" for people with disabilities with its humanistic care and cultural fruits. Through the translations and conversions between audio-visual elements and creating a barrier-free environment in the field of culture and art, people with disabilities are allowed to enjoy the same cultural nourishment and artistic interests as the able-bodied person. This is one step forward towards the satisfaction of the higher-level cultural needs of people with disabilities and is the source of the value and meaning of barrier-free films.

(2) Talent Training: the New Force of Barrier-free Audiovisual Communication

With the development of the barrier-free film industry, the public has more expectations for technical quality, artistic effects, and the depth and breadth of the descriptions of barrier-free movies. How to break through the limitations of Live Audio Description, improve the aesthetics of image descriptions, and optimize the quality of accessible audio-visual works has become a must-answer question for the innovative development of accessible films and television.

In the process of content production, dissemination, and promotion of barrier-free films in China, young students from media colleges, universities, and related majors, with the Communication University of China being a key representative, out of their social responsibilities exert their professional strengths, playing active roles in promoting the equality of human rights and the spirit of humanitarianism. Through the education of the concept of accessibility and the practice of creating accessible films, colleges and universities gradually cultivate students' awareness of human rights, dedication, social responsibility, and professional abilities, creating a good cultural atmosphere of accessibility in the whole society, contributing youth power to social progress and human civilization.

At the end of 2017, Communication University of China, Beijing Gehua CATV Network, and Oriental Jiaying, jointly launched the charitable barrier-free film project Guangming Cinema. From one-time live audio description services to reproducible audio-visual cultural products that can be mass disseminated, Guangming Cinema has gradually expanded the values of accessible audio-visual communication through practice and innovation, providing innovative solutions to improving professional content production, as well as the operability of screening and promotion of accessible audio-visual works.

On professional content production, more than 500 volunteer teachers and students of film and television have brought more possibilities to the practice, innovation, product services, and academic research to accessible audio-visual productions through their work in grasping cinematic language, deciphering visual content, understanding deeper meanings, and script writing. On the operability of screening and promotions, Guangming Cinema has formed a set of national coverage systems based on cooperation with provincial level Associations of the Blind, working with schools for the blind, libraries, communities, cinemas, and film festivals. First, while improving the efficiency of product production and promotion, Guangming Cinema keeps in touch with the Disabled Persons' Federations and the Associations of the Blind, regularly holding seminars and screening feedback meetings, constantly taking creative ideas and service suggestions. Second, in the process of continuous optimization and adjustment according to the needs of the audience and user feedback, Guangming Cinema tries not to divorce with reality, achieving two-way interaction with the visually impaired. Third, in travelling nationwide for screenings and promotions, Guangming Cinema organically combines the professional advantages of colleges and universities, the resource advantages of enterprises, and the platform advantages of media organizations, condensing the strengths of various parties of all sectors of society, and ensuring the consistency and sustainability of visual description services.

(3) A Common Pursuit: A New Chapter in the Development of the Cause of the Disabled

On December 13, 2006, the United Nations General Assembly adopted the Convention of the Rights of Persons with Disabilities (hereinafter referred to as the "Convention"). The Convention aims to promote, protect, and ensure the full and equal enjoyment of all human rights and fundamental freedoms by all persons with disabilities and to promote respect for the inherent dignity of persons with disabilities. As one of the first signatories of the Convention, China revised the Law on the Protection of Persons with Disabilities in 2008 to bring the domestic law on track with the Convention, showing the firm determination of the Chinese government to actively promote the cause of persons with disabilities.

In July 2019, the State Council of China released the white paper "Equality, Participation and Sharing: 70 Years of Protection of the Rights and Interests of Persons with Disabilities in New China", which clearly points out that it is necessary to care for groups with special difficulties, respect the wishes of the people with disabilities, protect the rights of people with disabilities and pay attention to social involvement of people with disabilities. The white paper sees it as the country's undeniable obligation and the absolute requirement of the socialist system with Chinese characteristics, to "enable people with disabilities to fully participate in social life with equal status and equal opportunities, and share the achievements of material and spiritual civilization" and to strive to help those with disabilities to gain full rights, as well as to participate in, contribute to, and share in economic and social development.

3. Obstacles and Breakthroughs in Barrier-free Movies

(1) Marrakesh Treaty: Restrictions and Breakthroughs in Film Copyright

The current barrier-free film creation process is to translate, supplement, and re-edit the audio-visual language of the original film and television works by adding subtitles for the hearing-impaired, sign language, and video descriptions. Therefore, the first thing faced in the process of production is copyright protection in the film industry.

Back in 2009, the World Federation of the Blind, Brazil, Ecuador, and Paraguay proposed a World Intellectual Property Organization treaty to help alleviate the worldwide shortage of books. At the time, less than 1% of barrier-free books were available in developing countries, and only about 7% in the most developed countries[3]. After four years of hard work, on June 28, 2013, the World Intellectual Property Organization concluded the Marrakesh Treaty[4], which specifically protects the reading rights of the visually impaired. The successful conclusion of this international treaty has made it possible for the visually impaired to obtain works in accessible formats and enjoy the right to read like those without impairments.

On June 1, 2021, the newly revised Copyright Law of the People's Republic of China (hereinafter referred to as the New Copyright Law) came into effect. The revision of the New Copyright Law has been discussed in many editions for many years, and has finally been formed into legislation that condenses the consensus of all walks of life at the current stage and reflects the greatest common denominator. It vigorously strengthens the protection of copyright, and puts forward effective enforcement measures in a targeted manner, which fully reflects the spirit of Chinese society to respect and encourage originality and protect innovation. More importantly, with the development of China's 5G technology and audio-visual industry, the New Copyright Law expands "The concept of "Braille" in (1)2, Paragraph 12, Article 22 of the 2010 Copyright Law and (2)3, Article 6 of the Regulations on the Protection of Information Network Dissemination Right - from "written works" to "in a barrier-free way that can be perceived by people with reading challenges".

---

[3] World Blind Union. Press Release WIPO Negotiations Treaty for Blind people [EB/OL]. http://www.worldblindunion.org/English/news/Pages/Press-Release-WIPO-Negotiations-Treaty-for-Blind-people.aspx,2016-11-29.

[4] Cui Wangwei. Domestic Status, International Perspective and Legislative Improvement of the Protection of Reading Rights for the Visually Impaired: The Third Amendment of China's Copyright Law from the Perspective of the Marrakesh Treaty[J] Research in Library Science, 2018(03):90-95+24. 崔汪卫.视障者阅读权保障的国内现状、国际视角与立法完善——基于《马拉喀什条约》视域下我国《著作权法》第三次修订[J].图书馆学研究,2018(03):90-95+24.

And the beneficiary groups have been expanded from the blind, to other visually impaired people, as well as hearing impaired people, people with intellectual disabilities, people with limb disabilities, and other groups with reading challenges. It also expands the notion of "text" from plain text to audio, video, and perceptible tactile forms, solving the issue that existing regulations do not cover accessible reading methods in the digital environment, and providing a legal basis for the implementation of the Marrakesh Treaty.

In February 2022, China submitted the ratification of the Marrakesh Treaty to the World Intellectual Property Organization. According to its terms, the treaty will enter into force for China in May 2022. The conclusion and implementation of the treaty will provide a larger platform and more possibilities for the development of China's barrier-free film industry.

(2) Oasis in the Desert: Coverage and Promotion of Public Welfare Services

Improving the coverage of accessible films in China is like building an oasis in the "cultural desert" for people with disabilities, which requires both "precision drip irrigation" and "sources of living water". "Precision drip irrigation" means more accurate positioning of service objects under limited conditions. Being aware of commercial operation and investment, "source of living water" means to utilize the public welfare nature of barrier-free films to cooperate with film companies and commercial theater chains to build barrier-free public welfare theater chains for people with disabilities, so that public welfare and market forces can work together for an industry breakthrough in barrier-free movies.

With the purpose to serve, China's barrier-free film industry is gradually achieving nationwide coverage and continues to improve the range of public welfare services for common development. The first is the scalability of the service objects, from the visually impaired, to the people who are both visually and hearing impaired, to the elderly who find it inconvenient to watch movies – these all may become the service objects of barrier-free films. The second is the extension of service content, from accessible films, to accessible documentaries, TV dramas, and interpretations of major events, etc. The content of accessible cultural services will continue to be enriched with people's increasingly diverse cultural needs. The third is the extension of service forms, from the creation of barrier-free film and television works to their public welfare screenings, from screenings on specific anniversary days to activities on a regular basis, from offline screening to online disseminations, from public welfare barrier-free screenings to barrier-free social and cultural service activities. With the continuous development of China's barrier-free films, barrier-free audio-visual cultural services will surely have a broader space for development and a brighter prospect.

In terms of creating accessible versions of film and television works, with the rollouts of the "Proposal on the Development of Barrier-free Film Industry in China" and "Proposal on Releasing Copyrights and Promoting the Development of Accessible Films", the social value and public welfare attributes of accessible film and television works have been increasingly recognized and supported by the industry. Many copyright owners of films and TV series are willing to release some copyrights for experimental creations and promotions of barrier-free works, ensuring the continuous and stable development of barrier-free films in quantity and quality. This creates more possibilities for the production and dissemination of barrier-free films in terms of subject matter, genre, content, and style.

In June 2021, with the strong support of Tencent Pictures, for the first time the Guangming Cinema public welfare project team of Communication University of China simultaneously completed the production of the barrier-free version of a movie, in lockstep with the original version for the theater chain. This enabled the premiere of the barrier-free version of the new film to be screened in the theater chain, simultaneously with the original version - the first time in Beijing. This means that visually impaired friends can really "walk into the same cinema and watch the same movie", and enjoy the barrier-free movie works of the same schedule together with able-bodied people. From movies to TV dramas, cartoons, military parades, from the production of films that have already been released to the realization of simultaneous viewing at the premiere, from all going their own way to formulating group standards and industry standards, China's barrier-free film production has come to provide more extensive and dynamic choices in content, as well as more reliable and feasible standards in quality.

(3) Barrier-Free Cinema: Integrating into Society, "Seeing" the World

At the Beijing Winter Paralympics, a Chinese athlete who is visually impaired said after the game: I can't see the world, but I want the world to see me. When visually impaired people are given the same love and respect as able-bodied people, they can do as well as able-bodied people. Society needs to give people with disabilities full understanding and respect, and the same trust and expectations, as to able-bodied people.

With the production and dissemination of barrier-free films, the visually impaired, like the able-bodied, are enabled to obtain visual information in a timely and accurate manner, thus receiving emotional comfort and meeting aesthetic needs, which in turn give them a greater sense of social participation and assimilation, as well as the sense of shared values. This is an important aspect for people with disabilities to enhance their sense of gain, happiness, and security. It is also an important direction for the development of the barrier-free film industry.

Watching movies is as much an entertainment activity as a social activity. Sitting in the theater is like walking into a miniature society. While enjoying the same film work, participating in exchanges and discussions with the people around them - for people with disabilities, the equal and free collective atmosphere is much more attractive to them than the barrier-free film itself.

Going to the cinema to watch a movie is not only leisure, but also a sense of ceremony. While steadily producing barrier-free films, building barrier-free cinemas so that the visually impaired can have the same movie viewing experience as the able-bodied person is an inevitable requirement for the development of barrier-free film industry, and also provides opportunities for visually impaired persons to integrate into social life and participate in social activities.

A barrier-free cinema does not mean a cinema only for people with disabilities. Its final form should be a cinema with barrier-free infrastructure, built for both people with disabilities and able-bodied people to watch movies at the same time. At present, China is accelerating the development of barrier-free movie-related equipment and channels, making it possible for people with and without disabilities to watch the same movie at the same time and place. The visually impaired utilize the barrier-free movie viewing activities as an opportunity to leave their homes, enter society, and participate in social life; through barrier-free movies, they not only "see" the stories in the images, but also "see" the colorful world.

4. Conclusion

In the process of building a barrier-free environment, cultural empowerment for the visually impaired is as important as empowerment for their daily physical life.

The production and promotion of barrier-free films is a full manifestation of China's humanitarian spirit and humanistic care, an effective way to safeguard and protect the legitimate rights and interests of people with disabilities, and an important channel to help visually impaired people integrate into society and become self-reliant. With the gradual advancement of national policies and relevant legislation, more people will pay attention to the difficulties and obstacles faced by people with disabilities, a socially disadvantaged group in the cultural field. Let light and shadow have sound, let culture be unimpeded. The development of China's barrier-free film industry is a great cause and a long journey. It deserves attention and much expectation.

SUBVERSION AND REBUILDING: MEDIA USE IN A GROUP OF VISUALLY IMPAIRED PEOPLE AGAINST THE BACKGROUND OF MEDIA CONVERGENCE

Qin Yuming and Song Junyi

Abstract: In today's 5G era, the Internet is part of daily life for visually impaired people. Wide and frequent use of media has transformed and reshaped the identity and interpersonal relationships of visually impaired groups, enhanced their social participation, and expanded the space for their social discourse, and plays a significant role in boosting their integration into society. Although all of this is based on the rapid development of digital technology, we need to stay alert of the trap of "technology only". Technology and social media use by visually impaired people are impacted by multiple mechanisms such as social institutions, legislation, content production, distribution and acquisition, information technology, as well as consumer psychology. A deep understanding of the complexity of the media environment and the visually impaired group are needed to effectively improve the group's media use experience.

Keywords: Media Convergence, Visually Impaired People, Media Use, Accessibility

The development of information technology has provided technical support for the visually impaired group to realize the conversion of information symbols. According to the "Online Social Networking Report for Visually Impaired Persons" jointly released by the Accessibility Research Association and Tencent QQ in 2019, 90% of visually impaired respondents believe that they need the Internet in their lives, and that it can help them gain more equal access to information and its utilization in the Internet age[1]. Largely consistent with the evolution of information technology, the behavior in internet issue of visually impaired groups has also undergone a transition from PC to mobile. With the rapid development of the mobile Internet, the usage environment of smartphones is becoming more and more complex. For this reason, at the beginning of research, development, and design, in addition to the usual text input, many smart phones and related software have gradually added functions such as voice input and two-way conversion of voice and text, such as iPhone's "voiceover", WeChat's voice input, and the two-way conversion of voice and text by iFLYTEK, etc. These not only meet the needs of able-bodied people, but also inadvertently provide a more convenient choice for the visually impaired to access media. A survey conducted by Communication University of China on the students at the Beijing School for the Blind in 2018 shows that mobile phones and Braille books have become the main media for visually impaired students to obtain information, with mobile phones accounting for 44.44%. TV programs, radio programs, and computers are also effective ways for visually impaired students to obtain information.

It can be seen that compared with traditional media with a weak reach, new media technology provides more access opportunities for visually impaired groups, especially with the advent of the 5G era and the continuous update of app design, mobile phones undoubtedly boast broader space for development in improving cultural and spiritual life of visually impaired groups. Wide and frequent use of media has transformed and reshaped the identity and interpersonal relationships of visually impaired groups, enhanced their social participation, and expanded the space for their social discourse, eventually boosting their integration into society.

---

[1] Accessibility Research Association. Online Social Networking Report for Visually Impaired Persons [EB/OL]. (2019-10-15) [2019-11-30]. https://www.siaa.org.cn/knowledge. 信息无障碍研究会.视障人士在线社交报告

Social integration is a process of social action in which the subject in a disadvantaged position actively interacts with individuals and groups in a specific community in a reflective and continuous manner[2]. Having a social identity is the premise of participating in social life. How the visually impaired person positions him or herself in social life and gets along with others is fundamentally about the establishment of one's group identity relating to self-identity and belonging, and the answer is often the result of multiple factors. These factors include not only social relationships (such as kinship, geographical and professional relationships) and economic status of the visually impaired individual, but also the values of the society in which they live (such as people's cognition of visually impaired diseases) and the degree of inclusiveness (such as accessible facilities and public opinions), etc. These factors subtly affect the categorization of "I", "us" and "them", and then affect the construction of self-identity and group identity[3].

Based on the differential mode of association in traditional Chinese society, visually impaired individuals exist in many social relationships determined by kinship and geographical relationships composed of able-bodied people. The contrast between "special and normal" is both obvious and profound. In addition, as an important platform for reproducing and disseminating the above-mentioned parameters of identity, the mass media often find it challenging when they try to guide visually impaired groups to interpret and judge their self and group identities. On the one hand, as mass media, traditional media must observe and present the visually impaired from the perspective of a larger proportion of society – those without impairments, that is, a perspective of others; on the other hand, the coverage scope of traditional media is also limited to a certain extent, which limits the length and strength of coverage on visually impaired groups, with the changes in social attitudes and inclusiveness slow and tortuous. The visually impaired who receive a lot of negative feedback

---

[2] Jin Hengjiang, Zhang Guoliang. The influence of WeChat Use on Social Integration of International Students in China: Based on a Survey at Five Universities in Shanghai [J]. Modern Communication (Journal of Communication University of China), 2017, 01: 145-151. 金恒江,张国良.微信使用对在华留学生社会融入的影响——基于上海市五所高校的调查研究[J].现代传播(中国传媒大学学报)

[3] Wu Yao, Wei Miao. Subversion and Reshaping: Identity in Digital Reading [J]. Editorial Friend, 2018, 11: 5-10+15. 吴瑶,韦妙.颠覆与重塑:数字阅读中的身份认同[J].编辑之友

from others and society are easily influenced by negative emotions in a state of embarrassment, therefore internalizing certain stereotypes about groups of people with disabilities, and coming to have a relatively negative attitude towards personal development prospects, which influences their social identity and social life.

Today's fusion media, based on digital technology, while impacting the public by its virtual, vertical, massive features and other characteristics of new media platforms, also subverts and reshapes the interpretation and judgment of the self-identity of the visually impaired, as an increasingly primary reference tool for them to establish their identity. First, the massive carrying capacity of new media platforms, with its rich and diverse content, allows the societal attention to visually impaired groups to no longer to be limited by capacity. Big data shows that in the five years from 2013 to 2018, the total number of online news items related to "blind people" and "visually impaired" exceeded 50,000, which was 26 times greather than the sum in the first ten years from 2003 to 2012[4]. The massive amount of information enables visually impaired groups to accurately receive feedback from others in social interactions, and adjust their own behavior in a timely manner. For example, a large number of new media reports about Zheng Rongquan, the first visually impaired person in China to take the general college entrance examination to enter a university, not only rekindled the hope of visually impaired children to study for college, but also let visually impaired people see career paths other than becoming masseuses and tuners, and that they have the same right to social participation and discourse as able-bodied people. Not only that, a large quantity of reports on visually impaired groups have also led to changes in social values and improved the level of tolerance and civilization of the entire society. Secondly, online social networking hides the defects of visually impaired groups, weakens the contrast between "special and normal", and enables them to "start anew" on the Internet, reshaping their main assets. Finally, fragmented and vertical new media platforms encourage people with common characteristics to "re-tribalize" and advocate self-help acquisition, self-writing, and active dissemination of information. Through active self-writing and active dissemination within the group, the

---

[4] Founder Zhisi Internet Big Data Information Service Platform [EB/OL].[2019-05-15]. http://59.108.111.23/c_login.jsp. 方正智思互联网大数据信息服务平台

18

visually impaired groups can eliminate traditional self-cognition and view their own defects objectively. Combined with a series of offline activities organized by federations for people with disabilities, foundations, public welfare associations and other social organizations such as the "Visually Impaired Service Team's Grassroots Project" organized by the Disabled Persons' Federation in Dongcheng District, Beijing, the visually impaired have gradually realized they have the same opportunities and power as able-bodied people, and have found a way to reflect their own worth. The subject consciousness reshaped by the Internet is further recognized and consolidated with in-person social life. With the help of new media technology, visually impaired groups are undergoing a transformation of their identities, as they confirm themselves, adjust themselves, and actualize themselves, gradually realizing the beautiful shift from relying on "social supply" to "self-supply" and promoting social development at the same time, and finally integrating into the society themselves.

The improvement of self-identity or social identity accelerates social integration, and also affects the construction and development of social network. In the process of social integration, individual social interaction is as important as information reception. Compared with the closed-loop acquaintance circle within the differential mode of association, mobile Internet breaks the blockade of blood and geographical relations, and reshapes the interpersonal network and information exchange method for visually impaired groups. The two-way automatic conversion function between speech and text symbols helps the visually impaired to hide their "defects" in the virtual network, and conducts cross-time-and-space communication, freely shuttling between various social tools just like people without visual impairments. In this environment of equal communication, visually impaired people are more likely to actively socialize in various forums or communities, expressing opinions like able-bodied people with more self-confidence, and thus readily participating in social life. Not only that, their media use, known for its positive feedback, is conducive to organically merging strong and weak relationships in interpersonal network, and unwittingly reshaping the social relations of the visually impaired. On one hand, the expansion of online relationships, coupled with extending in-person relationships over the cyberspace, expands one's relationship network; on the other hand, the online social networking plays a positive role in building strong relationships: due to its virtuality and immediacy, it is easy for the visually impaired to establish indiscriminate social interactions; and also because online social interaction is more lively and relaxing than offline, thus is better in shortening the distance in time and space and deepening mutual understanding. The new media platform has expanded the scope of communication and through this connecting all aspects of life, improving the social relationship capital of the visually impaired through expansion, connection, and interaction.

It is undeniable that these radical changes and reshaping can only happen with brand new media experience brought by digital technology to the visually impaired. In the process of socialist modernization, high-speed mobile internet technology is an emerging force to ensure that people with disabilities enjoy human rights and basic freedoms, and a catalyst to eliminate information barriers and promote social integration. Its increasingly accessible strategic significance is becoming more and more prominent in facilitating equal information reception, education, obtaining employment, integrating into social life, and enjoyment of culture and art, for people both with or without disabilities.

However, in the process of understanding and realizing the significance of media use by visually impaired groups, people's attention is transfixed by technology, with blind devotion to improving the ease of media use. Some scholars believe that the use of technology to bridge barriers of media use for different users (especially people with audio-visual disabilities) has become the top priority for optimizing the media experience of visually impaired groups, while communication subjects, media differences, media use behavior, institutional environment and many other factors, are all ignored.

What's more fatal is that when the barrier-free system in traditional media is not yet complete, the rapid advent of high-speed Internet technology has made it seem easier to solve the problems lingering in the traditional media era. Thus, the research of barrier-free media use has jumped on the bandwagon, concentrated in the fields of applied sciences such as information science and mechanical automation. However, they are blindfolded by technology. In fact, ignoring factors such as communicators, communication content, communication targets and other factors while filtering things from the lens of technologicalism, have not achieved optimal results in barrier-free media use research. In fact, "accessible" technology does not mean "smooth" communication[5].

For mobile Internet, with hardware technology being vigorously popularized, soft factors such as human factors, institutional factors, and social factors in the process of barrier-free communication have gradually become stumbling blocks for visually impaired groups in their media use. For example, the voice navigation system provided by Apple's mobile phone is more professional than previous mobile phones especially designed for the blind, but its high price discourages ordinary visually impaired people; screen-reading software can conduct the primary recognition function, but it has no emotion – its interpretation of visual, cultural, and artistic work cannot bring a pleasant experience to the viewer, and even fails in basic semantic expression. At this time, human intervention is required – those professionals who master the basic picture language and have the ability to "encode and decode" – to complete the auditory transformation of visual elements, such as TV programs with descriptive soundtracks, and barrier-free movie commentaries, etc. Like other countries in the world, China is also practicing public cultural services, such as the Beijing Hongdandan Visually Impaired Cultural Service, Shanghai's "Sound of Light and Shadow", Communication University of China's Guangming Cinema and other barrier-free film public welfare interpretation services, ensuring that visually impaired groups are to the maximum extent able to have the same opportunities for media use and the right to appreciate arts as able-bodied people. Thus, the research on media use for visually impaired groups is a wide-ranging issue that is closely integrated with social mechanisms, legislative guarantees, content production, distribution and acquisition, and audience psychology, etc. Only through a multi-angle observation to understand the complexity of converged media platforms can we improve the media use experience of visually impaired groups.

Compared with content production and optimization at a specific level, building a barrier-free media environment is the primary issue to improve the media experience of visually impaired groups. In the West, telecommunications and terminal service providers often become the main

---

[5] Li Dongxiao, Xiong Mengqi. After "Accessibility": Research and Reflections on Barrier-Free Communication with The New Media [J]. Zhejiang Academic Journal, 2017, 06: 199-206. 李东晓, 熊梦琪. "可及" 之后:新媒体的无障碍传播研究与反思[J].浙江学刊

forces playing a positive and constructive role in promoting the production and dissemination of barrier-free film and television works under the supervision of law and society, The 21st Century Communications and Video Accessibility Act of 2010 in the United States stipulates that all software, hardware, and service providers that provide telecommunications and terminal services in the United States need to be accessible, and that beginning the year 2011, the four major broadcasting networks and the five major cable channels must provide four hours of unobstructed film and television services per week, and gradually expand the scope of services to fully cover the United States in a few years. In countries such as the UK, no less than 20% of TV programs on mainstream TV channels with public service obligations feature narration services. In China, most of the bodies that promote barrier-free dissemination of media are governments, schools, libraries, and other social and public service institutions, while the cable television networks, commercial websites, and cultural product suppliers that directly face the audience and provide cultural content are for the time being free to follow their own corporate ethics in this respect, and their content for the visually impaired group is far less than that of the able-bodied public, and the levels of services vary between different industries, enterprises, and products. Questions like whether the supply of content should be encouraged as a public welfare behavior or be required in a mandatory manner, and whether the service's public welfare or its commercialization should be more emphasized, are still waiting to be answered.

The construction of a barrier-free media environment first requires a strong legal foundation. During the "two sessions" in 2022, the issue of promoting the barrier-free environment through legislation won more support of the representatives, and many deputies to the National People's Congress, and members of the Chinese People's Political Consultative Conference from various industries have on their own accord put forward the motion of "suggesting making a law for a barrier-free environment", and stated that it is imminent to do so. This on one hand calls for physical spaces and places to be made barrier-free, on the other hand, it includes the barrier-free development of "soft environments" such as media culture. As early as 2019, film director Jia Zhangke, a deputy of the National People's Congress, signed jointly with 32 representatives the

"Proposal on the Development of Barrier-free Film Industry in China" and submitted it to the conference, with a conceptual plan for Barrier-free films' legislation, copyright delineations, and service improvement, and called on society to pay attention to the top-level design of the media environment for visually impaired groups. In addition, formulating national technical standards on information accessibility and promoting the popularization of Internet accessibility are also the focus of building a barrier-free media environment. In 2019, the State Council Information Office released "Equality, Participation, and Sharing: White Paper on 70 Years of Protection of the Rights and Interests of Persons with Disabilities in New China", which emphasized the need to strengthen the building of information accessibility standards - national and industry standards which will facilitate the use of communication equipment, Internet information access, and auxiliary devices use for persons with disabilities[6]. In January 2022, 227 websites and apps across the country completed the first batch of aging-friendly and barrier-free information modifications under the guidance of the "Special Action Plan for Aging and Barrier-Free Modifications of Internet Applications " issued by the Ministry of Industry and Information Technology in 2021. They launched a variety of distinctive functions such as font enlargement, voice guidance, "one-key direct connection to human customer service", and underwent a comprehensive evaluation under the ageing and barrier-free evaluation system for Internet applications established by the China Academy of Information and Communications Technology, the Internet Society of China, and other organizations. The evaluation system aims to provide users with disabilities with more comprehensive, considerate, and direct facilitation services, helping them fully enjoy the convenience brought by intelligent technologies such as the Internet, and share the achievements of scientific and technological development on an equal and barrier-free footing.

The production and distribution of media content suitable for visually impaired groups have become another important problem overshadowed

---

[6] State Council Information Office. Equality, Participation, and Sharing: White Paper on 70 Years of Protection of the Rights and Interests of Persons with Disabilities in New China [EB/OL]. (2019-07-25) [2019-11-30]. http://www.scio.gov.cn/zfbps/ndhf/39911/Document/1660531/1660531.htm. 国务院新闻办公室.平等、参与、共享: 新中国残疾人权益保障70年白皮书

by the development of information technology. Although different forms of information symbols can be freely converted with the help of digital technology and new media platforms and visually impaired people seem to have the same opportunities to access information as able-bodied people, the shortage of suitable content has not made the two groups truly equal. From a statistical point of view, the barrier-free supply of media content in the converged media environment has had little improvement compared to the era of traditional media, and the cultural products that visually impaired groups can choose are still limited to Braille books and TV. According to survey data on the media usage habits of students at Beijing School for the Blind, only 9.26% of the students have the habit of watching movies, and four people have not listened to or "watched" movies at all. Some visually impaired people say that TV is easier to operate than new media platforms, that online content lacks accessible versions and that the search path is cumbersome, so it is better to "watch" TV. It can be seen that although the Internet provides a convenient and rich way to obtain media products, for the visually impaired group, the increase of media channels does not mean the increase of available content, which in essence has pulled back the visually challenged people who are about to march on to the information age. Therefore, the construction of barrier-free content still requires the support and efforts of many parties, in the setting up of special projects, integrating the strengths of film and television institutions, universities, technology companies and social groups, deeply tapping into the potential of digital information technology to fully meet the spiritual and cultural needs of visually impaired groups, and effectively promoting accessible audiovisual content production.

The Guangming Cinema project of the Communication University of China may provide a shareable example for this. The film interpretation work in this project is jointly carried out by teachers and students of Communication University, with the film source and broadcast channel provided by Beijing Gehua Cable TV Network Co., Ltd., and Oriental Jiaying Media Co. Ltd., with an emphasis that the supply of accessible versions of films should be professional, sustainable and expandable. The project's professionalism lies in the participation of professional film and television personnel from Communication University of China. Barrier-free films and television are different from ordinary recording and editing:

the key is to decompose the scenes, and in the gaps of dialogues and sounds, use the language that the visually impaired can understand to tell the picture information and the emotions and meanings behind it, so as to convey emotions and disseminate cultural values. The participation of teachers and students majoring in film and television and the development of related academic research help to formulate guidelines for the production of barrier-free film soundtracks and improve the professional level of the interpretation services. Sustainability lies in the fact that this project model integrates multiple forces, including the professional and personnel advantages of the university, the resource advantages of telecommunications and new media companies in film sources and communication channels - the effective combination of personnel, film sources, and platforms makes this barrier-free service sustainable. Expandability lies in four dimensions: first, service objects can be expanded - blind people, people with severe visual impairments, and people who want to understand the content of the programs without looking at the screen are the target audience; second, the participating institutions can be expanded - all new media companies can participate, which is also the social responsibility of commercial companies in the new media era; third, service content can be expanded - barrier-free movies are just the beginning - the corresponding model can be extended to oral narration services of audio-visual content on mainstream channels and government websites; fourth, education and employment of the disabled youth can be expanded - public welfare film narration is attracting more and more visually impaired groups to join in, becoming a new path for them to receive education and achieve employment.

The above practices are all based on the premise of a comprehensive understanding and accurate grasp of visually impaired people, a specific user group. However, in today's widespread application of big data, this understanding is still not fully complete. First of all, in terms of user portraits, a global survey on the basic data of visually impaired groups is still in progress. All kinds of studies are based on local visually impaired groups as the research targets to conduct sample surveys, leaving many blind spots in the understanding of visually impaired groups, while data update is slower than the speed of changes in social and media environments, struggling to meet the urgent needs of scientific research and government decision-making. Secondly, in audience behavior research, most of the current studies are limited to questionnaires and experimental methods to define and classify the media usage habits, psychology and usage disorders of visually impaired groups in a simple manner, while media usage trends of visually impaired groups amid changing information technology are not fully reflected in a timely manner. On new media platforms with significant interactive features, visually impaired people have long ceased to passively receive information, but this change has not been paid attention to and examined in accessible communication research. Finally, in sociological research, the visually impaired group is still a study blind spot, and the research on the media rights of the visually impaired group is still in the stage of "three blanks": the query into the localized empowerment of new media for the visually impaired group is still blank, research on audio-visual media behavior of visually impaired groups is still blank, and the theoretical and systematic research on the accessibility of audio-visual content is still blank. When visually impaired groups use digital technology to break through the barriers set by visual information symbols and can express and write "freely", will the social roles of these groups change? Is this group sensitive to the speed of digital technology development? How will the arrival of 5G affect them? Can technological empowerment be demonstrated in this group of people? The inquiries of these questions may once again confirm that China's building of barrier-free media still has a long way to go.

(Qin Yuming, Professor, Doctoral Supervisor, Communication University of China. Qin's main research fields: media integration and documentary visuals; Song Junyi, 2019 doctoral student of Radio and Television at Communication University of China.)

THE NEW-ERA LANDSCAPE OF BARRIER-FREE FILMS AND TELEVISION: GENRE TRENDS, RESEARCH DIRECTIONS, AND THE CHINESE MODEL

Wu Weihua, Wang Nian, and Gao Yinfeng

Abstract: By attaching descriptive soundtracks and sign language, barrier-free productions provide new visual and audio channels for countless visually impaired and hearing-impaired people around the world to appreciate movies and television shows. The study on barrier-free movies and television is an interdisciplinary field linking audiovisual communication, media sociology, and disability research. Based on literature review and the analysis of current media environment, this paper maps out this industry's development and its Chinese model, in order to contribute to the studies of the characteristics and cultural functions of barrier-free films and television.

Keywords: Barrier-Free Films and Television, Audio-Visual Communication, Developing Trends, Chinese Model

Barrier-free films and television is a composite concept formed based on the concepts of barrier-free information and the cultural realm of film and television communication. It refers to films, television, and other audio-visual cultural forms and entertainment consumer products serving

27

people with disabilities. It answers policy advocacy from the perspective of the social practice of barrier-free communication, and reflects the profound equality, openness and fairness of barrier-free social participation and cultural applications. The dissemination practice of barrier-free films and television is more closely related to the information accessibility of the disabled and the efficiency of their consumption of cultural products. It is a key indicator of the effectiveness, modernity, and equality of information processing, communication, and feedback between persons with disabilities, the society, and media.

The main target groups of accessible films and television are the people with disabilities who are marginalized in cultural, informative and communicative scenarios due to physical disabilities, as well as some people with low learning abilities and cognition, and culturally marginalized groups, such as the elderly, children, and healthy people affected by certain environmental conditions. On the one hand, it focuses on the abilities, literacy, rights, etc., of people with disabilities in the current society, culture, and media use. On the other hand, it also examines the establishment and applicability of the multi-dimensional support system of policy, society, market, and public. In the past 20 years, driven by the ideas of information accessibility, the ideals of international information accessibility and bridging the information gap for people with disabilities have been continuously promoted. An interactive, diverse model, led by the government, driven by technology, participated in by the public, is gradually taking shape, while the application, research, and educational development of barrier-free films and television continue to grow

Accessible films and television, as one of the important categories of information accessibility and cultural equal rights, has shown a diversified, sustainable, quasi-professional and standardized development trend in the past 30 years. It has become an important endeavor to ensure that people with disabilities enjoy equal cultural rights, share the fruits of social development, and integrate into the social order.

1. The Evolutions of the Forms and Genres of Barrier-Free Films and Television

Barrier-free films and television presents itself as the most unique, service-oriented cultural carrier and communication mode in the practice and research of audio-visual communication. The customized model of serving specific groups of people and its purpose of promoting social and cultural services for public welfare and equal rights, have since its inception "made it an important part of public cultural services, and an important embodiment of information equality and cultural equality, ensuring the rights of people with disabilities."[1]

Barrier-free films and television, and its purpose in barrier-free capacity building and inclusive participation of information, culture, and communication, were once only charitable advocacy and services by non-governmental organizations and scientific research institutions. But since 2000, it has become a top-down, multi-party collaborative cause, jointly promoted by those in politics, economy, science, and education, in all countries in the world. From the formulation and implementation of laws and regulations to the requirements of technical and ethical norms, it has morphed into a global driving force, and has also shown the international community's ideals of humanistic care, knowledge equality, and the goals of people's livelihood. Affected by the popularization of global Internet and mobile communication technologies, the social landscape, cultural space and media carrier of barrier-free films and television have also undergone earth-shaking changes. The consumption and appreciation of barrier-free films and television "is the basic cultural right of the hearing-impaired."[2] It has become the most important component in the construction of an inclusive, open, and diverse information society, bringing the arts and humanities digitally, and it is an indicator of bridging cultural, digital, and information gaps, for building a fair and inclusive knowledge and education eco-system.

[1] Pan Xianghui, Li Dongxiao. Pictures and Colors: The Development Status and Prospects of China's Barrier-Free Films. Zhejiang Academic Journal, No. 4, 2013, p189-199. 潘祥辉, 李东晓:《绘声绘色:中国无障碍电影的发展现状及展望》,《浙江学刊》
[2] Ma Bo. Universal Accessible Film Promotion Model. China Press Publication Radio Film and Television Journal, September 10, 2015. 马波:《普及型无障碍电影推广模式》,《中国新闻出版广电报》

When a vertical view from the perspective of its cultural morphology, barrier-free films and television could mean barrier-free drama performances in the wider sense, and in day-to-day life entails barrier-free contact and participatory communication of audio-visual new media in the cybersphere.

Since 2000, barrier-free theatre performances and barrier-free films and television have complemented each other and developed in an integrated manner, presenting a coordinated, diversified, sustainable, quasi-professional, and standardized global public welfare development trend. Specifically:

1) The barrier-free cultural service model, in the form of public welfare activities, still exists. They are mainly temporary tours and on-site activities run by non-profit organizations and public welfare organizations for people with disabilities. For example, deaf theater performances are equipped with sign language commentaries and special subtitles next to the stage; and movie screening with live interpretation for the hearing impaired. This type of barrier-free cultural activity often relies on event funds and cultural performance resources that the organizer can raise, and also requires volunteers contributing their artistic sign language expression and film language oral description ability. This model is mostly seen in the world map of accessible cultural communication activities in a charitable and self-organized form, which is relatively scattered and difficult to maintain. "The Theatre Interpreter Initiative" in Slovenia is a recent successful barrier-free theater activity. Quasi-professional sign language interpreters are trained and positioned on the stage. They simultaneously perform sign language interpretations in congruence with performance onstage.

2) Quasi-professional "sign language" theatrical performances (for the hearing impaired) and film and television performances with audio descriptions (for the visually impaired) have become a sustainable model for barrier-free cultural communication services. The relatively standardized "sign language" drama training organizes professional drama and stage performers and hearing-impaired performers to provide more relaxed, understandable, and

MEDIA STUDY FRONTIERS IN CHINA

appreciable public performance services for the hearing-impaired group, and has gradually become an international routine for deaf stage performances and theatrical performances, with European and American models having already been developed. The European model is carried out in the form of The Deaf Theatre Network Europe, which was established at the Vienna Deaf Theatre Congress in 2001 with the hope of uniting the scattered deaf theatre organizations in Europe, exploring the history and heritage of European deaf theatre, holding special performances of European and international deaf theatre festivals, and cooperating with professional institutions to develop a series of deaf theatre training courses. The Mimics and Gesture Theatre in Ariadne, Russia, in cooperation with the Ukrainian Society of the Deaf, developed a sign language and performance play version of Shakespeare's "The Taming of the Shrew". In the performance, actors not only need to express themselves in sign language, but also need to use oral language, facial expressions, and body language in the performance. On June 1, 2019, after the successful premiere of "The Taming of the Shrew" in Kharkiv, it quickly entered a national tour, striving to deliver a wonderful combination of sign language communication and stage performance to hearing-impaired people all over Ukraine. The Soviet Deaf Theatre has a long-standing tradition, and its cultural heritage has been scattered to Russia, Ukraine and other countries since the 1990s. Whether it's the old Soviet Deaf Theatre or the ongoing (nearly 50-year-old) Kyiv "Rainbow" theatre, as well as a wide variety of small troupes, such as Tomsk's "Indigo", the "Gesture" troupe in Novosibirsk, the "Slov.net" troupe in Rostov, or the "Piano" theater for deaf children in Nizhny Novgorod, all commit to serving the hearing-impaired, producing barrier-free theatre for public performances. However, many struggle to sustain due to finances, manpower, and space constraints. Barrier-free theaters finds it difficult to survive in difficult situations, constrained by various factors such as politics, society, the economy, and volunteers. Looking at the history of barrier-free theater on the European continent, we can clearly see its difficult road of self-struggle. The British

Theatre of the Deaf was disbanded due to poor management, and the DeafForum Theatre carried on the baton; the Swedish Tyst Teater survived for more than 50 years and developed its own TV show. The International Visual Theatre in France was founded in 1977, but it was not until 2004 that it had its own theater for the deaf in Grand-Guignol, Paris. In other countries, such as Spain, there are five deaf theaters in Madrid alone, and programs have been launched all year round; Finland, through the community theater under the jurisdiction of the national cultural department, sets up an annual deaf theater project to serve the hearing-impaired in the community; Germany, in the form of cooperation with the German Deaf Theatre Group, started the development of barrier-free theater projects. In recent years, outside the The Deaf Theatre Network Europe, accessible theater professionals from other European countries such as Finland, Belgium, Bulgaria, Croatia, Finland, and Portugal have proposed the concept of "bilingual theater" and established "Sign & Sound Theatre Europe", to promote education development, information sharing, and cooperative performances of barrier-free theater in the form of non-governmental cooperation.

Theater	Country	Founded	Genre
3D Derby Deaf Drama	UK	2002	Drama, Musical
Ariadne Mimics and Gesture Theatre	Russia		Drama, Musical
Australian Theatre of the Deaf	Australia	1979	Drama, Musical
China Disabled People's Arts Troupe	China	1987	Musical
Common Ground Sign Dance Theatre	UK	1986	Musical
Das Deutsche Gehörlosen Theater	Germany		Drama, Musical
Deaf West Theatre	California, USA	1991	Drama, Musical
Deafinitely Theatre	UK	2002	Drama, Musical
Quest	Maryland, USA	1997	Drama, Musical
International Visual Theatre	France		Drama, Musical

National Theatre of the Deaf	USA	1967	Drama, Musical
Seña y Verbo	Mexico	1993	Drama, Musical
ONA-ON	Slovenia	Unknown	Sign language interpretation
Rayduha	Ukraine	Unknown	Drama, Musical
Signdance Collective	UK, Netherlands	2001	Drama, Musical
Theatre Hand in the Eye	Belgium	2006	Drama, Musical
TOYS Theater	Russia	1985	Drama, Musical
Tyst	Sweden		Drama, Musical
The New York Deaf Theatre	USA	1979	Drama, Musical

Table 2-3-4: Internationally Famous Theatres
for the Deaf (not conclusive)

The leader in accessible theater in the United States is the National Theatre of the Deaf (NTD). Founded in 1967, it is one of the oldest theater companies in the United States. NTD has won numerous awards at U.S. and international theater festivals and theater for the deaf festivals. To date, it has had over 10,000 performances world-wide. Barrier-free dramas it has developed combine various forms such as performance, oral language, American Sign Language and lip language to provide hearing-impaired people with the opportunity to appreciate theatrical performances. They also promote the concept of accessible theater to the public, allowing more members of the public to understand and access sign language and, through accessible theater, promote the concept of accessible art communication. NTD created the American oral accessible theater model and became a leader in this field, leading a group of small and experimental theater organizations and theater houses in the United States to join a franchise-style development and performance cooperation of accessible theater. These include Chicago Theatre for the Deaf, Children's Theatre of the Deaf, Circuit Playhouse Theatre of the Deaf, Dayton Community Theatre of the Deaf, Lights On! Deaf Theatre (Rochester, NY), Minnesota Theatre of the Deaf, Music Theatre Company, New Dominion Theatre of the Deaf, North Carolina Theatre of Gesture, Quiet Zone Theatre, Readers Theatre for the Deaf, Sign of the Times Community Theatre Group (Springfield, Massachusetts), Spectrum Deaf Theatre, Sunshine Too, and more. There are also some short-lived accessible theater groups, such as The Black Deaf Theater Group, which was active in New York in the 1990s, and The New York Deaf Theater, all of which made important contributions to the development of American accessible theater.

3) Since the beginning of the new millennium, barrier-free films for the hearing impaired and barrier-free films for the visually impaired have been developed in many countries. From the perspective of film and television typology, the following two development trends are overserved.

First, sign language, lip language, and subtitle-style films and TV programs serving the hearing-impaired population[3] are integrated into the field of mass communication, forming a normal and daily trend of information accessibility services. In China, barrier-free TV programs for hearing-impaired people started in 1978 with "Learn a Little Sign Language" on Shanghai TV's Channel 2, followed by "Sign Language Program for the Deaf" on Guangdong TV in 1984; Sign language TV programs are the main shows for this genre of barrier-free works, and there are few film works that insert sign language on the screen; in the 40 years since 1978, the production and dissemination of Chinese sign language programs, especially sign language news programs, are also constantly being explored. However, due to the different expressions of sign language due to differences in regions, dialects and ethnic groups, the popularization and promotion of the common language of sign language is even more difficult, making it difficult for sign language films and television to make a breakthrough.

Second, descriptive films, and TV programs serving the visually impaired are gradually becoming more diverse and richer, adhering to the tradition of barrier-free theater-style with accompanying narration, they have developed a standardized, broadcast-grade production form. In China, a long-term, effective, and sustainable model has been developed through nationwide campaigns such as the Guangming Cinema project, the joining of public welfare screening theaters, and the progress of cultural projects in poverty alleviation. In China, barrier-free film and television service for the visually impaired was born in 2003, which was launched by the China Braille Press, who started by interpretating movies for the blind.

---

[3] Wu Xinxun. Sign Language TV Programs in Developing Countries of the World, Disability in China, No. 9, 1996, p22-24. 吴信训:《发展中的世界各国手语电视节目》,《中国残疾人》

After that, non-profit organizations in Beijing, Shanghai, Guangzhou, Wuhan, Hong Kong and other places followed suit. Events aimed at assisting people with disabilities were held and there were on-site oral movie interpretation services by volunteers, which helped some visually impaired people experience and understand movies. In 2009, Shanghai Film Publishing House began to produce barrier-free films. This type of barrier-free films and television mainly includes descriptive films (there were few TV programs), and some scholars also call them "oral visual art"[4] or " oral image for the visually impaired"[5]. In this paper, "barrier-free films and television" refers to movies and television works, and " barrier-free films" specifically refers to movie works. In the following, we will mainly review the world experience and local practice in the production, dissemination and public welfare advocacy of barrier-free films and television for visually impaired people.

According to Ma Bo's description of the social positioning of barrier-free films and television, its "public welfare positioning is clear. The public welfare positioning can effectively protect the green channel of (its) development and ensure the rights and interests of the visually impaired". The advocacy and promotion of barrier-free film and television services is also a response to the new requirements and demands of national public cultural services, which calls for gradually incorporating barrier-free film and television services into China's developmental path, featuring a "public welfare publication supply system, rationally allocating public cultural resources" and " equalization of public cultural services"[6], in accordance with the requirements of public welfare, universal coverage, equality, and convenience. At the same time, barrier-free films and television also require cooperation between government departments, civil organizations, technology companies, and education and scientific research departments, striving for more cultural rights in this service for people with disabilities, combining the strengths of governments, society, the public, and different

---

[4] Ma Bo. On Barrier-Free Films. Contemporary TV. No. 5, 2016, p110-111. 马波：《浅议无障碍电影》,《当代电视》

[5] Wu Zongyi, Xie Zhenzhen. Development Status of Visually Impaired Oral Video Description Services in China and its Promotion in Mainland China. Journal of News Research, Vol. 6, No. 10, 2015, p20-21. 吴宗艺,谢桢桢：《中国视障口述影像服务的发展现状与大陆推广》,《新闻研究导刊》

[6] Ibid.

groups, and the vision of "technology popularization-application, adaptability-literacy improvement".

2. The Development Trend of Barrier-Free Films and Television

In the international community, with the active advocacy of the United Nations and the response of many countries, the production and development of accessible films have grown significantly in the past 30 years, showing a trend of diversity, sustainability, quasi-professionalization, and standardization. On the one hand, with the attention paid to people with disabilities in publication and anti-discrimination laws of various countries, the United Kingdom, France, Germany, the United States, Canada, Spain, Australia, New Zealand, and other countries have gradually developed a series of standardized barrier-free film and television services. On the other hand, with the signing of and push by the Convention on the Rights of Persons with Disabilities passed by the United Nations General Assembly and the international community's Marrakesh Treaty, discussions and actions on safeguarding the rights of the visually impaired have gradually developed into an international consensus, increasingly affecting the formulation and implementation of national barrier-free film and television rules of various countries. Specifically, western countries have incorporated the production, dissemination, and consumption of barrier-free films and television into the public television service system, and barrier-free films have evolved rapidly with the empowerment of Internet technology.

The evolution trend is summarized as follows:

1) The advocacy by disabled associations has become the mainstream, and the enforcement of government legislation has gradually become a trend.

The visually impaired and handicapped associations in western developed countries play a mainstream advocacy and constructive role in promoting the production and dissemination of accessible films and television. The Royal National Institute of Blind People (RNIB), The National Federation of the Blind (NFB), Canadian National Institute for the Blind (CNIB), the Confédération Française Pour La Promotion Sociale Des Aveugles Et Amblyopes (CFPSAA) and other institutions actively cooperate with governments to push for adding copyright exceptions and mandatory production time limits for accessible films and television in relevant publishing laws, anti-discrimination laws, and laws protecting people with disabilities. The push of legislation is mainly in two aspects, one of which is copyright exceptions. For example, Article 121 of the U.S. Copyright Law "Limitations on exclusive rights" specifically includes "Reproduction for blind or other people with disabilities", and Article 37 of the Japanese Copyright Law on limiting copy rights in "reproduction for visually impaired persons, etc.", Article 45a of the German Copyright Act "persons with disabilities", and others all refer to the copyright exceptions for visual and audio works. The second is the guarantee of the duration of accessible films and television. The Disability Discrimination Act 1995 of the UK clearly stipulates that TV networks must guarantee a 10% annual production rate of accessible films and television. The Federal Communications Commission of the US has specifically issued a rule of "50 hours of video description" per calendar quarter, requiring public television channels to ensure 50 hours of TV programming with audio descriptions every quarter to serve the visually impaired viewers. In 2011, public television channels were told to expand this time limit to four hours per week of accessible service.

2) Accessible TV becomes mainstream, and accessible movies are updated rapidly.

With the mandatory push of government legislation, the production, dissemination and consumption of barrier-free films and television in western developed countries are mainly concentrated in public television services. Accessible TV has gone mainstream, and accessible movies are updated rapidly. Traditional broadcasting networks are the main marketing and dissemination platforms for accessible TV, such as the nine major public broadcasting networks in the United States and nearly 100 TV channels in the UK. In recent years, popular online audio and video service providers have become the main market for accessible films. As of June 2019, Apple's iTunes online store had launched 1049 accessible movies (data from June 8th); Netflix, the largest online movie rental provider in the United States, launched 975 accessible movies (statistics from June 21st). They respectively feature original web series, documentaries, TV series and children's programs, etc.; Amazon video service had also launched 529 accessible film and television works (data from June 8th). For the American film and television industry and Internet service providers, the production, provision and dissemination of accessible films and television have become routine work for equal rights, in striving to not break the law. As for content provision, most accessible film and television works are limited by the copyright restrictions of popular film and television works, content restrictions, and the difficulty of public welfare production of descriptive soundtracks, showing signs of aging and inactivity, in sharp contrast with the hustle and bustle of the developed American Hollywood film and television industry. At the level of consumption and dissemination, positioning of persons with disabilities, public awareness, consumer behavior guidance, and cultural derivatives have not been fully developed; barrier-free films and television only cater to individual viewing and family consumption, while group cinema viewing and film cultural activities are relatively weak.

3. The Research Path of Barrier-Free Film and Television Services

With the development of the creation and dissemination of accessible films and television, research in this area has gradually sprung up, and the following research paths have gradually formed:

First, based on the traditional research framework of audio-visual communication, research and analysis of the audio-visual narrative, creation mode, and production of barrier-free films and television are carried out; this type of research is mostly based on observation of phenomena, and scene description, presenting a mode of situational research and observational notes. Polish scholar Agnieszka Walczak's "Creative Description: Audio Describing Artistic Films for Individuals with Visual Impairments", published in the Journal of Visual Impairment & Blindness, in a form of a theoretical essay, describes the conditions of a creative narrative in accessible filmmaking[7]. Liu Yang, Xiong Yanyinzi, and Huang Tianshu, in the form of analysis of film production and selection, discuss the issue of cultural adaptability in the adaptation and screening of barrier-free films. They argue that visuals and narratives should be properly considered in a comprehensive manner together with the selection and production of barrier-free movies, to meet the horizon of expectation of visually impaired people to a greater extent[8]. After interviewing and tracing the creative jounrey of Jiang Hongyuan, China's first-generation barrier-free film creator, in Zeng Guangchang presented the collision of ideas and experimental explorations in the early days of barrier-free films in a line-drawing style[9]. Wu Zongyi and Xie Zhenzhen tried to extract a localized barrier-free film promotion model in China from looking at the history of barrier-free movies[10].

Second, academic interactions between the development of barrier-free films and television, and communication research. Gao Xiaohong and Chen Xingang argue that "meeting the basic information demands of people with disabilities is the main content of barrier-free communication work; satisfying the artistic, aesthetic demands of people with disabilities is, however, a difficulty in barrier-free communication. Reproduced as an audio-visual product by narrating the pictures, barrier-free films need to solve the three major obstacles of film and television works for the blind - movement barriers, information barriers, and cultural barriers." The barrier-free film and television works "present the exact same listening time as the original film, and the purpose is to ensure that the blind group can enjoy the equal rights of art and aesthetics to the greatest extent. The conversion is actually the whole process from visual language, to written language, and then to auditory expressions, finally presenting to the blind

---

[7] Walczak, Agnieszka. Creative Description: Audio Describing Artistic Films for Individuals with Visual Impairments. Journal of Visual Impairment & Blindness, 2017, Issue 4, p387–391.

[8] Liu Yang, Xiong Yanyinzi, Huang Tianshu. On the Choice and Way out of Barrier-Free Movies for the Blind. Home Drama, No.5, 2016, p133-133. 刘扬，熊闫寅子，黄天书:《浅谈盲人无障碍电影的选择与出路》,《戏剧之家》

[9] Zeng Guangchang. The Development of Barrier-Free Films. Movie Review, No. 9, 2012. 曾广昌:《无障碍电影在发展》,《电影评介》

[10] Ibid.

audience an audio recording with a sense of imagery."[11] Pablo Romero-Fresco and Louise Fryer explored the relationship between accessible descriptive soundtracks and audio-guided audiobooks from an audience research perspective[12]. Li Dongxiao's "Hearing and Seeing: Research on Barrier-Free Communication in Film and Television Media" is a relatively complete and comprehensive work of research on barrier-free audio-visual communication, which outlines the current landscape of barrier-free film and television development. The work includes chapters on the concepts, objects, and practice of film and television media accessibility, the needs and usage habits of film and television media for hearing and visually impaired audiences, the evolution of practices of the world's barrier-free film and television communication, the supply and promotion strategies of barrier-free content on China's TV media, etc[13].

The third is the search for a public service model of barrier-free films and television with Chinese characteristics. The main content demonstrated in this research path is the coordination and cooperation between Chinese non-profit organizations, teaching and research institutions, public libraries, as well as news, film, and television publishing institutions. Wang Yu[14], Xia Xiongfei[15], Qu Dapeng, Wang Jingbo[16], Lu Ning[17] and others

---

[11] Gao Xiaohong, Chen Xingang. Guangming Cinema: Research and Practice of Barrier-Free Audiovisual Communication. Chinese Editors Journal, 2019(03):4-7. 高晓虹,陈欣钢:《光明影院:无障碍视听传播的研究与实践》,《中国编辑》

[12] Romero-Fresco,Pablo, Fryer, Louise. Could Audio-Described Films Benefit from Audio Introductions? An Audience Response Study. Journal of Visual Impairment & Blindness, Issue 4, 2019, p287–295.

[13] Li Dongxiao. Hearing and Seeing: A Study of Barrier-Free Communication in Film and Television Media, Zhejiang University Press, Zhejiang, 2013. 李东晓:《听见 看见:影视媒体的无障碍传播研究》,浙江大学出版社

[14] Wang Yu. Barrier-Free Films: Promoting Public Welfare and Benefiting the Disabled. National Bibliography, No. 5, 2011, p40-41. 王瑜:《"无障碍电影":推动公益事业 惠及残障人士》,《全国新书目》

[15] Xia Xiongfei. The Promotion of Barrier-Free Films Should Be Increased. Youth Journalist, No. 19, 2018, p62. 夏熊飞:《应加大无障碍电影推广力度》,《青年记者》

[16] Qu Dapeng, Wang Jingbo. Doing Warm Things with "Good Voice" - Public Welfare Activities of Barrier-Free Film Interpretation. China Radio, No. 1, 2017, p36-38. 曲大鹏,汪静波:《用"好声音"做温暖事——谈无障碍电影解说公益活动》,《中国广播》

[17] Lu Ning. Research on Government - School Cooperation in Carrying out Barrier-Free Video Cultural Services - Taking the Development of Barrier-Free Video Cultural Services in the Library of Nanjing Special Education Vocational and Technical College as an Example. The Science Education Article Collects (Early Issue), No. 11, 2014 Issue, p221-222. 陆宁:

have started to explore the public service model of barrier-free movies from the multi-party cooperation model of public welfare actions. Occasionally, some scholars try to rewrite the public welfare model of barrier-free movies, such as Chen Jiankai's discussion on the feasibility of marketization and industrialization of barrier-free movies.[18]

However, in general, most local studies on accessible films are characterized by their small sample sizes, obvious local features, and being case-oriented. Experimental and public welfare-style empirical observation and reflection, documenting and analysis of individual participation and scene reproduction, and discussion of balanced use of audio-visual language and the auditory accessibility of information have become the main textual components of this type of research.

4. Operation Guangming (Bright light): The Chinese Model of Barrier-Free Films

The development and dissemination of barrier-free film and television has become a practice and research field with interdisciplinary characteristics in the past 30 years of gradual development. This provides the disabled with equal access to information and the possibility of cultural participation and exchange, fully enjoying and integrating into the current all-media society, fully grasping the opportunities of knowledge acquisition and information dissemination as much as possible, and participating more actively in building the society, and cultural development. This has become the social development goal of governments all over the world.

The development of barrier-free films in China marks a new starting point for Chinese cultural assistance activities for the disabled, and it is also a new direction for the extension of cultural services for the visually impaired in the country. After nearly ten years of development, China's barrier-free movies have gone from "community", "library", "telling movies

《政校合作开展无障碍视频文化服务的研究——以南京特殊教育职业技术学院图书馆开展无障碍视频文化服务为例》,《科教文汇(上旬刊)》

[18] Chen Jiankai. The "Barriers" of Barrier-Free Films: An Analysis of the Current Situation of "Barrier-Free Films" in Shanghai and Exploration of the Way Out. Journal of News Research, No. 7, 2015, p33-34. 陈建凯:《无障碍电影的"障碍"——上海市"无障碍电影"现状分析及出路探究》,《新闻研究导刊》

to blind people ", deliveries of barrier-free DVDs, and barrier-free movie viewing activities, to "Xinmu Cinema" and Guangming Cinema. The development shows changes from small-scale oral films to barrier-free multimedia publications, from public cultural spaces of communities and libraries to cinemas and film festivals, from serving a narrow and special group of people to being publicly known with public participation in the new era. The creation and dissemination modes of Chinese barrier-free movies are in the following three forms.

1) The rise of the non-governmental public welfare model and the service model that is scattered, community-centered, and on the grass-roots level, raising the voices of people with disabilities,

The Voice of Light and Shadow - Shanghai Barrier-free Film and Television Culture Development Center's "grassroots NGO + public welfare" non-governmental production model has become the leading form of non-governmental non-profit barrier-free film services. It has always been difficult for grassroots NGOs to intervene in the production and screening of barrier-free films. With the support of the Shanghai Disabled Persons' Federation, the Shanghai Barrier-Free Film and Television Culture Development Center has been operating for many years, and has trained its own management team, narration manuscript writing and review team, and barrier-free film dubbing team from volunteers. They have successfully completed the production and screening of more than 50 high-quality barrier-free films. This model of the Shanghai Barrier-Free Film and Television Culture Development Center can also be seen in Beijing, Hangzhou, Guangzhou and other big cities, relying on the advocacy and leadership of grassroots non-profit organizations, public welfare groups, public libraries, and libraries for the blind, forming a scattered, community-based, grass-roots service form.

In the past 20 years, non-governmental non-profit organizations have emerged rapidly in China and have played an important role in helping the poor and disadvantaged groups to improve their survival and development conditions. The productions, screenings, and tours of barrier-free films that have spawned under the non-governmental public welfare model are a manifestation of the active participation of Chinese non-governmental forces in the cultural undertakings of helping people with disabilities.

2) With the help of a Braille audio-visual publishing platform, developing a barrier-free film publishing model of "copyright + public welfare"

The "copyright + public welfare" barrier-free film publishing model committed to by China Braille Press and Shanghai Film and Audio Publishing House is the mainstream model of barrier-free film production and publishing in China. These two publishing houses are the pioneers of China's barrier-free film publishing. They have long been committed to the pursuit of copyright exceptions for barrier-free films, professional productions, and public welfare delivery services. Their barrier-free film services reach and benefit the whole country.

In recent years, China Braille Press has increased the production of barrier-free films, and promoted barrier-free film projects into the national major audio-visual publishing projects of the "Twelfth Five-Year Plan" and "Thirteenth Five-Year Plan", China Excellent Publication Award and The National Press and Publication Reform and Development Project. It has thus developed exploratory barrier-free film and television productions and publications into a popular project aimed at benefiting the cultural and entertainment life of marginal groups such as those with hearing and visual disabilities, the physically handicapped, the elderly, and minors. During the "Twelfth Five-Year Plan" period, the Braille Press has produced 119 barrier-free film and television works, and during the "Thirteenth Five-Year Plan" period, the production of barrier-free films will be elevated to a rate of 100 per year.

Thus, a sustainable publishing model has been developed based on the Braille audio-visual publishing platform, with help by the China Disabled Persons' Federation, grass-roots volunteer liaison stations providing assistance to people with disabilities, and disabled service clubs (stations), forming a barrier-free film delivery service network – a successful Chinese model of the publication and release of barrier-free films.

3) Exploring new models that incorporate ideological and political content in courses, building a new platform for cultural public welfare, and integration of universities, publishing and public welfare services.

In addition to the non-governmental public welfare and publishing and distribution models, the School of Television of Communication University of China, based on the Marxist view of journalism in practice, explores combining ideological and political content with public welfare communication practices, with the scientific methodology of "practice, cognition, and innovation" as a reference, and has created a new model of barrier-free film service in the new era: Guangming Cinema.

Guangming Cinema takes action research as the method, the Marxist journalism view as the theoretical framework, and is guided by the educational strategy that combines ideological and political teachings with cultural public welfare. Its "Barrier-free Documentary Writing" (for undergraduates), and "Barrier-free Documentary Writing Studies" (for postgraduates) - creative writing workshops and writing courses are closely integrated with barrier-free film production, national public welfare screenings, and the building of barrier-free film platforms for international film festivals, creatively breaking the invisible barriers between ideological and political education and professional courses, building a new channel of ideological and political education for young students to love and commit to learning. At the symposium of teachers of ideological and political theory courses, General Secretary Xi Jinping, in view of the overall situation of the development of the Party and the country, pointed out that "We must make good use of classroom teaching as the main channel, ideological and political theory teaching must be strengthened while being improved. Ideological and political theory education must improve its affinity and pertinence to meet the needs and expectations of students' growth and development. All other courses must guard and cultivate their own fields, so that various courses and ideological and political theory courses can go in the same direction and form a synergistic effect."[19] Guangming Cinema

---

[19] Xi Jinping. Xi Jinping's Important Speech at the Symposium of Teachers of Ideological and Political Theory in Schools, 2019. 习近平:《习近平在学校思想政治理论课教师座谈会重要讲话》

is an educational model that uses courses to lead on-the-ground practices, promote public welfare, and teach ideology, politics and ethics. "It assists in helping students solve confusions in ideology, values, and sentiments, and inspire their enthusiasm and motivation to study for the country and the nation, helping them clarify their own values and social positioning in the process of creating values for the society."[20]

Since its launch in 2018, Guangming Cinema has completed more than 100 barrier-free films such as " Hello, Mr. Billionaire ", "Wolf Warrior II", "The Founding of an Army", "My War", " Forever Young" and "The Piano in a Factory" and donated them to blind schools and university libraries across the country. With the vision of "70 films in 70 years" and "104 films in One Year", Guangming Cinema has worked with Gehua Cable and China Braille Press to deliver two films a week to visually impaired people - simple and sincere public welfare actions and a gift to China's 70th anniversary of its founding.

Guangming Cinema is not only a new method, new thinking and new practice combining ideological and political teachings with media education, but also a new platform for cultural public welfare with Chinese characteristics in the new era. It advocates bringing visually impaired people to the best cinemas, creating accessible film works that can be reproduced and disseminate, so as to build a more professional, public service-oriented "cultural tactile paving " and promote a stage of equal rights for cultural sharing. The movie viewing activity led by Guangming Cinema is a very distinctive public welfare activity of the Beijing International Film Festival. For the first time, visually impaired people in China were brought to the cultural space of the International Film Festival, extending the social value and cultural significance of the film festival and even film itself, while also reflecting the social responsibility and public welfare responsibility of the film industry in its continuous development. During the Two Sessions in 2019, Director Jia Zhangke, a deputy of the National People's Congress, put forward the "Proposal on the Development of Barrier-free Film Industry in China", suggesting that the state legislate for barrier-free films, establish barrier-free film standards, reduce copyright restrictions on

---

[20] Xu Tao. Constructing an Educational System of Ideological and Political Teachings. Guangming Daily, October 18, 2019, 15th edition. 许涛：《构建课程思政的育人大格局》，《光明日报》

barrier-free films, and improve barrier-free facilities in cinemas. It affirmed the achievements of the Guangming Cinema project, and called on all sectors of society to support barrier-free movies, enrich the cultural life of people with disabilities, encourage them to integrate into and participate in society, and improve the level of civility in social development.

Conclusion

The public welfare paradigm of barrier-free film and television communication has been gradually established. After thirty years of practices and explorations in the development of barrier-free film and television based on the concepts of human rights equality, cultural and technological rights equality, and education equity, countries around the world have found policy advocacy and public service strategies that have adapted to their own national conditions and social characteristics.

China's barrier-free film and television, especially barrier-free films for the visually impaired, presents a dual development track of both theoretical research and actual practices. At the practical level, China's barrier-free film and television is a multi-layered structure, with co-participation and co-construction for a cultural tactile paving. At the cognitive level, the development of China's barrier-free film and television is rooted in local national conditions and social and cultural foundation, reflecting the strong cultural empathy of the Chinese nation and the mainstream values of public welfare participation.

The development of barrier-free film and television is an important milestone in the history of human rights, film and television copyright, and public welfare communication. It will play an important role in safeguarding the cultural rights, cultural participation, and national cultural identity of the visually impaired. As one of the developing countries with a large visually impaired population, we have a duty to constantly promote the practice of the Chinese model of barrier-free film and television, safeguard the legitimate rights and interests of people with disabilities, and embrace the new landscape of disability assistance services created by barrier-free film and television. This is not only the barrier-free ideal and consensus of the international community in the search for cultural equity, information sharing and inclusive education in the past 20 years, but also the goal of China's information barrier-free construction in the new era. Only by realizing a more comprehensive, three-dimensional, standardized and sustainable barrier-free cultural information dissemination standard, channel, application, and service model can we truly bridge the disability information gap and promote the development of the equality of knowledge, information, science, and technology for people with disabilities, answering the call of the times for social innovation and cultural construction in the new millennium.

(Wu Weihua, Professor, Communication University of China; Wang Nian, PhD student, Communication University of China)

* Fund support: This paper is a research milestone of the Key Art Project "Research on Cyber Culture and Security" of the 2019 National Social Science Fund. It is supported by the State Key Laboratory of Media Convergence and Communication. Project approval number: 19ZD12.

EMPOWERMENT WITH TECHNOLOGY AND ALLEVIATION OF KNOWLEDGE SHORTAGE: INFORMATION ACCESSIBILITY AND NEW DEVELOPMENT IN COMMUNICATION FOR DEVELOPMENT

Hu Fang and Liu Wen

Abstract: Communication for Development has always been committed to researching and solving development problems, especially the problem of unbalanced development. Mankind is constantly facing new development problems with the growth and progress of society, and the theory and paradigms of Communication for Development are also updated continuously, amid scrutiny and critiques. In the 21st century, rapid development of Internet and digital technology has led to dramatic changes in media ecology. More and more information is presented visually and depends on visual perception systems. A "digital gap" has become a serious problem for the global society. How to use technology to "empower" people with disabilities and eliminate the gap between rich and the poor in the field of knowledge and information has become a new question for Communication for Development in the new era.

Keywords: UN, Digital Gap, Technology Empowerment, Equality for Persons with Disabilities, Guangming Cinema

It can be said that the study of Communication for Development started at the same time as the establishment of the United Nations. Communication for Development's full name is "Communication for Development and Social Change" - a social process whose essence lies in the sharing of knowledge, the exchange of ideas, and the establishment of consensus. Development is the goal and communication is the tool. Communication for Development studies how to use communication theory to promote social progress, including material progress and intellectual progress, and bring about development and achieve wider equality and greater degree of freedom through communication technologies.

For more than 70 years after the end of World War II, the development goals of the United Nations and various agencies have been continuously adjusted and developed. Projects have been updated, ranging from the requirements of newly established countries to achieve national independence and self-determination, to the voices of the southern countries to eliminate poverty and narrow the development gap; from improving material poverty, to the improvement of intangible (information, knowledge) poverty; from issues such as agriculture, health, economy, education, and technology, to the return of issues like human rights, culture, needs, and capabilities, the development goals of the United Nations and various agencies are being adjusted and development projects updated. The connotation of "development" is constantly evolving, and the research paradigm of Communication for Development has also undergone several changes with the progress of the times.

"People" are born to pursue equality. Since its birth, Communication for Development has been committed to researching and solving development problems, especially the problems of uneven development, such as narrowing the gap between the rich and the poor between countries and people, as well as the problem of unfair distribution of power and rights. As long as there is inequality in any field and in any form, Communication for Development will proceed with its disciplinary significance and update its research agenda. However, with the rapid iteration of communication technology, the gap of knowledge and information between the rich and the poor has also appeared in human society, and the contrasts between "strong countries" and "weak countries" in information, the "rich" and the "poor" in knowledge are deepening day by day; In terms of mastering knowledge and obtaining information, the differences between people with disabilities and able-bodied people, between young people and middle-aged and elderly people, and between people with different educational levels are becoming increasingly large. The knowledge gap represented by printing technology as the medium has developed into the digital divide represented by the medium of information technology.

The term "digital divide" is derived from the "knowledge gap hypothesis", a well-known early research result of communication studies. Digital divide refers to the fact that due to the development of information technology, the gap in people's ability to receive and use information has created an insurmountable divide in society, resulting in the "digital information Matthew effect". There are about 70 million people with disabilities in China (which directly impacts the lives of 200 million people), including 17.32 million visually impaired people. Since the development of information technology has mostly occurred in the direction of vision, this has significantly affected the life and development of all visually impaired people. The digital divide has become an almost insurmountable barrier for the visually impaired. This kind of inconvenience caused by the iteration of media technology to people with disabilities is generally called "information barrier". It is in this development context that the barrier-free dissemination of information has become an important global issue. The UN Convention on the Rights of Persons with Disabilities recognizes, "...the importance of accessibility to the physical, social, economic and cultural environment, to health and education and to information and communication, in enabling persons with disabilities to fully enjoy all human rights and fundamental freedoms."

In China, since the 1990s, the attempt of " barrier-free information" has been started. In April 2008, the Standing Committee of the Chinese People's Congress organized the revision of the Law of the People's Republic of China on the Protection of Persons with Disabilities, and added in Article 52 of Chapter VII "Barrier-Free Environment" that the state and society should take measures to "promote accessibility in information exchange". Since then, Chinese persons with disabilities have begun to enjoy the right to barrier-free information exchange (referred to as the "right to barrier-free information") in addition to the right to barrier-free facilities (also known as the "right to barrier-free material environment").

In June 2011, the State Council of China promulgated the "Regulations on the Construction of Barrier-Free Environments", the third chapter of which is "Accessible Information Exchange". The so-called "barrier-free information" means that any individual (whether able-bodied or with disabilities, young or old), under any circumstances, can obtain and use information in an equal, convenient and barrier-free manner.

Yang Fei, a Chinese scholar, gave a clear explanation on the information accessibility rights of people with disabilities, "The information accessibility rights of people with disabilities refer to the rights of persons with disabilities to obtain, receive, and transmit information in an equal, convenient, and barrier-free manner. Rights, in addition to rights to traditional barrier-free information exchange services such as text prompts (such as subtitles), Braille, sign language, and voice, in the information age also include rights to electronic and information technology accessibility, Internet accessibility, and others."[1] Promoting "barrier-free information" and providing equal opportunities for all individuals, including persons with disabilities, to share information technology achievements, has become a common goal of the United Nations, international organizations, and governments since the beginning of the new century.

Through the development of the theoretical research and promotion of "barrier-free information" in the international community and in China, we can get a glimpse of the new progress of Communication for Development in the 21st century and the subject's localized process in China.

1. Paradigm Changes in Communication for Development Studies

Communication for Development, as the name implies, studies how to "promote development through communication". In a broad sense, the essence of this theory is about researching and practicing how to make media technology realize its powerful functions in developing

---

[1] Yang Fei. On Information Accessibility Rights of Persons with Disabilities [J]. Journal of Henan University of Economics and Law, 2013(2): 118-124. 杨飞. 论残疾人的信息无障碍权【J】.河南财经政法大学学报

countries. "Communication for Development can be interpreted as: the use of modern and traditional communication techniques to promote and strengthen the processes of socioeconomic, political, and cultural changes."[2] American scholar Godwin C. Chu finds, "the works of Daniel Lerner, Wilbur Schranm, Everett Rogers and others helped establish the notion that communication has a role to play in the process of social and economic development."[3]

The early theories of Communication for Development were mainly put forward by Daniel Lerner based on a set of experimental data, with "empathy" as the core theory, and then developed into the theory of media function by Wilbur Schramm, mainly emphasizing that the function of the media in society is relatively decisive, which can be regarded as the social and economic expression of the Bullet Theory. In 1969, Everett M. Rogers published an academic monograph titled " Modernization Among Peasants: The Impact of Communication" based on his research on media and modernity of more than 200 farmers in Colombia and proposed the famous theory of communication – the Diffusion of Innovation Theory, which academically defined Communication for Development. The theory of innovation diffusion amplifies the transformative function of the media in third world countries. It has not only been highly valued by the governments of various countries, but also widely recognized by academic circles: the International Communication Association (ICA) has officially included Communication for Development in the academic field of communication.

Chinese scholar Pan Yupeng made a fairly pertinent evaluation of early Communication for Development in 1989. He pointed out, "Communication for Development is a kind of purposeful communication. In other words, it is a communication process with a special purpose set up by development communicators. In this process, the purpose of Communication for Development is related to the expected changes and

---

[2] Xu Huiming. Research Status of Communication for Development in China [J], Contemporary Communication, 2003 (2): 18-20. 徐晖明. 我国发展传播学研究状况【J】, 当代传播

[3] Chu, G. C. (1986). Development communication in 2000 - future trends and directions. In AMIC-WACC-WIF Consultation on Beyond Development Communication, Singapore, Nov 18-22, 1986. Singapore: Asian Mass Communication Research & Information Centre.

goals."[4] It can be seen that at its very beginning, Communication for Development was actually a discipline with a clear political purpose.

With Communication for Development put into practice, it struggled to adapt to local conditions in Asia, Africa, Latin America and other countries and regions. The main symptoms were: on one hand, development projects were first disseminated to people of Asia, Africa, and Latin America through the media in the mode of "combining rigidity and softness", in accordance with the Diffusion of Innovation Theory. This top-down communication not only failed to achieve the expected diffusion effect, but was resisted to varying degrees in various countries and regions; on the other hand, the cultural diffusion promoted by the interaction of media technology and media content (mainly news) could not adapt to the cultural characteristics of developing countries. After the early theoretical formation of Communication for Development, it encountered a "Waterloo" in practice, which also led to numerous questions in academic circles.

When analyzing the reasons for the incongruity between the theory and practice of early Communication for Development, American scholar Andrew A. Moemeka proposed, "the pioneer researchers in the field of development communication saw economic growth as the final goal of development and geared all their efforts toward using communication to help achieve this goal in the developing societies.[5]" Developed countries' understanding of the media situation in developing countries does not match with the economic foundations of those countries. In other words, when the economic development of developing countries does not reach a certain level, it is difficult for the cultures from developed countries to penetrate and be accepted there. This is the deep, underlying reason why development communication suffered setbacks in the early stages there.

Of course, there is another kind of analysis in the academic world. Professor Zhi Tingrong, a Chinese scholar, commented on early development communication: "'development communication', which

---

[4] Pan Yupeng. Introduction to Development Communication [J]. Journalism Bimonthly潘玉鹏. 发展传播学简介【J】. 新闻大学

[5] Moemeka, Andrew A., Communicating for Development: A New Pan-disciplinary Perspective. United States, State University of New York Press, 1994. 6【美】安德鲁·A.莫米卡（Andrew A.Moemeka）.发展传播学: 历史与观念的回顾【J】.彭娟、程悦,译. 李兴亮, 译校.新闻研究导刊, 2012（12）: 32-34.

has been marked with a deep historical imprint, has finally come to an end... After all, development communication is a theory within a historical landscape with a north-south wealth divide, and an aim to study communication and development in the Third World, and the goal to maintain this status-quo, that is, the international domination of capital.... It is actually derived from colonial theory, even the critical theory school is no exception."[6] Here, Professor Zhi Tingrong said that Communication for Development has "come to its end", because if we look at the pattern of international communication, the function and practice of media acting on society advocated by Communication for Development at that time indeed possessed the meaning of colonial theory. From the view of political economy, early Communication for Development did not play its aspiring role in the development of countries, races, and civilizations.

Later, at the conference in Honolulu, Everett M. Rogers, a major contributor to development communication theory, also had to admit its failure in practice. "Rogers was one of the first scholars to acknowledge the problems of early development communication models and theories, and his 'Communication and Development: The Passing of the Dominant Paradigm' (Rogers, 1976), based on a review and criticism of the modern paradigm, argued that by the mid-1970s it could be concluded with some certainty that the dominant paradigm had disappeared, or at least in Asia, Africa, and Latin America, it had become obsolete as the dominant development model. Rogers pointed out the weaknesses of previous research: first, ignoring social structure variables, second, only the individual is the unit of analysis."[7]

Today, when we stand at the forefront of the 21st century and look back at the theories and practices of developing communication in the 20th century, we will naturally have new insights. To be fair, the ups and downs in the early development of communication studies are not only due to internal reasons. After World War II, global economic development was extremely unbalanced, the political and economic structures were facing huge adjustments, the two poles were competing for hegemony, and the

---

[6] Zhi Tingrong. The Rise and Fall of Development Communication [J]. Journalism Bimonthly. 1996 (4): 4-7. 支庭荣. 由盛转衰的发展传播学【J】. 新闻大学

[7] Han Hong. Research Shifts and Theory Transformation of Development Communication in the Past 30 Years [J]. Chinese Journal of Journalism & Communication, 2014(7): 99-112. 韩鸿. 发展传播学近三十余年的学术流变与理论转型【J】. 国际新闻界

international situation changed dramatically, which made for certain that theories of Communication for Development could not adapt to turbulent social development at that time. At the beginning of its establishment, Communication for Development indeed stood at the forefront of the times and became a trend-setter, but it failed to keep up with rapid changes. Keeping pace with the times is the mainstay of development. However, it cannot therefore be asserted that early development communication failed, because despite this, its contribution to the discipline of communication is still remarkable. Communication for Development reminds people that the media can play a certain role in the uneven development of regions, and theoretically extends a series of important achievements that are still of academic value today.

After Communication for Development was questioned, some scholars from developing countries have made reflections in line with the actual situation based on their local experience. Their main direction is what kind of development communication theory is needed to guide practice at different stages of development.

Chinese scholar Han Hong has conducted a detailed study on this. "Latin American phenomenologist Pasquali believes that knowledge about development needs to be generated through phenomenology, that is, to 'suspend' the notion of development without preconditions, allowing knowledge to be generated in intentional actions within real conditions, not in the study rooms of scholars and the subjective imagination of Western heads of government. This fundamentally criticizes the modernization paradigm that divides the subjective and the objective, the promoters of development and the beneficiaries of development."[8] "A.G. Dagron (2001) argues that the purpose of communication is firstly to promote participatory decision-making, action and 'conscientization', and secondly to help people acquire new knowledge and new skills, and thirdly to use communication to promote better coordination and cooperation between governments and NFOs related to development projects. The above emphasis on the subjectivity and agency of the stakeholder has shifted the focus of development communication theory from information diffusion to participation. Encouraging participation, stimulating critical thinking, and emphasizing 'process rather than result' are regarded as the main tasks

---

[8] Ibid.

of development communication."[9] Kronenburg believes that the premise of participatory development is that human beings have an endogenous ability to create knowledge, and this ability is not the prerogative of experts; it is common among members of society, including being able to identify the needs of community development, diagnose obstacles hindering development, find solutions, and put them into practice.[10] It can be seen that the localization of development communication has already become an important basis for the re-emergence of this discipline.

Viewing culture in combination with material foundations, researching theories based on local practices, and using different methods in different countries according to local conditions - this concept of development communication with the dialectics of Marxist materialism began to become mainstream at the end of the 20th century. Development communication theory has developed from media diffusion to participatory empowerment in various ways, and has gradually moved from a macroscopic national perspective to a community perspective. Professor Hu Yiqing of Nanjing University, China, who has long been devoted to the study of the history of communication studies, has also keenly discovered the fundamental of this change - localization. "Localization of communication studies should be a diverse academic requirement, which can generally be described as critical thinking on the part of Chinese scholars in the process of dialogue with Western academics."[11]

Since the 21st century, the characteristics of localization, community, diversity, and participation have become the key for development communication to return to academic hotspots. China has "started to apply the theoretical framework of development communication in researching the Chinese local situation. Some valuable investigations, and some large-scale projects have been carried out, and fruitful results have been obtained. The main papers in this area are: 'The Influence of Mass Media on Concept Modernization' 大众媒介对观念现代化的影响 (Wang

---

[9] Ibid.

[10] Srinivas R.Melkote, H.Leslie Steeves: Communication for Development in the Third World: Theory and Practices for Empowerment (2nd Edition) [M], New Delhi: SAGE Publications India Pvt. Ltd., 2001.

[11] Hu Yiqing, Chai Ju. Criticism of Development Communication: Rethinking the Localization of Communication [J]. Contemporar Communication, 2013(1): 12-15. 胡翼青,柴菊. 发展传播学批判: 传播学本土化的再思考【J】. 当代传播

Yihong, in Journalism Research Materials, Vol. 50, 1990), 'Research on the Correlation between Urban and Rural Areas in Zhejiang Province' 浙江省城乡的相关性研究 (Min Dahong and Chen Chongshan, in Journalism Research Materials, Vol. 55, 1991), and 'An Empirical Analysis of the Effectiveness of News Communication' 新闻传播效力的一项实证分析 (Zhang Xuehong, in 'Journalism Research Materials' Vol. 57, 1992), etc. Books in this area include *Journalism and China's Modernization* 新闻事业与中国现代化, *Mass Communication and China's Rural Development* 大众传播与中国乡村发展, *People, Media, and Modernization* 人·媒介·现代化, *Communication and National Development* 传播与民族发展, and so on."[12]

Today, most scholars in China and abroad have reached a consensus on the nature of development communication. That is, the study of development communication is to study the process of social development, and its essence lies in the sharing of knowledge, the improvement of abilities, the satisfaction of needs and interests, and is based on different levels of social development, finally realizing the sustainable development of all mankind.[13] In this process, media and information communication technology are important tools to promote social development and social transformation. At different stages of development, the focus of theoretical research of development communication is also different. When a research paradigm of a specific development stage faces a new development period with new difficulties and challenges, problems of inapplicability of theory and insufficient explanatory power will inevitably occur. Therefore, the critique of existing paradigms and the demand for new perspectives, new frameworks, and new concepts also continue to emerge with the progress of the times and social development, which promotes the self-development and evolution of development communication.

---

[12] Xu Huiming. Research Status of Communication for Development in China [J], Contemporary Communication, 2003 (2): 18-20. 徐晖明. 我国发展传播学研究状况【J】, 当代传播

[13] Jan Servaes, Patchanee Malikhao, translated by Zhang Ling. Communication for Social Change. Wuhan: Wuhan University Press, 2014:21 【比】瑟韦斯,【泰】玛丽考. 发展传播学【M】. 张凌,译. 武汉:武汉大学出版社

2. New Development Issues Brought by Communication Technology - Digital Divide

Human society has always faced different problems at different stages of development, from the self-determination of emerging countries after the end of World War II, to the elimination of poverty and disease; from backward countries replicating the development model of developed countries in pursuit of rapid economic growth, to third world countries seeking political independence and exploring multiple development models; from promoting the popularization of education and bridging the knowledge "gap", to demanding the elimination of all forms of inequality, especially differences in the enjoyment of modern scientific and technological achievements and access to information. In addition, there are some fundamental problems that have been running through all stages of development since the beginning of human society, but they will only be presented or exposed in certain ways in different periods or under the catalysis of specific historical events. In the 21st century, development communication continues to study and respond to new topics with the development of the new era.

From the paradigm shift of "dependency theory" to "innovation diffusion" theory, to the proposal and promotion of participatory development concepts and models, the objects of research and analysis of development communication are concentrated on the communication process of development projects in various fields such as economy, society and culture. However, in the process of research and development, and promotion of all new technologies, consideration given to persons with disabilities and groups with different educational levels, attention paid to barrier-free dissemination of information and everyone's right to access information, and the consideration of equal participation of different groups of people in every field of social development and social life - these issues cannot be solved by any top-down development project or by relying on bottom-up participation and promotion. These issues are not new problems faced by development communication in the new era, they are the essence of "human development", and they are permanent yet ever-renewing concerns that have always existed in the development of human civilization. However, the acceleration of scientific and technological development is increasingly surpassing the speed of "human development", making the dichotomy between efficiency and equality more and more difficult to resolve, and therefore digital divide has become a new problem that needs to be solved in the new era.

In recent years, academic circles have paid more and more attention to digital divide. As of April 10, 2022, 4,645 documents were retrieved on CNKI with the search terms of "digital divide"数字鸿沟.

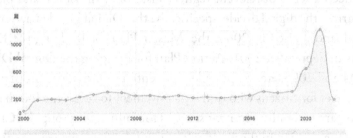

Figure 1 Number of studies on the theme of "digital divide" 数字鸿沟 from 2000 to 2022 (CNKI search results)

Today, "digital divide" has become the focus of social and academic research. The reason for this is the inverse correlation between the ability to use information technology and one's physical capabilities. Information communication is the interaction between human senses and symbols. The main challenge faced by human beings in the information age is that in the absence of changes in the sensory organs, the way in which information symbols are presented is constantly shifting to digitalization and visualization. Information reception needs to rely more and more on human beings' visual sense. For people with visual impairments, this broadens the digital divide by adding greater obstacles and difficulties in obtaining information.

In the period when print media prevailed, knowledge gap mainly came from text symbols, and the way to overcome obstacles was to use touch to liberate vision; in the era of broadcast media, information reception was relatively friendly to visually impaired people, and there were fewer obstacles; TV media came to dominate, the digital divide began to appear and deepen. Because TV media needed to rely on sound and light to present content, for visually impaired groups, there were great obstacles to the reception of information; Moving forward to the Internet-based new media ear, a greater amount of information, especially visual information has explosively appeared, been transmitted, and been stored. For the visually impaired, the more media technology develops, the deeper the digital divide these people face and the more difficult it is to bridge.

In order to bridge the digital divide brought about by the advancement of the media, many countries have begun to introduce corresponding measures and policies, and have made various attempts. "South Korea has introduced a series of relevant regulations, policy measures, and plans to help narrow the digital divide, specifically: the 'Digital Divide Law' enacted in 2001 and revised in 2002, the 'Master Plan for Bridging the Digital Divide' in September 2001, 'Action Plan for Bridging the Digital Divide ' of 2004 and 2005, etc., to provide preferential information infrastructure and services for citizens who find it inconvenient to access the Internet, and provide targeted online content services for vulnerable groups."[14] China is also among the first in the world to carry out development communication research and practice. In protecting the information rights of people with disabilities, the whole Chinese society is making unremitting efforts, from the central government to grassroots organizations, from enterprises to universities, from various institutions to every citizen.

In order to protect the audio-visual cultural rights and promote social participation and cultural sharing of the visually impaired, the School of Television at Communication University of China established the Guangming Cinema project at the end of 2017, making use of the advantages of journalism and communication to produce accessible films for the visually impaired. The School is committed to improving the accessibility of cinemas and researching standards and quality systems for accessible film production. In addition, many local Chinese high-tech brands have always been committed to the development and production of high-tech products that can help people with disabilities to access information.

---

[14] Ren Guisheng. Measures and Lessons of South Korea in Narrowing the Digital Divide [J]. Management World, 2006(7):157-158任贵生. 韩国缩小数字鸿沟的举措及启示【J】. 管理世界

3. Looking at Development Communication from the Perspective of Barrier-free Information

The original intention of technological development should be to better "empower" human beings. Therefore, while improving the efficiency of society, creating more economic benefits, and pursuing GDP, we should also take into account people with disabilities, the elderly, the extremely poor, as well as uneducated groups, and other marginalized groups that have been neglected and have lagged behind. We should have preferential policies for them, taking equality into account. The 2030 Sustainable Development Goals proposed by the United Nations in 2015 after the Millennium Development Goals, promised to "End poverty in all its forms everywhere" and "leave no one behind" in the development process.

Just as Michel Foucault put forward the notion that "knowledge is power", in the context of the rapid development of emerging contemporary technologies, "information is power", and the uneven access to information has led to a new form of "disparity between the rich and the poor" on a global scale. With the progress of society and the development of civilization, people's awareness of rights is also awakening. The pursuit of development is no longer just to eliminate poverty and disease, protect basic human rights, etc., but to improve everyone's "happiness index". With the rapid progress of science and technology, the social landscape has undergone earth-shaking changes, and development communication has also shown many new changes and new developments in terms of research objects, development goals, communication methods, and theoretical paradigms.

The research object of development communication is no longer just the communication and promotion of one development project after another, or bottom-up social participation, but the renewal and reshaping of mindset from decision-making centers of countries and organizations to each participant of society. This is a structural and constructivist change.

The development goals of human society have also risen from eliminating poverty and disease, eliminating gender discrimination, and protecting the environment to more diverse, three-dimensional and deepened sustainable development goals such as promoting all-round development of people and improving people's "happiness index". "Empowerment" by technology and "poverty alleviation" by knowledge have become the most urgent development goals to be achieved. Countries around the world have begun to shift from the improvement of infrastructure to the promotion of barrier-free information in their response to the issues involving population aging society and people with disabilities. The development doesn't stop at caring for and satisfying the physical and material needs of special groups, but also pays more attention to the satisfaction of their intellectual needs.

"In 1998, U.S. President Bill Clinton signed into law an amendment to the Labor Rehabilitation Act of 1973. Section 508 to the Act stipulates that electronic and information technology products developed or purchased by the federal government and department must be accessible to people with disabilities."[15] In the same year, the Spanish government introduced the Computer Accessibility Regulations; in 2003, the Netherlands enacted the Internet Accessibility Regulations; in 2004, Switzerland also enacted Accessibility Regulations for Government and Public Utility[16]. In 2005, the second phase of the World Summit on the Information Society (WSIS) adopted the Tunis Commitment, declaring: "We shall strive unremittingly, therefore, to promote universal, ubiquitous, equitable and affordable access to ICTs, including universal design and assistive technologies, for all people, especially those with disabilities, everywhere, to ensure that the benefits are more evenly distributed between and within societies, and to bridge the digital divide in order to create digital opportunities for all and benefit from the potential offered by ICTs for development."

Since the beginning of the 21st century, China has paid attention to information accessibility, and has attached great importance to the convenience for people with disabilities in obtaining information. The report of the 17th National Congress of the Communist Party of China emphasized the importance to "carry forward the spirit of humanitarianism, develop the cause for people with disabilities, promote the work of barrier-free information, and minimize or even eliminate the barriers in the

---

[15] Qian Xiaolong, Zou Xia. Overview of the Development of Information Accessibility in the United States: Interpretation of Section 508 [J]. Research in Electronic Education, 2007(12): 88-93. 钱小龙，邹霞．美国信息无障碍事业发展概况：Section 508解读【J】．电化教育研究

[16] Yang Fei. Information Accessibility Rights of Persons with Disabilities [J]. Journal of Henan University of Economics and Law, 2013(2): 118-124. 杨飞．论残疾人的信息无障碍权【J】．河南财经政法大学学报

exchange of information among people with disabilities, as well as between people with disabilities and able-bodied people. It is a sure requirement for the new era as it develops to a certain stage, a concrete manifestation of social and humanistic care, and it is also an important part in building a well-off society in an all-round manner and a harmonious socialist society." In 2004, China held the first Information Accessibility Forum, which has thus far been successfully held 16 times, continuously striving for the attention and investment of the whole society in the cause of information accessibility, because "the cause of information accessibility can help people with disabilities to cross the digital divide, share in the information civilization, and it is an important part of safeguarding the rights and interests of persons with disabilities, and is pertinent to the well-being of millions of persons with disabilities." [17] At the 14th Information Accessibility Forum held in July 2019, the "White Paper on the Development of China's Information Accessibility (2019)" was officially released, which included in-depth discussions of the models and methods of promoting information accessibility in China, analysis of future development trend of information accessibility, and put forward policy recommendations to promote information accessibility in China.

Chinese scholar Pan Yupeng summarized the communication channels and the functions of development communication as follows: "In a developing country, what is the role of communication channels? There are roughly four points: (1) Dissemination of knowledge to inform people of major events, opportunities, dangers, and changes in communities, nations, and the world; (2) provide a forum in which to speak about national or community life; (3) teach skills and ideas that people need to make their lives better; (4) create and maintain a base of public opinion."[18]

"Information accessibility" is a new goal in the new stage of human society development. The realization of such development goals has also undergone many changes in the way of communication, and the composition and emphasis of communication methods. In addition to the communication power of mass media, the realization of new goals also

---

[17] The 11th China Information Accessibility Forum was held in Beijing [J]. Research on Disabled Persons, 2015(4): 7. 第十一届中国信息无障碍论坛在北京举行【J】. 残疾人研究
[18] Pan Yupeng. Introduction to Development Communication [J]. Journalism Bimonthly, 1989(4): 47-49. 潘玉鹏. 发展传播学简介【J】. 新闻大学

needs to again rely on the development of interpersonal communication. For example, in the traditional social landscape, the inheritance of culture and the transmission of knowledge are achieved through one-way communication from parents, elders, and teachers to students; while in the contemporary information society, the younger generation is more capable than the older generation in quickly and efficiently absorbing new knowledge, acquiring new information, and mastering new skills. Interpersonal communication plays a more important role than in the past in promoting development, and has seen a change in intergenerational direction.

Technology "empowerment" and knowledge "poverty alleviation" not only require the United Nations, international organizations, and governments around the world to better perform their respective responsibilities in the field of development, but also require the awakening of the sense of responsibility of enterprises, communities, and in fact, all people. In the information society, every technology research and development institution should take into account the level of benefit and acceptability for different groups, including persons with disabilities and the elderly, when developing and designing new technologies. The same goes for information producers when producing and processing content. Theories and paradigms of development communication, based on localized studies, also need to improve the explanatory power of new phenomena and trends including "information accessibility", and the ability to predict future social development, in order to rejuvenate themselves in the new era.

(Hu Fang, Researcher, Master's Supervisor, Communication University of China; Liu Wen, Lecturer, Postdoctoral Fellow, School of Television, Communication University of China)

THE ROLE OF BARRIER-FREE FILMS ON THE "VIEWING RIGHTS" OF THE VISUALLY IMPAIRED — A CASE STUDY ON CUC'S GUANGMING CINEMA

Daniel Long Zhang, Sisy Xijing
Zhao, and Chenshan Rong

Abstract: In a recent barrier-free communication practice in China, Guangming Cinema uses audio translation to help restore the enjoyment of watching movies for the visually impaired to stimulate their socialization process. By working together with both academia and industry, this paper uses case studies, questionnaire surveys, and interviews to understand how these Audio Description (AD) movies help the visually impaired audience have an equal experience to any able-bodied person, resulting in a positive effect on their social life and cultural understanding. The Guangming Cinema also makes use of advanced media technology to make sure that the visually impaired can have access to these resources conveniently.

Keywords: Barrier-Free Communication, Audio Description, Socialization

Introduction

Every day, people with disabilities face barriers that restrict them from being full participants in society like others. For those who are visually impaired, they are facing even larger obstacles in life. For example, they cannot move freely without others' help. They cannot go to general schools, or enjoy entertainment like sighted people.

The United Nations indicates accessibility as one of the basic human rights. It also states that people with disabilities should have equal rights to social and cultural activities. As one of the most popular cultural activities today, movies have become an increasingly important enjoyment of modern life.

The film industry has been booming in China in recent years. Since movie box offices took off in 2006, China has become the second-largest film market in the world beginning in 2012.[1] In 2018, China's box office receipts hit a new record at 8.87 billion USD, with domestic films' recorded receipts accounting for 62% of total sales.[2]

Yet people who are visually impaired have very few opportunities to enjoy the movies, which with economic progress, is an ever-growing market. With more and more advanced technology and awareness concerning the visually impaired, the Guangming Cinema decided to provide barrier-free movies for the visually impaired people in China. This paper uses case studies, questionnaire surveys, and interviews to understand the meaning of barrier-free films to the visually impaired. How does the Guangming Cinema satisfy their movie appreciation needs? What difference can barrier-free films bring to their life?

---

[1] BBC News. China Becomes World's Second-Biggest Movie Market. [EB/OL]. (2013-03-22) [2019-02-20] https://www.bbc.com/news/business-21891631.
[2] Tan, Jason. Another Record Year for China's Box Office, But Growth Slows. [EB/OL]. （2019-01-02) [2019-02-21] https://www.caixinglobal.com/2019-01-02/another-record-year-for-chinas-box-office-101365697.html.

Understanding Barrier-Free Film

Rights of the Disabled

On October 15, 1984, through the union of the International Federation of the Blind (IFB) and the World Council for the Welfare of the Blind (WCWB), the World Blind Union (WBU) was formed in Riyadh, Saudi Arabia. It represented the 253 million visually impaired persons in 190 countries, with the aim to make a world where visually impaired people can participate fully in any aspect of life they choose.[3]

The Convention on the Rights of Persons with Disabilities was adopted in 2006 and came into force in 2008.[4] It was the first international treaty to specifically determine the rights of persons with disabilities. In Article 21, it announced the rights of receiving information, encouraging the mass media and other information providers to make their service accessible to people with disabilities. Article 30 states that persons with disabilities have the right to equally take part in cultural life, not only to have but also to enjoy access to television programs, films, theater, and other cultural activities in accessible formats.[5]

The current *Law of the People's Republic of China on the Protection of Disabled Persons* was adopted at the 17th Meeting of the Standing Committee of the Seventh National People's Congress on December 28, 1990. In 1994, the *Regulation on the Education of the Disabled* was introduced. In 2007, China became a Party member to The Convention on the Rights of Persons with Disabilities. Henceforth, China has released several regulations to protect the rights of the disabled. In 2007, the *Regulation on the Employment of the Disabled* was released. In 2012, the State Council published the *Regulation on the Construction of Barrier-free Environments*. In 2017, the *Regulations on Disability Prevention and Recovery of the Disabled* was released.

[3] WBU. About WBU [EB/OL]. (n.d.) [2019-02-20] http://www.worldblindunion.org/English/about-wbu/Pages/default.aspx.
[4] OHCHR. Human Rights of Persons with Disabilities [EB/OL]. (n.d.) [2019-02-20] https://www.ohchr.org/en/issues/disability/pages/disabilityindex.aspx.
[5] OHCHR. Convention on the rights of persons with disabilities [EB/OL]. (n.d.) [2019-02-20] https://www.ohchr.org/EN/HRBodies/CRPD/Pages/ConventionRightsPersonsWithDisabilities.aspx#21.

Movies' Function in Socialization

Socialization is a two-way interaction between people and society. It not only refers to the process of people obtaining their unique personality and picking up various social norms, but also includes how people exert influence on the society. As Xi Congqing defined, one's socialization includes learning knowledge, techniques, norms, and other social culture, adapting to the society as well as influencing society and creating new culture.[6]

According to the theory of broad and narrow socialization, there are seven principle socialization agents—family, peers, school, community, the legal system, the cultural belief system, and the media.[7] As Tan wrote in *Mass Communication: Theories and Research*, mass media is an important socialization agent, and it shapes our attitudes, values, behaviors, and perceptions of social reality.[8]

Since the foundation of Communication, many scholars have done plenty of studies on the functions of mass media. In a book published in 1948, *The Structure and Function of Communication in Society*, Harold Lasswell posits that there are mainly three functions of mass media - social environment surveillance, social relation adjustment, and social heritage inheritor.[9] In 1959, from the perspective of sociology, Charles Wright added entertainment as the fourth function of mass media.[10] In *Mass communication, popular taste, and organized social action*, Lazarsfeld and Merton put forward three mass media functions—status conferral, social norms enforcement, and narcotizing dysfunction.[11]

---

[6] Xi Congqing (1993). *Sociology of The Disabled* [M]. Beijing: Huaxia Press, P57-59.

[7] Arnett, Jeffrey Jensen (1995). *Adolescents' Uses of Media for Self-Socialization* [J]. In *Journal of Youth and Adolescence*, Vol. 24, No. 5, P519–533.

[8] Tan, Alexis S. (1985). *Mass Communication: Theories and Research* [M]. London: Macmillan Publishing Company. P243.

[9] Lasswell, Harold. (1948). *The Structure and Function of Communication in Society* [M]. New York: Harper & Bros. P217.

[10] Fourie, Pieter Jacobus (2007). *Media Studies: Media History, Media and Society* [M]. Cape Town: Juta and Company Ltd. P186.

[11] Lazarsfeld, P. F. & Merton, R. K. (2004). *Mass Communication, Popular Taste and Organized Social Action* [M], Peters, J. D. & Simonson, P. (Eds.) In *Mass Communication and American Social Thought: Key Texts, 1919-1968*, New York: Rowman & Littlefield Publishers, Inc., P230.

As one of the most popular art forms, there were also research studies on the functions of movies. According to Liu Ming, movies can nurture the human mind, increase the audience's moral and aesthetic level, and form ideological acknowledgment.[12] Movies are considered as "equipment for living" as the audience applies its understanding of the films into everyday life.[13] Plenty of research studies are done about movie effects. Movies can exert influence on people's behavior. Many scholars studied the relationship between violence in movies and in reality. Experiments in psychology found that media violence increases real aggression in a short period.[14] Watching movies can also change people's beliefs in the real world. When exposed to certain narration, people's attitudes see significant changes.[15] When physically disabled teenagers watch inspirational movies, their self-esteem will be raised, and they will feel less anxious when interacting with other people.[16] As most people do not interact with people with disabilities, movie representations about them will shape people's understanding of life of persons with disabilities.[17] Going to the cinema itself is good for people. The visual stimulation of films can provoke an emotive response which is therapeutic and promotes well-being.[18]

As adolescents are at the crossroad of teenage years and adulthood, their socialization attracts many scholars. Birkök found that in terms of transferring knowledge, movies are the most effective tools.[19] Arnett studied

[12] Liu, Ming (2015). *On Movies' Social Functions* [J]. In *Media*, Issue 1, P75–76.

[13] Young, Stephen Dine (2000). *Movies as equipment for living: A developmental analysis of the importance of film in everyday life* [J]. In *Critical Studies in Media Communication*, Vol 7, Issue 4. P447–468.

[14] Dahl, G., & DellaVigna, S. (2009). *Does Movie Violence Increase Violent Crime?* [J] In *The Quarterly Journal of Economics*, Vol 124, Issue 2, P677–734.

[15] Igartua, J. J., & Barrios, I. (2012). *Changing Real-World Beliefs with Controversial Movies: Processes and Mechanisms of Narrative Persuasion* [J]. In *Journal of Communication*, Vol 62, Issue 3, P514–531.

[16] Jin, Haixin (2009). *Using Films to Conduct Psychological Intervention on Physically Disabled Teenagers - Take Inspirational Films About the Disabled as an Example* [J]. In *Art Education*, Issue 11, P60-63.

[17] Harris, Leslie (2002). *Disabled Sex and the Movies* [J]. In *Disability Studies Quarterly*, Vol 22, Issue 4, P144-162.

[18] Uhrig, S. C. Noah (2005). *Cinema is Good for You: The Effects of Cinema Attendance on Self Reported Anxiety or Depression and "happiness"*. ISER Working Paper Series, 2005–14, Institute for Social and Economic Research.

[19] Mehmet Cüneyt Birkök, (2008). *Alternate Media Usage in Education as a Socialization Tool: Movies* [J], In *Journal of Human Sciences*, Vol. 5, No. 2, P1-12.

how adolescents use media for self-socialization and found that adolescents have greater control over the choices of media than that compared with other socialization sources such as family and friends, as they can choose the materials that suit them best.[20] Political socialization is also one of the themes examined by scholars. Mass media provides content that is essential to develop political values.[21] Active citizenship is an indirect result of news media use, interpersonal communication, and social participation.[22] As one of the mass media, movies are the most enjoyable and understandable political socialization tool.[23]

People with disabilities, as a special group of social members, have unique characteristics when it comes to socialization. First of all, due to the various physical deficits, their socialization is much more difficult than that of able-bodied people. The socialization process can also be very complicated due to different social environments as well as their own attitudes. People with disabilities show higher motivation to integrate their own ability to serve the society in order to feel a sense of value.[24]

For those who have disabilities, the goals of socialization are mainly in five domains—acquire living skills, psychological adaptation, set life goals, adopt social norms, and form social roles.[25]

From Barrier-free to Audio Translation

"Barrier-free" or "accessibility" mainly describe the condition that public facilities serve people with disabilities in everyday life. It was not until the 1960s, with the efforts of international organizations and social groups fighting for the fundamental rights of people with disabilities in Europe and America that the concept of "barrier-free" began to take

---

[20] Arnett, Jeffrey Jensen (1995). *Adolescents' Uses of Media for Self-Socialization* [J]. In *Journal of Youth and Adolescence*, Vol. 24, No. 5, P519–533.

[21] Hanna Adoni, (1979) *The Functions of Mass Media in the Political Socialization of Adolescents*. In *Communication Research*, Vol. 6, No. 1, P84–106.

[22] McLeod, Jack M. (2000). *Media and Civic Socialization of Youth* [J]. In *Journal of Adolescent Health*, Vol.27, No. 2, P45–51.

[23] Song Zhen (2010). *The Features and Function of Political Socialization in Movie Media* [J]. In *Hebei Academic Journal*, Issue 2, P236-238.

[24] Xi Congqing, (1993). *Sociology of The Disabled* [M]. Beijing: Huaxia Press, P59-61.

[25] Xi Congqing, (1993). *Sociology of The Disabled* [M]. Beijing: Huaxia Press, P70-74.

shape.[26] It took root in the concept of "normalization" raised by N.E. Bank-Mikkelsen of Denmark, who proposed "to let the mentally retarded obtain an existence as close to the normal as possible".[27]

In the area of communication, the term "barrier-free" or "accessibility" means that everyone in any circumstances can obtain and use information equally, conveniently, and without obstacles. In a world where media is omnipresent, "cinematography... has become one of the most widely-spread and influential form of arts".[28] Yet, people who are physically disabled have difficulties gaining access to it. There are different ways to help people with disabilities appreciate cinematography. One of the efforts to gain media accessibility is through audiovisual translation (AVT), which is also referred to as film translation, TV translation, screen translation, multimedia translation, and many others.[29]

In actuality, AVT was not initially designed for people with disabilities. It flourished when the number of TV channels, programs, dramas, film festivals, and other media or media activities increased exponentially. As mentioned by Diaz-Cintas and Anderman (2008), "Traditionally ignored in academic exchanges, subtitling for the deaf and hard-of-hearing (SDH) and audio description for the blind and the partially sighted (AD) are becoming part of our daily audiovisual landscape and attracting the interest of many scholars and practitioners.[30]" At the same time, people witnessed rapid development in the field of media accessibility for those with sensory impairments.

[26] How the Concept of "Barrier-Free" Comes into Being [J]. In Outlook, Issue 17, P20.

[27] NIRJE B. (1969). The Normalization Principle and its Human Management Implications [M]. In KUGEL R. & WOLFENSBERGER W.Changing Patterns in Residential Services for the Mentally retarded. Washington, D.C.: President's Committee on Mental Retardation. (1969-01-10)

[28] Matkivska, Nataliia (2014). Audiovisual Translation: Conception, Types, Characters' Speech and Translation Strategies Applied [J]. In Kalbų Studijos, No. 25, P38-44.

[29] CHO S-E. Basic Concepts in the Theory of Audiovisual Translation [EB/OL]. (2014-06-21) [2019-02-20]. Hankuk University of Foreign Studies. http://builder.hufs.ac.kr/user/ibas/No31/15.pdf .2014:P377-396.

[30] Cintas, J. D., & Anderman, G. (Eds.) (2008). Audiovisual Translation: Language Transfer on Screen [M]. Hampshire: Palgrave Macmillan, P2.

Previous Studies on Audio Translation

Most of the work in the field of AVT had been in the discipline of translation. In translation studies, researchers tend to provide the theoretical background and frameworks for performing AVT, from linguistic perspectives to managing possible strategies to overcome current challenges, "while some other areas of AVT remain unexplored"[31], such as translation for the visually impaired.

For people with visual disability, they have obvious difficulties accessing artistic entertainment forms such as movies and operas. The sounds and dialogues they perceive are not enough for them to fully experience the film or play. In order to help them associate the image to what they hear, audio description (AD) was invented. AD or descriptive video service (DVS) is a more recent development within the concept of AVT. It can be described as "an additional narration that fits in the silences between dialogue and describes action, body language, facial expressions and anything that will help people with visual impairment follow what is happening on screen or on stage" [32].

Since visually impaired people are not able to see or see clearly, audio means a lot to them. Taiwanese scholar Chao Ya-ly investigated media usage and motivation of the visually impaired in Taiwan through questionnaire surveys and phone interviews. She found that no matter the degree of visual impairment, the motivation to use broadcast media is comparable to those with normal sight.[33] Similarly, in 1994, a nation-wide interview was carried out in the United Kingdom involving 320 visually impaired people. The results showed that visually impaired people were keen to keep abreast of the news, and audio cassettes played an important role. They not only provide information, but also companionship, purpose, and meaning.[34]

[31] Hernández-Bartolomé, A., & Mendiluce-Cabrera, G. (2004). *Audesc: Translating Images into Words for Spanish Visually Impaired People* [J]. In *Meta: Journal des traducteurs / Meta: Translators' Journal*, Vol 49, Issue 2, P264–277.

[32] Cintas, J. D., & Anderman, G. (Eds.). (2008). *Audiovisual Translation: Language Transfer on Screen* [M]. Hampshire: Palgrave Macmillan, P6.

[33] Chao, Ya-Ly. (2001). *A Survey on the Media Uses and Motivations of the Visually Impaired in Taiwan* [J]. In *Mass Communication Research*, Vol 66, P61–96.

[34] Marsland, D., Leoussi, A. S., & Norcross, P. (1994). *Disability Abated: Audio-Cassettes for the Visually Impaired* [J]. In *Journal of the Royal Society of Health*, Vol 114, Issue 1, P29–32.

There are also studies examining how helpful AD can be to the visually impaired. In a field trial of Audio Described Television, conducted by RNIB in 1994, researchers examined television viewing patterns of a sample of 100 visually impaired people to determine the barriers they meet in accessing television, and the impact of AD in removing these barriers. The results indicated that AD significantly improved television accessibility by enabling visually impaired people to "watch" programs which had previously been inaccessible. The partially sighted people's experience of regularly "watched" programs was also improved.[35]

Emilie Schmeidler and Corinne Kirchneer examined the impact of AD by involving 111 adults with blindness to watch television science programs with and without AD. Research results indicated that AD made the program more enjoyable, interesting, and informative.[36]

Researchers also examined how AD with different traits can have varied influence on its audience. Susanne Johanna Jekat, along with two other researchers, used the semantic differential method to compare visually impaired subjects' reception to AD films with those of the sighted viewers to the corresponding original versions. They found that if the AD is concrete, the two target audiences often perceive the main characters and the film concepts in similar ways.[37]

In mainland China, both the practice and academic study of AVT and AD are relatively slow. Few academic research studies have been done. According to the study by Li Dongxiao, there is no AD service provided by television stations in mainland China, and the demands for media access of the visually impaired are largely neglected.[38] In another study, Li Dongxiao and Pan Xianghui investigated the development of barrier-free films in China. The results showed that although barrier-free film has seen

---

[35] Pettitt, B., Sharpe, K., & Cooper, S. (1996). *AUDETEL: Enhancing Television for Visually Impaired People* [J]. In *British Journal of Visual Impairment*, Vol 14, Issue 2, P48–52.

[36] Kirchner, C., & Schmeidler, E. (2001). *Adding Audio Description: Does It Make a Difference?* [J] In *Journal of Visual Impairment & Blindness*, Vol 95, Issue 4, P197–212.

[37] Jekat, S. J., Prontera, D., & Bale, R. J. (2015). *On the Perception of Audio Description: developing a model to compare films and their audio described versions* [J]. In *Trans-kom*, Vol 8, Issue 2, P446–464.

[38] Li, Dongxiao. (2013). *The Present Situation of Barrier-free Development of China's Television, Problems and Suggestions* [J]. In *Modern Communication*, Vol 35, Issue 5, P7–13.

great improvements, it still faces obstacles like imbalanced development, lack of supply, low production standards, etc.[39]

Visually Impaired People in China and Guangming Cinema

Status Quo of the Visually Impaired in China

China has the largest population of people with disabilities in the world. According to a report released in 2018, there are more than 85 million people with disabilities in China, of which more than 17.5 million are visually impaired.[40] Since older people are the fastest-growing age group in China, the number of blind and visually impaired people is expected to increase. Their demand for audiovisual arts, like movies, is non-negligible, and should be placed on the agendas of the government and social service groups.

With the development of economy, increasing effort has been devoted to help the visually impaired live a better life. Achievements can be seen in city services, education, employment, rehabilitation, etc. News coverage of the visually impaired has also increased rapidly, which indicates that the Chinese society is paying more attention to this group of people.

---

[39] Pan, X. & Li, D. (2013). *Development and Prospect of Barrier-free Films in China* [J]. In *Zhejiang Academic Journal*, Issue 4, P188–198.

[40] ASSEMBLES G. (2018). China Country Report to World Blind Union Asia Pacific, General Assembly, Ulaanbaatar, Mongolia [EB/OL]. (n.d.) [2019-02-21] http://wbuap.org/archives/1416.

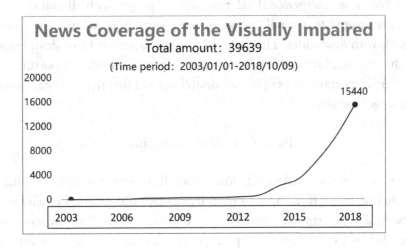

China Association of the Blind (CAB) puts much emphasis on information accessibility. It set up the Information Accessibility Promotion Committee, and took the lead in drafting several national standards on information accessibility, such as in mobile terminals and banking services. CAB has also organized trainings in computer and smart phone use each year to promote the information technology knowledge of the visually impaired. It also values the role of the Internet to provide services for visually impaired persons.

Despite these efforts, compared with the large number of visually impaired persons, this group of people is still facing many barriers in their social life. The first problem is education. According to a national survey in 2006, the illiteracy rate of the visually impaired who are 15 years or older was 43.29%.[41] Even those who enter schools for the blind cannot properly communicate with the non-visually impaired. Secondly, visually impaired persons do not have many choices in terms of their career. 63% of the visually impaired learn Chinese massage skills to earn a living. Most of them do not have high salaries. The third problem is participation in public life. Although the visually impaired form a large group in China, people do not usually see them in public space. Many of them do not want to cause trouble for other people, so they try to stay at home as much as

---

[41] China Disabled Federation. *Thirteenth "Five-Year Plan" for Disabled Illiterate Young Adults* [EB/OL]. http://www.cdpf.org.cn/hcxm/ggjy/201801/t20180105_616106.shtml

possible. The interpersonal relationships of people with disabilities are usually limited to a small enclosure—to their family members or other people with disabilities. Their activities usually occur within a small range of their village, town, or city. Thus, creating communication opportunities are very important for people with disabilities as a first step to engage with the larger society.

Barrier-free Movies in China

Compared with America and other European countries, China's (including Hong Kong and Taiwan) barrier-free films started much later. The Audio Description Development Association from Taiwan was only founded in 2002.[42] It aims to promote the development of AD with the help of AD technology and professionals from the culture, communication, and other related fields. In 2009, the first volunteer group of movie guides for the visually impaired was set up in Hong Kong by the Hong Kong Society for the Blind (HKSB). It organized its first film seminar in 2010, with around 130 people participating.[43]

It was not until the beginning of the 21st century that barrier-free movies for the visually impaired made their debut in mainland China. At first it was not in the form of film, but in the form of narration. China Braille Press organized volunteers to narrate movies to the visually impaired every weekend beginning in 2003.[44] In 2005, Xinmu Cinema was founded by Wang Weili and his wife in Beijing.[45] It was a small-scale cinema located in a courtyard home. Volunteers came every weekend to narrate alongside the films. In other cities like Shanghai, Guangzhou, Wuhan, and Hong

---

[42] Audio Description Development Association [EB/OL]. http://www.dvs.org.tw/.

[43] HKSB. Audio Descriptive Movie Show for the Visually Impaired at AMC [EB/OL]. (n.d.)[2019-02-21] https://www.hksb.org.hk/en/newsDetail/106561/%E8% A7%86%E9%9A%9C%E4%BA%BA%E5%A3%AB%E7%94%B5%E5%BD%B1 %E5%AF%BC%E8%B5%8F%E6%96%B0%E9%A2%86%E5%9F%9F%E7%A0 %B4%E5%A4%A9%E8%8D%92%E9%A6%96%E6%AC%A1%E8%BF%9B%E 5%86%9B%E7%94%B5%E5%BD%B1%E9%99%A2%E6%AC%A3%E8%B5% 8F%E7%94%B5%E5%BD%B1/.

[44] Ma, Bo (2016). *On Barrier-free Movies* [J]. In *Contemporary TV*, Issue 5, P110–111.

[45] CHENG L, CHU Y. & ZHANG M Z. Feature: Chinese Cinema Lights up World for Blind Movie-goers [EB/OL]. (2018-02-07) [2019-02-21] http://www.xinhuanet.com/english/2018-02/07/c_136956808.htm.

Kong, volunteer activities of narrating movies also emerged. However, there was no AD film then. The first AD film *Examination 1977* was released in the Shanghai Library in 2009. On its release day, the first movie studio for barrier-free movies was established. In 2011, China Braille Library was founded. One department was specifically set up for AD film making and had released 116 barrier-free films. However, because it was only a library with few communication channels, the influence of those films was limited. As of today, out of the 34 provinces in China, only about 10 provinces provide barrier-free movie service with government support.

Today, there are still many obstacles in the development of barrier-free film for the visually impaired. From the central government to the local government, there is no identified department looking into barrier-free film production currently. The development of barrier-free film is unbalanced. The more developed a place is, the more resources able to be devoted to developing barrier-free films, which usually means more and better-quality film production. There are also no national standards for barrier-free films. Although there is support from the state level, the barrier-free industry has not been well-developed. It is led mostly by the government or NGOs. One of the problems is the lack of investment as a result of little market engagement, which generates even fewer barrier-free movies. There are also problems with copyright. Movies whose copyright can be easily obtained are usually old movies. It is difficult for the visually impaired to get access to the latest movies. In addition, the quality of barrier-free movies is not high due to the lack of professionals producing them. Most of the barrier-free movie makers are volunteers and only a few of them have professional training.

Guangming Cinema

The Guangming Cinema is a project co-sponsored by the Communication University of China (CUC), Beijing Gehua CATV Network co. Ltd (Gehua), and Dongfang Jiaying Cinema Line Media co. Ltd. (Dongfang). This project aims to produce barrier-free films for the visually impaired by combining the resources of both academia and the industry.

CUC is a state university directly affiliated with the Ministry of

Education of China. It is famous in information and communication studies, and is known as the cradle of radio and television media talents in China. CUC has high-quality talents in the fields of sound recording, broadcasting, and audio production. It also has leading capabilities in radio/video research and production. Gehua is a state-owned listed company recognized by the Beijing municipal government, and it is the only cable network operator in Beijing. Dongfang is a relatively young company, with Gehua as its largest shareholder. As a new media company, Dongfang works with 16 other network operators and high-technology companies such as Alibaba Group to combine the Internet with radio and television networks, and to bring film products to thousands of households.

The Guangming Cinema was officially launched in February 2018. The first five barrier-free movies were made as sample films, including *Qian Xuesen*, *Wolf Warriors 2*, and *The Founding of an Army*. On the 28th National Handicapped Day on 20 May, 2018, 50 visually impaired persons were invited to be the first audiences. By May 13, 2019, the project completed audio translations of 104 films and has donated all the films to 19 special schools for the blind, 20 blind associations, and 68 libraries. More than 10 charity screenings were carried out all around China. By the end of 2021, the project completed audio translations of 416 films and has screened the films for over 2 million visually impaired people in 31 provinces, autonomous regions, and municipalities in China.

There are three main service modes of the Guangming Cinema. The first one is through HiTV. As a giant network operator, Gehua provides network platforms in Beijing and Xinjiang, and owns the China TV Cinema line. A sub-channel of Guangming Cinema will be added when the quantity of barrier-free films reaches a certain amount. With the help of intelligent voice remote control, the visually impaired can access barrier-free films through HiTV at home. In the near future, Gehua will also be cooperating with internet giants such as Baidu and Iqiyi to broaden the access options for barrier-free films. The second form of service mode is through community cinemas. Supported by Beijing's municipal government, Gehua has built several community cinemas in Beijing, each of which has an area of about 80 to 150 square meters. With some technical renovation, these cinemas can screen barrier-free films. The third way is through audio applications. By cooperating with professional audio apps such as Himalaya FM, a new avenue of Guangming Cinema will be established. Visually impaired people can then gain access to these films without any payment.

Grant Viewing Rights

Large number, high illiteracy, low income, and low social participation are four characteristics of visually impaired people in China. Guangming Cinema aims to provide them with equal chances for art appreciation as well as more social engagement opportunities.

When a person loses sight, there are three kinds of barriers he or she faces. The first barrier is action, or movement. It is difficult to live in a world where you cannot tell where you are, where objects are, and where other people are. The second barrier lies in obtaining information. 80% of the information we receive from our environment is visual.[46] Being unable to see means living in a desert of information, shielded in a castle built by darkness. The third barrier is cultural. Without information, the visually impaired cannot understand the culture although they are living in it. Using technical and artistic means, visual cultural implications can be transformed into information that the visually impaired can use to understand the mainstream culture and interact with it. Just like tactile paving leads to every corner of the city, there should also be cultural tactile paving to lead the visually impaired to the palace of art.

According to Maslow's hierarchy of needs theory, there are five tiers of human needs, namely physiological, safety, love and belonging, esteem, and self-actualization.[47] Although China has made great achievements in poverty reduction, people's basic needs still need to be fulfilled. Most needs of the visually impaired are psychological, like intimacy, friendship, prestige, etc. Watching films with friends and family is a common activity in our social life. More chances for communication and social participation should be created for the visually impaired.

---

[46] Kaplan, Melvin (2006). *Seeing Through New Eyes: Changing the Lives of Children with Autism, Asperger Syndrome and Other Developmental Disabilities Through Vision Therapy* [M]. London: Jessica Kingsley Publishers, P15.
[47] MCLEOD S. Maslow's Hierarchy of Needs [EB/OL]. (2018-12-20)[2019-02-25] https://www.simplypsychology.org/maslow.html

Barrier-free to Appreciate Arts

Although many efforts to help the visually impaired enjoy films were made before, the majority of them still seldom have the chance to see films. According to one volunteer student, Geng Chuqing, an old lady was so excited to see a film for the first time in her life, that she woke up very early that day and could not fall asleep again.

After the first five barrier-free films' production, two surveys were carried out. The first one was done after the screening of the film *Wolf Warriors 2* to retired visually impaired people. The second one was done in the special school for the blind in Beijing.

These two groups of people were identified because of the difference in their usage of Braille. Most of the retired audience cannot read or seldom read Braille, while the students have learned Braille and obtain most of their information from it.

After listening to the movie, 96% of the retired audience said that they can totally understand or understand most of the movie. 83.3% of the students can totally understand or understand most of the movie. This shows that with narration, they can get much more information from the film. During group interviews, many visually impaired people also mentioned that when they listen to the same film without narration, they usually feel confused about the relationships and actions of the characters. While watching barrier-free films, they do not feel lost.

When asked how much they enjoyed watching the film in AD, all the retired people said they quite enjoyed it or enjoyed it very much. 83.3% of the students said they enjoyed it.

When asked whether the narration spoiled the fun of the movie, 65% of the retired audience indicated that they loved the narration parts best. 68.5% of the students loved the dialogues while 66.67% of them loved the narration.

The Guangming Cinema enabled participants to do the following three things to make sure that the visually impaired can truly feel that they are watching movies.

Firstly, the fundamental and also the core value of Guangming Cinema is the pursuit of an equal aesthetic experience. Before the existence of barrier-free movies, radio stations used to broadcast edited versions of movie recordings. It is an edited version because it usually alters the film length and adjusts original scenes and audio. Hence, a lot of information was deleted. In order to ensure that the visually impaired have the same aesthetic experience, the movie lengths under the Guangming Cinema were kept exactly the same as the original ones. As a public welfare program, Guangming Cinema tried its best to "add" information instead of "delete", so that the visually impaired can experience the movies as much as normal people.

Secondly, professional skills are the key to successful AD films. A good command of basic visual language is the prerequisite for audiovisual translation. While doing audio translations for a 120-minute movie, the script of narration should be accurate to one second, so that the narration would not overlap with dialogues, synchronized voice, and other important soundtracks. The narration transcript of a movie would consist of dozens of pages, some even longer than 100 pages. Every single paragraph is carefully weighed and considered. According to one of the volunteers, Li Yingyi, her team discussed for a long time even on how to describe a pile of money. Should they say the money piled up to half a meter high or as long as one's arm, or as high as 10 bricks. Besides, movies of different genres and artistic styles should be treated differently. Action movies and war movies like *Wolf Warriors 2*, should add more detailed descriptions of the scenes. While watching these kinds of movies, visual representation is an important experience. Thus, the audio translation should be from vision to text, then from text to audio, and the final work should enable their listeners to experience a vivid scene.

Lastly, understanding the target audience is also crucial. Before AD of movies, the Guangming Cinema did some surveys on their target audience. They found that the visually impaired got to know the world in a totally different way than able-bodied people, especially those who were born blind. They construct the world through senses of hearing, touch, and taste. They also build their concept of abstract things like color and beauty in a similar way. Once the AD translators have this knowledge in mind, they can then avoid obscure descriptions like "there are white clouds in the blue sky". During interviews with some visually impaired people, they said that visions would be created in their minds as they listen to the narrations. If the narrator gives fewer details, the movie in their mind would be less vivid. In the interview, the students of Beijing School for the Blind said that when the volunteer talked about running under the blue sky on horseback, what he thought was that there was a four-legged animal running, and there should be a chair on the back of the horse for the rider to sit on. But is that the truth? They hope that the narrator can not only tell the story clearly, but also focus on describing the objects and circumstances on the screen. Furthermore, if the description is detailed, they may even be able to smell the scents in the scene.

Barrier-free to Social Culture

Without AD, visually impaired people can listen to movies by hearing the dialogues and sound effects in the movies. However, much information will be missing. If they ask their family members or friends to add descriptions while watching movies together, there may also be problems. One problem is that their narrator might not be professional and they do not have experience in determining which part of the image should be described. The other problem is that it is a joy spoiler for those narrators. When one is narrating during a movie, there will occasionally be intense dialogues or scenes that change too fast for the narrator to follow. If they continue their narration, the narrator themself would miss out on certain information in the movie. Usually, the narrators would stop adding descriptions, leaving the visually impaired at a loss. Thus, it is quite common that the visually impaired do not enjoy the movie as much while sitting with their family and friends.

The barrier-free movies produced by Guangming Cinema can solve this problem. On the one hand, the narrations in the movies are made by professionals with a clear understanding of audio representation. On the other hand, the barrier-free movies are not just audio recordings. The visual elements from the original movies are kept, which also makes it available for sighted people to watch the barrier-free films alongside the visually impaired. Therefore, the visually impaired can enjoy the same movie with other people and have discussions about it instead of being excluded from this social experience. He Chuan, chairman of the Beijing Blind Association, highly praised the barrier-free films of Guangming. In an interview with the media, he said that visually impaired people couldn't see films in the past. Now we can enter the cinema to see films through barrier-free films. We feel that we have synchronized with the society and can smoothly and equally participate in social and cultural life and enjoy cultural and artistic achievements. I think this is a very happy thing.

From another perspective, going to the cinema itself has a strong sense of ceremony. The first step of getting involved in the society is going out of one's home. Watching films provides them a good reason to go outside. The screenings are all organized by the community cinema or library and the local blind association. On the way to the cinema, the visually impaired people always talk with each other. During the screening of the film, it is common to see them discussing in a low voice with people nearby, regardless if they are acquainted or not. In the cinema, an elderly blind man said that in order to come to the cinema to see barrier-free movies, he got up at six in the morning. It is one of the happiest things to go into the cinema and watch a movie like a sighted person. The volunteers also play an important part in their social activities. One of the reasons that people with disabilities do not want to go outside is because of the discrimination from other people. The volunteers are not only ones that the visually impaired can talk with, but also represent the care from the society. Letting the visually impaired feel that they are not excluded from the society can be of great help to their socialization.

Movies are imbedded with rich cultural elements. Through narration, the visually impaired can get to know the cultural meaning of certain gestures, symbols, customs, etc. At the beginning of each movie, narrators will introduce the main actors and directors. The narrator will also help the audience understand common social gestures. For example, in the movie *Qian Xuesen*, when Qian Xuesen was proposing to the lead actress, he put her hand on his heart. With AD, the audience can understand that this gesture means promise and seriousness. Also, when Qian Xuesen was eating a traditional Chinese dish Beggar's Chicken, the narrator described that the dish was covered with clay. Through such detailed descriptions, the visually impaired can imagine what such a dish looks like. Similarly, during the survey, many students said they learned several new phrases or gained knowledge from the barrier-free film they saw.

Barrier-free to Accessibility

Before Guangming Cinema was introduced, barrier-free movies were shown mainly in local libraries or unions for the disabled. For those living in remote areas of a province, it's not convenient for them to go to the cinema. Thus, the number of people who have access to the service is limited. The evolution of media form and technology has improved the communication and aesthetic experience for the visually impaired. Internet technology has provided a powerful tool to innovate barrier-free communication. "Duplicable" and "accessible" are two goals of the Guangming Cinema. It not only provides as many barrier-free movies for the visually impaired as possible, it also satisfies the needs of the visually impaired by fully utilizing the potential of media technology.

In terms of the current service mode, Guangming Cinema has established a communication system by integrating cinema lines and community, online and offline, traditional radio and television, and an interactive network. With an extensive and diverse communication method, these barrier-free movies can reach as many visually impaired people as possible. In the future, the Guangming Cinema plans to produce 104 movies every year, so that the visually impaired in China can enjoy 2 movies per week, which is equal to or even higher than able-bodied people. It will also provide audio translations for Chinese documentaries, classic television programs, and other genres of AD products according to the various needs and preferences of the visually impaired.

Guangming Cinema has made full use of new technology to improve the accessibility of visually impaired people. The promotion of barrier-free movies can be combined with mobile media, artificial intelligence, virtual reality, big data, cloud computing, etc. Currently, internet companies like Baidu, Tencent, and iFLYTEK have begun their programs to promote barrier-free communication. In the future, a networked public service platform will be built for the visually impaired, with intelligent systems as the core. Intelligent voice technology will be applied to terminals like mobile phones, apps, wearable devices, and other devices. The visually impaired will be able to type without actually seeing, and enjoy barrier-free products. With the help of new media technology, the visually impaired will share the same information environment as everyone else.

The Guangming Cinema also calls on the establishment of laws and regulations for barrier-free products. The practice of barrier-free communication in China has emerged rather late in comparison to developed countries. In a fast-changing world with a new media environment, it is urgent to construct barrier-free communication channels and build a barrier-free communication environment for the visually impaired. Guangming Cinema has tried to start with barrier-free movies and television productions, formulating China's technical standards and promoting legislation in related areas.

Conclusion

Access to information is a basic human right. Movies, as one of the most popular forms of mass media, have significant influence on human society and individual development. China has the largest number of visually impaired people in the world. Usually with issues such as high illiteracy, low income, and low social participation, the visually impaired have a growing need for social and cultural development. Guangming Cinema is a charity program aiming to promote barrier-free movies in China for the visually impaired to help with their socialization process.

In China, the practice of barrier-free communication started later than in developed countries. Guangming Cinema has made AD movies for the visually impaired to provide them with an enhanced movie-watching experience. Different from previous edited movie recordings, AD movies add information rather than delete them from the original movies. The producers of the Guangming Cinema are people with professional visual knowledge. They understand how to deal with various genres of movies. A background survey was also carried out to understand how the visually impaired construct the world. Questionnaire surveys showed that AD movies are welcomed among visually impaired people. The narration has helped them to have a better understanding of the movie.

AD films also provide the visually impaired with an opportunity to enjoy movies with their family and friends, hence increasing their social involvement with others. Furthermore, AD movies also help the visually impaired to better understand and appreciate different cultures.

Movies are really barrier-free only when they are easily accessible to the visually impaired. The Guangming Cinema is different from previous barrier-free communication practices in that it made good use of advanced media technology. The barrier-free products are duplicable and accessible through HiTV, audio applications, and community cinema. With the help of intelligent voice, the visually impaired can type and choose the channel they want to watch. In the future, a networked platform will serve even more visually impaired people. Moving forward, the Guangming Cinema should be a good avenue to set up barrier-free movie standards for the industry and promote legislation in related areas.

Of course, barrier-free communication practice has a long way to go. Unbalanced economic development results in unequal social services. In relatively more developed cities, the visually impaired will tend to have more chances to access barrier-free movies, as well as new media technologies. People of different age groups also have different needs. As a pioneer in barrier-free communication, the Guangming Cinema is working hard to provide the visually impaired with viewing rights and satisfy their need for art appreciation.

(Zhang Long, Director, Professor, Doctoral Supervisor, Department of International Journalism and Communication, School of Television, Communication University of China; Zhao Xijing, Director, Lecturer, Academic Research Office, School of Television, Communication University of China; Rong Chenshan, postgraduate student, International Journalism and Communication Reserve Talent Class, School of Television, Communication University of China)

SOCIAL VALUES AND AESTHETIC ORIENTATIONS OF BARRIER-FREE FILMS

Fu Haizheng and Pan Yue

Abstract: Barrier-free movies, as a public cultural service specially provided for persons with disabilities, promotes information equality and cultural sharing in the whole society. This article takes the Guangming Cinema public welfare project established by Communication University of China in 2017 as an innovative case to discuss the humanistic care, social values, and aesthetic orientations embodied in the development of barrier-free films, through theoretical research and summarizing practical experiences, contributing to enhancing the sense of gain, happiness, and security of people with disabilities and the development of China's barrier-free cause.

Keywords: Barrier-Free Movies, Guangming Cinema, Audio-Visual Communication

"Accessibility" was originally an architectural design concept aiming to provide a convenient and safe space for people with disabilities. In the 1950s, Danish scholar N.E. Bank-Mikkelsen proposed "the normalization principle", hoping to help people with disabilities to return to mainstream society like able-bodied people. In 1969, Bengt Nirje of Sweden first theoretically explained the "normalization principle"[1]. Since then, the

---

[1] NIRJE B. The Normalization Principle and Its Human Management Implications[J]. The International Social Role Valorization Journal,1994,1(2):19-23.

"normalization principle" has become the basic principle for the formulation of accessibility standards[2], and the target audience has been expanded from people with intellectual disabilities to all persons with disabilities.

Providing persons with disabilities with equal opportunities to participate in social life is an inevitable requirement for the development of the cause for persons with disabilities. Entering the new era, the main issue in our society has been shifted to the dissonance between the people's ever-growing needs for a better life, and their unbalanced and inadequate development. In addition to the construction of a barrier-free environment at the physical level, the construction of a barrier-free culture at the intellectual level has attracted more and more attention from all walks of life. How to build a "cultural tactile paving" that goes straight to the soul while laying the physical tactile paving, so that persons with disabilities can fully participate in social life with equal status and equal opportunities, and share the achievements of material and intellectual civilization, has become an important topic in national strategies and public welfare.

On December 17, 2017, China's first barrier-free film production and dissemination project with college teachers and students as volunteers, Guangming Cinema was established. The project, jointly launched by Communication University of China, Beijing Gehua Cable and Oriental Jiaying, aims to optimize the service mode of oral video description, improve the quality of accessible film works, create a more professional and service-oriented "cultural tactile paving", through high-quality production and large-scale launch of films, allowing more visually impaired people to enter the colorful world of films and share in the cultural achievements of the new era.

1. Barrier-free Movies: Public Cultural Services Specially Provided for Disabled Groups

Barrier-free movies generally refer to movies that translate, split, and transform the audiovisual language of the movie by adding sign language, subtitles, or narration on the basis of the original movie, so that the visually

---

[2] Duan Peijun, et al. National Strategy for Accessibility [M]. Shenyang: Liaoning People's Publishing House, 2019: 2. 段培君, 等. 无障碍国家战略[M]. 沈阳: 辽宁人民出版社

impaired or hearing impaired can enjoy it. Its purpose is to provide unique cultural services for specific groups of people, thereby promoting the rights of persons with disabilities to information equality, social participation, and cultural sharing.

There are currently 1 billion persons with disabilities in the world and more than 300 million visually impaired people. In recent years, the aging of the global population has accelerated, and China has nearly 250 million people aged 60 and above. In a narrow sense, the target audience of accessible films refers specifically to persons with visual or hearing impairments, but in a broad sense, all persons with disabilities are the audience of accessible films, including both visually and hearing impaired persons, as well as the elderly with limited mobility and reduced visual function.

According to the different service objects, barrier-free movies can be simply divided into two types: those for the visually impaired and those for the hearing-impaired, each with their corresponding ways of transforming the audio-visual elements. The transformation of "hearing → vision" is mainly realized through subtitles or sign language windows for the hearing-impaired, while the transformation of "vision → hearing" is mainly based on image description. Film is an audio-visual art based on vision. The sense of sight is an important source for human beings to obtain a film's information. Visually impaired people will encounter more obstacles than others when appreciating film and television works. Therefore, Guangming Cinema focuses its research and creation on barrier-free movies for the visually impaired, and brings a complete viewing experience to the visually impaired through image description.

(1) The Social Value of Barrier-free Films

Film is considered the "seventh art" that integrates architecture, music, painting, sculpture, poetry, and dance. Through visual creation, sound design, and scene editing, it makes the audience feel as if they are in the scene, but also seem to transcend the scene. It is rich in artistic value. As a popular leisure and entertainment activity, film also has a wide range of cultural values and social significance. Through the remaking of the real world and the creation of the virtual world, film constantly arouses the audience's thoughts about current life, reflection on human nature and life, and creates more topics for cultural exchange and thought discussions for the public.

At present, China has made remarkable achievements in the construction of a barrier-free environment, and the construction of barrier-free culture is accelerating. In the era of new audio-visual media, the production and promotion of accessible films has become a new direction for the extension of accessible cultural services. Through image description visually impaired people can understand and enjoy a movie fully just like people with normal vision. This is not only an expansion of visually impaired people's artistic life, but also a satisfaction of their intellectual and cultural needs. Through the art form of film, the visually impaired can resonate with the characters in the film, and then, just like people with normal vision, through virtual stories, they can enrich their real life, broaden the breadth of life, obtain spiritual enlightenment, and have more topics for communication with others, which in turn lead them to actively participate in social life.

Barrier-free movies provide more choices for the intellectual and cultural life of the visually impaired. For a long time, visually impaired groups have been greatly restricted in their access to and selection of audio-visual culture, due to a lack of the visual sense. As an important carrier of cultural communication, film is an important channel for people to enjoy intellectual and cultural life. It is the basic cultural right of the visually impaired to consume and enjoy movies just like able-bodied people[3]. Guangming Cinema creates favorable conditions for visually impaired people to access audio-visual media through image description, allowing them to have as many cultural choices as people with normal vision in addition to Braille, radio, and audiobooks, so that they can feast on audio-visual content and share in cultural achievements together.

Accessible films create more opportunities for visually impaired people to participate in social life. Maintaining social relationships with diverse groups of people is an important condition for individuals to receive social support.[4] In real life, limited by visual impairment, the level of social

[3] Ma Bo. Universal Accessible Film Promotion Model. China Press Publication Radio Film and Television Journal, September 10, 2015. 马波：《普及型无障碍电影推广模式》，《中国新闻出版广电报》
[4] He Zhaiping. A Review of Foreign Social Support Network Research [J]. Foreign Social Sciences, 2001(1):76-82. 贺寨平. 国外社会支持网研究综述[J]. 国外社会科学

participation of the visually impaired is low. According to the Report on Online Socialization of the Visually Impaired, 74% of them go online to socialize and find a common language with others[5]. Watching movies together can not only create an active and interactive group social space for the visually impaired, but also allow the visually impaired and the able-bodied to have more common topics. There are many family members and friends of visually impaired people at each Guangming Cinema public welfare screening event. During the viewing of the movie, the visually impaired will communicate with the people around them very naturally and actively; after the movie is over, they will comment and discuss the plot and connotation of the movie in groups of three or five. Barrier-free movie viewing activities provide a good platform and environment for people with disabilities to build confidence in social participation and gain social recognition in the interaction with able-bodied people, not only shortening people's social distance physically, but also promoting deep spiritual communication between people, with the good platform and environment provided by the viewing activities.

(2) Development Process of Barrier-free Films

Video description, a method of converting visual images into sound descriptions, was born in the United States in the 1970s, and is also known as descriptive video[6]. In the early 1990s, American television stations began to roll out audio-assisted channels for video description services for people with disabilities[7]. Since 2016, Netflix, the world's largest paid video site, has begun to provide audio descriptions for all content in its streaming library, aiming to provide visually impaired users with the same search and movie viewing functions as sighted users. Compared with developed countries in Europe and America, China's video description service started relatively late. In 2002, Taiwan's "Video Description

[5] Accessibility Research Association. Online Social Networking Report for Visually Impaired Persons [EB/OL].(2019-10-17)[2020-05-31]. http://www.siaa.org.cn/qq-4. 信息无障碍研究会.视障人士在线社交报告
[6] Cronin B J, King S R. The Development of the Descriptive Video Service[J]. Journal of Visual Impairment and Blindness, 1990, 84(10): 503-506.
[7] Snyder J. Audio Description: The Visual Made Verbal[J]. International Congress Series,2005,1282:935-939.

Development Association" was established. In 2005, "Xinmu Cinema" was built in Beijing. In 2009, the Shanghai Disabled Persons' Federation, the Shanghai Library, and the Shanghai Film Critics Society planned to establish the "Barrier-Free Film Studio". In April of the same year, China's first barrier-free film "Gaokao 1977" premiered.

With the gradual launch of domestic barrier-free movie services, the problems and difficulties faced in the service process have gradually emerged. First, "video description" itself has the dual attributes of public service and professional creation, but there is a lack of theoretical research and effective evaluation methods home and abroad on how to effectively and properly describe images to visually impaired people, resulting in a lack of standardized and professional content production. Secondly, most of the video description service volunteers in the above projects are organized by the government or public welfare organizations and recruited from the larger society, the number of qualified volunteers is still small, and the quality of video description services is uneven. And due to probable conflicts of volunteers' schedules, it is difficult to guarantee the narration quality and screening times of accessible films. Based on the above limitations, we urgently need to explore a standardized and large-scale production mode of accessible films.

2. Guangming Cinema: Productions and Value Expansion of Barrier-Free Movies

Common video description service modes at home and abroad are divided into two types: live audio description and pre-recorded description. At present, the development of the former in China has relatively matured. In Beijing's "Xinmu Cinema" and Shanghai's "Sound of Light and Shadow", volunteers are invited to serve as narrators at the film screening site, explaining the film for the visually impaired on the spot. This is widely recognized by visually impaired people. On-site listening and real-time narration have brought more interaction and a sense of ceremony to the cultural activity of "movie watching". From one-way listening to the sound in the projector, to being able to communicate with warm-hearted people on the spot, and to feel the rhythmic flow of the narrator's narration and the original sound of the movie, live audio description brings more warmth and human touch to the barrier-free video service. In addition, the audience and the narrator are in the same physical space. The audience can more intuitively feel the narrator's emotions and resonate. This also helps to build a bridge of deep communication between the two sides, and establish an equal dialogue among the visually impaired, and between the visually impaired and the sighted people.

With the development of barrier-free movies, the public has expanded their expectations for the technical level, artistic effect, and the depth and breadth of video description services. How to break through the limitations of live narration, improve the artistic sense of video description, and optimize the quality of accessible films have become the key to the innovative development of accessible films. In order to solve the problems of service professionalism and project sustainability, at the end of 2017, Communication University of China launched the Guangming Cinema barrier-free film public welfare project. From one-time live description services to reproducible and disseminatable audio-visual cultural products, Guangming Cinema has completed the value expansion of barrier-free films through practical innovation. From the production and dissemination of product content to the sustainability and expandability of welfare actions, the project provides a professional and stable public welfare platform for the future development of China's barrier-free film industry.

(1) High-quality Content Production

Guangming Cinema uses the pre-recorded video description mode. Volunteers completed the recording of video description and the post-production work such as editing, mixing, and synthesis in advance in the studio, and burned the finished film into a USB flash drive or CD for subsequent screening and promotion. Although the production process is relatively complicated, the advantages are very obvious.

One is the accuracy of content description. How to obtain information is a problem that visually impaired people have to face when watching movies, and it is also a basic problem to be solved in the creation of barrier-free movies. How to capture the most important elements to transform from visual information to auditory information in a limited time has become an

CUI LIN AND WU MINSU

important topic that barrier-free film creators continue to explore. Whether it is live or pre-recorded, a narrative script with accurate content, complete information, and adequate understanding is the top priority of barrier-free film creation. The writing of the narration involves the interpretation of the camera language, the deciphering of the narrative logic, and the grasp of the plot content, all of which require volunteers to have high professional abilities. Relying on the help of the "double first-class" discipline project at Communication University of China, Guangming Cinema has built a barrier-free film creation team with more than 500 teachers and students in audiovisual communication, ensuring the quality of films with the volunteer team's professionalism and stability, and the efficiency of films with the scale of the team and number of volunteers. In the production process, Guangming Cinema strictly controls the quality and adopts a pre-recording mode that is easy to modify and adjust repeatedly. From writing, recording, editing, and synthesizing, every step is meticulously crafted and perfected. A 90-minute accessible movie often requires more than 300 hours of repeated deliberation. From the exact name of an item to the coherence of a scene, the project team always puts the accuracy of content description first, in order to provide accurate, professional, and adequate barrier-free services for visually impaired friends.

The second is in-depth interpretation of connotation. In the process of creation, Guangming Cinema not only accurately describes the content of the picture, but also deeply interprets the connotation and thought value of the story behind the picture, so that the visually impaired can not only understand "what is happening now" when enjoying the movie, but also the "cause of occurrence" and "the intention of plot development", so as to more fully recognize and feel a movie. For example, in "You and Me", it is introduced that the landlord's grandmother "will often twist her neck, like the little girl taught her". This detail is used to cleverly link the beginning and end of the film, so that one too can comprehend the plot design through listening. At the end of "Tunnel War", "the bronze bell hanging on the old tree was rung again. This time, it conveys the joy of victory and good blessings", the volunteers reasonably deducted the connotation of the visuals, skillfully integrating the ethos of the times and humanistic ideals.

The third is the high fidelity of sound quality and tone. The auditory sense is the most important channel for visually impaired people to receive information, and the auditory element plays the key role in barrier-free movies. From pure "visual art" to "audio-visual art" with both vision and audio, the ideographic function and artistic value of auditory elements in films have gradually become recognized by the public. An excellent barrier-free film should be understood and heard well, so that visually impaired people can enjoy the hearing. While "translating and reproducing"[8] the audio-visual elements, video description volunteers should also convey emotions to the audience and perform artistic presentation through sound modeling. There is an amount of uncertainty in live description of video. Different volunteers have a different grasp of the emotions of the video, and the status of the same volunteer in different sessions of service will inevitably fluctuate. Only fine sound editing and strict audio adjustment in accordance with the standardized production process can ensure the clarity and smoothness of the sound information of a barrier-free film, and realize the delicate coordination of the narrator's narration, the film's dialogue, and the original sound effects. Only by repeated adjustment and continuous polishing can the narrator's emotions always be full and his or her voice always contagious, and then through the narrator's leading in emotions, the emotions of the visually impaired can be stimulated, and the rippling effect of both parties' aesthetic emotions can be obtained[9]. The recording session of Guangming Cinema is carried out in a professional studio. Special recording engineers and monitoring personnel will be arranged for each recording to supervise the layers, texture, and appeal of the narrator's voice, so that the sound can touch the soul, ensuring that the narration and the film's soundtrack match naturally and harmoniously. After the recording, the post-production team will denoise and level the vocal track, and then mix and synthesize it with the original sound of the film, not only achieving high fidelity of sound quality and tone, but also making the sound elements of the film full of artistic beauty and aesthetic interest.

---

[8] Zhao Yali. Video Description: A Dialogue Between Perspectives of Translation and Representation [J]. Journalism Research, 2002(1):97-134. 赵雅丽. 口述影像: 一个翻译与再现观点的对话[J]. 新闻学研究

[9] Zhou Jing. Broadcasting Practice and Research of Audio Description under the Barrier-free Concept [J]. Journal of Jilin Academy of Arts, 2019(5):70-77. 周景. 无障碍理念下口述影像的播音实践与研究[J]. 吉林艺术学院学报

(2) Full Coverage, Multi-channel Dissemination of Works

Barrier-free movies are not only a kind of common audio-visual cultural product, but also a social public service for specific groups of people. The consumption, production and dissemination of such works have unique humanistic values and important social implications.

The fact that the content is copyable lays the groundwork for the widespread dissemination of accessible films. The barrier-free films produced by Guangming Cinema break through the limitations of on-site narration. Once the production is completed, it can be mass-produced and widely disseminated. On the one hand, compared to live narration, which can only invite a limited audience at a time, pre-recorded accessible movies have a wider audience. On the other hand, by copying their favorite movies, the visually impaired can enjoy movies anytime and anywhere, which further lowers the threshold for media access and expands the "accessibility" of audiovisual media. In addition, the pre-recording mode adopted by Guangming Cinema can well solve the contradiction between the current shortage of volunteers for video description services and the greater demand for viewing movies by the visually impaired, laying the foundation for the normalization of barrier-free film public welfare screenings, to benefit more visually impaired people.

The dissemination covers a wide range and helps persons with disabilities in cultural poverty alleviation. As of the end of 2019, Guangming Cinema has formed a unique communication model, referred to as the "five-enters" model: with the provincial blind associations as hubs, it has entered theaters, blind schools, libraries, communities, and a great number of families. Public welfare screenings and promotions of barrier-free films in 30 provinces, municipalities, and autonomous regions across the country have expanded the coverage of video description services from first-tier cities such as Beijing, Shanghai, Guangzhou, and Shenzhen to underdeveloped areas such as Xinjiang, Tibet, Qinghai, and Ningxia. Guangming Cinema travels to villages and households, and delivers movies to Daqingshan Revolutionary Area in Inner Mongolia, Liangshan Yi Autonomous Prefecture in Sichuan, Ningde in Fujian and other places, bringing cultural products to visually impaired people in poverty-stricken areas, and through the promotion and dissemination of barrier-free movies, achieving cultural poverty alleviation for visually impaired groups. Starting from the perspective of cultural communication, Guangming Cinema combines poverty alleviation with aspirational and intellectual support, and with the help of the film's subtle educational function, improves the quality of life and cultural literacy of visually impaired groups, inspiring persons with disabilities to overcome poverty and vigorously strive for a decisive victory in building a moderately prosperous society in an all-encompassing manner.

Diverse communication channels further expand the viewing space for the visually impaired. In the past three years, Guangming Cinema has continued to explore the dissemination channels of barrier-free movies: delivering barrier-free movies to the homes of persons with disabilities, opening up the "last mile" of barrier-free cultural dissemination. Guangming Cinema has cooperated with theaters around China to establish barrier-free screening halls, regularly organizing public welfare screenings of barrier-free movies offline, allowing visually impaired people to enter the cinema. Guangming Cinema works with urban radio and television media such as Beijing Gehua Cable to build an online barrier-free movie screening zone, making it possible for visually impaired people to watch movies without leaving home. It cooperates with online platforms to boost online promotion of barrier-free movies through partial authorization of copyright. Guangming Cinema has gradually established barrier-free movie viewing channels covering both online and offline viewing, providing more convenience and comfort to the "barrier-free viewing space" for the visually impaired.

(3) Public Service: Many Littles Make a Mickle

The promise of Guangming Cinema is to make 104 barrier-free films every year. This means that, in the 52 weeks of a year, visually impaired people can enjoy 2 barrier-free movies per week, reaching or even exceeding the viewing frequency of sighted people. After several years of practical experience accumulation and academic research, Guangming Cinema has produced 416 barrier-free films, and has gradually built a new university platform for public welfare.

Multi-party participation ensures the sustainability of public welfare projects. Guangming Cinema organically combines the professional advantages of colleges and universities, the resource advantages of enterprises, and the platform advantages of media. Through the joint efforts of many parties, the operation and management of barrier-free film services have been ensured to be professional, stable, and sustainable. In terms of the feedback mechanism, Guangming Cinema constantly adjusts the content according to the needs of the audience and user feedback; it keeps in touch with the disabled people's federations and blind associations, and regularly organizes seminars and movie viewing feedback meetings, so that visually-impaired friends can enjoy video description services while at the same time participating in content production and project optimization of barrier-free movies, realizing the two-way interaction between persons with disabilities and the able-bodied, and ensuring the healthy development of the project while promoting the "equality, participation, and sharing" of the visually impaired.

Shared stake holding ensures high expandability of a public service. As a public welfare project on dissemination of barrier-free audio-visual cultural products, Guangming Cinema is needed by many and has broad development prospects. From the narrow sense of accessibility for specific groups to the broad sense of accessibility that serves the whole society, the service objects of accessible films are constantly being expanded with the progress of the concept of accessibility. From barrier-free movies to barrier-free documentaries, TV dramas, and galas, etc., the service content of barrier-free cultural products is constantly enriched with the increasing diversity of people's cultural needs. From content creation to public welfare promotion, from event day viewing to normalized access, from offline screening to online dissemination, Guangming Cinema is founded on barrier-free movies, and continuously innovates its service forms, gradually developing into a barrier-free cultural brand covering barrier-free film production, barrier-free content dissemination, and barrier-free concept popularization.

3. Artistic Values and Aesthetic Education Values of Barrier-free Films

The reason why a fine product is "fine" lies in its profound thinking, exquisite art, and excellent production. From having nothing to having something, from having something to something good, and from something good to something perfect, barrier-free films have higher standards and more pursuits in terms of content production, artistic presentation and thought leadership.

(1) Artistic Values of Barrier-free Films

Aesthetics is a spiritual-cultural activity, and its core is life experience with aesthetic imagery as the object. In this experience, the human spirit transcends the limitation of "self" and obtains a kind of freedom and liberation[10]. This kind of aesthetic activity based on people's life experience and life observation plays an irreplaceable role in breaking through the shackles of sensory barriers and achieving self-realization and self-identification for the visually impaired.

Beauty is an aesthetic pleasure, and the production of this "pleasure" depends on subtle reactions of emotion and cognition[11]. The pleasure of watching movies for sighted people mainly comes from visual information, and for visually impaired people, it needs to be filled in with video descriptions. From film to culture to spirit, Guangming Cinema not only reproduces the artistic beauty of the film itself, but also tries to create an artistic world that allows visually impaired people to experience the beauty of culture on an equal footing, leaving them with a kind of imagination about the beauty of life and spirit.

1. *Space of Beauty*

Film is the art of light and shadow, a colorful and dazzling world. A qualified barrier-free film creator should become the builder, guide, and

---

[10] Ye Lang. Aesthetic Principles [M]. Beijing: Peking University Press, 2019: 15. 叶朗. 美学原理[M]. 北京: 北京大学出版社

[11] Armstrong T, Detweiler-Bedell B. Beauty as an Emotion: The Exhilarating Prospect of Mastering a Challenging World[J]. Review of General Psychology, 2008,12(4):305-329.

sharer of the barrier-free audio-visual aesthetic space[12]. From the choice of words and sentences in the narration, to the design choices of the storyline, to the description and shaping of the characters in the film, the barrier-free film must have beautiful content. From family and friendship, to love, from being friends and neighbors to serving the country and the people, from romantic love to love of family and country, barrier-free movies must portray beautiful emotions. From the expressiveness and appeal of the narrator's voice to the complementarity of the narrator's description and the film's original sound, accessible films must have beautiful forms. From the change of tone to the change of rhythm, to the sublimation of emotion, barrier-free movies must create a beautiful atmosphere. Barrier-free movies should provide the audience with the enjoyment of beauty through their creation, and allow the audience to discover and create beauty, and then through the movie, feel the beauty of life, discover the beauty of life, and feel the power of life in the movie.

2. *Beautiful Imagination*

Cinema is not just a real representation or a parody, but an art that involves mental activity, association, and imagination. Arnheim argues that once parts of the real event are removed, the lens's appeal is greatly enhanced[13]. For example, silent laughter in silent films is more artistically penetrating than vocal laughter, because it leaves people with endless space for imagination. "There are a thousand Hamlets in the eyes of a thousand viewers." Some blank space allows everyone to "personalize" their imagination based on their own life experience and understanding of the film. This positive choice and active "re-creation" give the film more artistic beauty and aesthetic value.

"Beauty does not stand on its own, something becomes beautiful when appreciated by people", without the reflection of the soul, there is no

[12] Zhou Jing. Broadcasting Practice and Research of Audio Description under the Barrier-free Concept [J]. Journal of Jilin Academy of Arts, 2019(5):70-77. 周景. 无障碍理念下口述影像的播音实践与研究[J]. 吉林艺术学院学报

[13] Arnheim, Rudolf. Film as Art. Nachdr. Berkeley: University of California Pr, 2000. (Page 91 in the Chinese version) 阿恩海姆. 电影作为艺术[M]. 杨跃，译. 北京：中国电影出版社，1981:91

beauty[14]. Guangming Cinema attempts to use the function of sound to convey emotions through creative description of the details of the pictures, so that the visually impaired can build an aesthetic system based on their own life experience through hearing and imagination. In "The Wandering Earth", "looking from space, the earth is like a crystal ball", this sentence not only vividly introduces the texture of the earth's surface with faint light lingering, but also through the connotations of fantasy and romance of the word "crystal ball" itself, arouses for people mysterious and beautiful imagenings.Forever Young", "The camera zoomed out at this time, and the plaque in the living room (of Shen Guangyao) said 'Three Generations and Five Generals'". By emphasizing the word "three generations and five generals", the narrator creates a voice image that obeys the style of the film and the overall emotional tone, so that the visually impaired can feel the Shen family's self-sacrificing love for the homeland through vocal modeling.

(2) Aesthetic Educational Value of Barrier-free Films

"Guangming Cinema" not only allows the visually impaired to "see" the film, but also expands the barrier-free film into an aesthetic educational activity. Through providing aesthetic clues which work together with the audiences' aesthetic experiences, Guangming Cinema aims to activate the audiences' own agency to foster one's aesthetic ability, refine one's temperament, and complete one's character while enjoying the movie.

Aesthetic ability mainly presents itself in the perception, understanding, and imagination of beauty, and its formation and cultivation are mostly done inadvertently. This kind of "inadvertent" process based on one's growth environment has caused an imbalance in aesthetic ability. For able-bodied people, aesthetics is a choice based on millions of sensory experiences. But for the visually impaired, due to limited senses, they can only perceive and explore their visual aesthetic ability through targeted training, the imagination of things, and the understanding of the both the outer and underlying meanings of the form. For this reason, Guangming Cinema deliberately added the explanation of the connotations of the story

[14] Zong Baihua. Aesthetic Walk [M]. Shanghai: Shanghai People's Press, 2005: 121.宗白华. 美学散步[M]. 上海: 上海人民出版社

and the description of important details when describing the images so that the surface information of the film is "knowable" and the deep meaning is "perceivable", so that the visually impaired can obtain equal levels of aesthetic experience as the sighted person while watching the movie.

The refinement of temperament and the improvement of character run through the barrier-free movie service. On the one hand, Guangming Cinema pays special attention to intellectual cultivation of visually impaired groups, adhering to and promoting the core values of socialism in the description of the images, showing and rallying the Chinese spirit, providing positive value guidance and spiritual guidance for the visually impaired. So that they will draw strength from movies, shape a wholesome character with self-esteem, self-love, self-reliance, and self-strength, and actively integrate into society and participate in social life. On the other hand, Guangming Cinema is committed to forming a public welfare atmosphere in the whole society, one of love and care that pays attention to the disabled groups, actively transmitting positive energy, so that they will have a more positive outlook on life and face life with an optimistic and sunny attitude; using barrier-free movies as the starting point, establishing a harmonious and beautiful relationship among individuals, and between people and society, promoting the integration of people with disabilities and the able-bodied, and promoting the progress of social civilization.

As a public cultural service specially provided for people with disabilities, barrier-free films not only share cultural achievements with them, but also provide fresh materials for human rights education and empathy cultivation of the able-bodied. With the help of the Guangming Cinema platform, Communication University of China combines public service and teaching practice, so that "cultivating people with morality" runs through from the beginning to the end; it unifies education of the whole person with talent cultivation, discovering a new model of "teaching ideology and politics in everyday classes". There is an organic integration of professional education, quality education, and aspirational education. While cultivating students' professional ability, the cultivation of their public welfare passion and love of home and country is also strengthened, achieving a well-rounded education throughout the whole process, for the whole person, and for everyone. Simultaneously during the training for barrier-free film creation, the volunteers will be educated on the popularization of barrier-free culture and universal barrier-free concepts, cultivating professional talents who "integrate knowledge and action" for the development of China's barrier-free cause, to serve national strategies, and fulfill social responsibility.

Barrier-free movies are an important part of the development of China's barrier-free culture and an important manifestation of the progress of human civilization and social modernization. In recent years, it has received extensive attention from all walks of life. During the two sessions in 2019, Director Jia Zhangke, a deputy of the National People's Congress, put forward the "Proposal on the Development of Barrier-free Film Industry in China", calling on all sectors of society to care about and support barrier-free films. At the third session of the 13th National Committee of the Chinese People's Political Consultative Conference held in May 2020, Li Qingzhong, member of the National Committee of the Chinese People's Political Consultative Conference and Chairman of the China Association of the Blind, submitted several proposals including the "Proposal on Including the Law on Building a Barrier-Free Environment in the Legislative Plan of the Standing Committee of the National People's Congress in 2021", and the "Proposal on Opening up Copyright and Promoting the Development of Barrier-Free Films"[15], helping people with disabilities to enjoy a well-off life in an all-round way and enrich the spiritual and cultural life of visually impaired people.

The essence of barrier-free culture is the spirit of humanity, the spirit of human rights, and the spirit of modernization[16]. "Guangming Cinema" uses barrier-free movies as a medium and public welfare actions as a bridge. While meeting the spiritual and cultural needs of persons with disabilities, it strengthens respect and protection for the visually impaired on the level of social acceptance, so that the socialist core values of "freedom, equality, justice, and the rule of law" are truly transformed into people's heart-felt identity and behavioral habits, promoting the integration of persons with disabilities and the able-bodied, and promoting equal rights in information,

[15] China Network. Member Li Qingzhong: Several Proposals that Speak Out for the Blind and Focus on Spiritual and Cultural Needs of Persons with Disabilities. [EB/OL]. (2020-05-27) [2020-06-04]. http://canjiren.china.com.cn/2020-05/27/content_41166035. html?f=pad&a=true. 中国网. 李庆忠委员: 多份提案为盲人发声关注残疾人精神文化需求
[16] Duan Peijun, et al. National Strategy in Accessibility [M]. Shenyang: Liaoning People's Publishing House, 2019: 80. 段培君, 等. 无障碍国家战略[M]. 沈阳: 辽宁人民出版社

culture and communication. From barrier-free movies to barrier-free culture, to the barrier-free cause that benefits all mankind, and guided by global vision, international standards, and Chinese characteristics, Guangming Cinema has discovered a national barrier-free development path. It is a vivid practice of building a community with a shared future for mankind, and a new direction and a new mission of cultural development in the new era.

TECHNOLOGIES AND DEVELOPMENT TRENDS OF NEW AUDIO-VISUAL COMMUNICATION

Wang Xiaohong

Looking back, the changes in the audiovisual communication industry have had a profound impact. It has not only brought about a "big video" landscape that comprises of radio and television, IPTV, video websites, self-media videos, etc., but also has fundamentally changed the viewing experience of human beings: people are no longer fixed, distanced, passive, but actively "watch" at any time, anywhere, and randomly; watching, discussing, and using have become important parts of audio-visual activities. And in this process, the originally closed audio-visual narrative has become a dynamically expanding process in open collaboration... Under such circumstances, audio-visual communication has developed a new functional attribute. What it builds is no longer just a viewing space, but also an activity space for maintaining communication, a discourse of self-expression.

The key question is not what happened, but how this happened and how the phenomena are interconnected. In my opinion, only by understanding why the above-mentioned changes are "new" and how they are possible, and "why they exist in such a way", can we see how they will grow in the future, and better understand the current changes, find the path of development, and even predict future directions.

1. What is "New": The Evolutionary Logic of Audiovisual Communication Forms

When online video appeared as a new audio-visual form, people had various vague descriptions for them, such as "video database", "my TV", "new screen", "supplementary medium for TV", etc. This situation is like the beginning of film and television. The film is called "new theater", " musical which can be screened", and television is called "small film" and "radio with images". Although new things are always inextricably linked with the past, and people are accustomed to using existing cultural patterns to describe emerging changes, today, both in theory and practice, these descriptions have big shortcomings. Online video is by no means a "supplementary medium" for TV, nor is it a translation of TV on the Internet. The two are completely different media forms. Taking communication relationship as the coordinate, American scholar Mark Poster defines the network audio-visual communication based on Internet technology as the second media age of mass communication, which is an integrated producer/seller/consumer system - a completely new configuration of the communication relationship, in which the boundaries between the three concepts of producer, seller and consumer are no longer clearly defined.[1]

This new configuration implies a fundamental change in communication relationship. That is, the subjectivization of communication, which is the premise for us to understand why this new form of audiovisual communication is "new".

If we further examine the development logic of human audiovisual communication, we may be able to understand the internal mechanism of the new audiovisual communication and its inevitable direction more clearly. Throughout the development of media, we can find that the use of each new technology builds a new relationship between people and the world, which reflects the pursuit of human communication on two levels: one is the constant pursuit of the re-presentation of the richness of bodily sensations; the second is to continuously pursue the deepening of exchanges and interactions.

---

[1] Poster, Mark, translated by Fan Jinghua. The Second Media Age. Nanjing University Press, 2001, pp. 3, 49. （美）马克·波斯特：《第二媒介时代》，范静哗译，南京大学出版社

1. Re-presentation of Bodily Sensations.

From mass communication to Internet communication, both people's social attributes and natural attributes unfold. From the early face-to-face interaction to the tying of knots as notes, to textual printing, to the birth of photography, to the successive emergence of film, radio, and television, the emergence of each medium is not only an overcoming of the limitations of the old medium, but also a re-presentation of perceptual richness of the human body. Specifically, photography overcomes the constraints of language and re-presents intuitive and subtle visual perception, but is limited by that "instant" moment; film overcomes the static state of photography and re-presents the richness of communication activities, but is limited by fictional narrative and space constraints; radio re-presents the sense of presence and intimacy of interpersonal communication, but is limited by only "listening" and not watching; TV re-presents the present scenes and enters the field of people's daily life, but is limited by one-way communication; only online video, especially webcast, truly re-presents "face-to-face" real-time interaction and the richness of perceptions.

2. Interactive Development of Transmission and Reception

Technological development leads to double-fold changes in the communication relationship: one is the change in the relationship between subject and object, and the other is the change in the way of interaction. Although TV strives to pursue interaction, it cannot fundamentally change the one-way nature of the subject-object dichotomy. Only in the Internet age can the subjectivization of communication and individual autonomy become possible. The power of video production and distribution is no longer in the hands of a few professionals, everyone can participate, everyone can broadcast, and everyone can be "an unlicensed TV station"[2]. From this angle, as an early application of online video, video-on-demand is a continuation of traditional media. Since then, with video sharing as the hallmark and mass participation as the core, audio-visual communication has become "new". It combines the characteristics of interpersonal interaction and mass communication. The more prominent

---

[2] Nicholas Negroponte: Being Digital, translated by Hu Yong and Fan Haiyan, Hainan Publishing House, 1997, p. 205 （美）尼葛洛庞帝:《数字化生存》,胡泳,范海燕译,海南出版社

and distinctive feature is that with it interpersonal communication is also mass communication; its attributes of mass communication are inherent in each occurrence of interpersonal communication, and the forms and relationships of human communication unfold in a diverse and three-dimensional way.

The significance of all changes in media technology and perception is not only in technology and perception themselves. They will inevitably lead to changes in people's sense of time and space, which means that people's activities and relationships are changing at the same time. After that, all new communication technologies will inevitably follow this path: through technology, further extending people's senses such as touch and smell; holographic technology, virtual reality, augmented reality technology and other applications have verified this; In terms of space, further expanding and deepening people's communication activities, from real space to virtual space, to all forms of mobile positioning, and then to human consciousness, imagination, and emotions, just as McLuhan predicted in 1964, that human existence seems to extend consciousness as an environment, and that with the advent of computers, the extension of consciousness has begun.[3]

Today, the progress and application of smart media, wearable devices, machine learning, big data analysis and precise push, as well as highly intelligent scene matching and emotional matching in the future, all reflect the ultimate re-presentation of human perception as well as the ultimate expansion of interactive communication. From this, it can be imagined that the development of future technology and the evolution of audio-visual communication will inevitably follow the path of how to better promote human experience, better meet human needs, and better expand human interactions. This also has implications for the direction of audiovisual communication practice.

[3] Marshall McLuhan. Understanding Media: The Extensions of Man, translated by He Daokuan, Commercial Press, 2003, p. 428, p. 431.（加）马歇尔·麦克卢汉:《理解媒介: 论人的延伸》, 何道宽译, 商务印书馆

2. How it is possible? The Structure and Mechanism of New Audiovisual Communication

When we are discussing new audio-visual communication or new audio-visual media, many unprecedented new functions such as socialization, instrumentalization, and contextualization inevitably enter our observation field, and the realization of these functions is inseparable from a new structure and mechanism: the "textualization of video".

I once proposed in the article "Video Textualization and its Technical Functions" that video textualization is the structure and mechanism that differentiates online video from TV. Because in Internet communication, video can be stripped into the smallest independent form, with the attribute of "vocabulary", which people can use and express freely. This means that online video text can be freely read and written by each individual without any barriers - a completely different structure and mechanism than TV "streaming". "Stream" is an important concept of television communication; it means that television expresses its meaning through an uninterrupted "stream" of video images. Video "stream" even exists in transitions between programs, to structure the information through a linear form. For programs that want to express their complete meanings, the editing rights of the video text are in the hands of professionals, and the audience cannot arbitrarily intercept the TV "stream" to make it independent. On the other hand, online video is completely different. The "textualized" structure and mechanism determines the uniqueness of online video in content production and dissemination, enabling people to actively participate in the construction of video meaning, and be "actively learning how to use a variety of functions, being not just a consumer anymore."

Therefore, whether we can gain insight into and activate the textualization mechanism and its technical potential in practice, as well as its various connections with social relations, directly affects the effectiveness of communication. In general, video textualization brings narrative changes and values in at least the following aspects.

(1) Breakable, Meaning Can Be Formed Independently.

Online video can be cut at will, as short as a single frame, or as long as you want. The cut content can obtain an independent form and its meaning regardless of the length. This technical feature directly brings three new narrative values:

1. *Value push of "fragment reference"*. Fragment cutting is a rhetorical strategy with prominent significance, which implies the amplification and push of value points. Through the forwarding and recommendations of netizens, independent clips that are out of its holistic context come to grab people's attention, helping people to quickly grasp the core and pay attention to the key points. In public events, "fragment references" are especially important.

2. *The Emphasized Details of "Messaging through Screenshot"*. With the video textualization mechanism, the detailed pictures that were originally fleeting or even had no clear meaning have become discourse symbols with independent meaning, which can be examined repeatedly to strengthen their meaning. Take the example of a popular short video: Amid the high-rise buildings in the most prosperous area of Beijing, smog comes from afar to near, changing from being shallow to thick, blowing up right to the face. Just a time-lapse shot presents the "Trauma of Smog" very profoundly, making it unforgettable.

3. *Meanings Created by "Multi-Screen Juxtaposition"*. The juxtaposition of different screenshots can say a thousand words without explicitly saying a single word. Similar examples are common.

The technical function, namely that the video can be cut, not only meets the needs of fragmented reading, but also creates new narrative value. How to cut out valuable information, amplify and disseminate value points, and let the content jump out and be "seen" in the ocean of information has become a new capability requirement.

(2) Can be Embedded and Seamlessly Connected

Online video can be embedded and spread through all media, such as embedded text reports, emails, instant messaging, Weibo, WeChat, H5, etc., showing the characteristics including seamless connection, ubiquity, and mobile access. There is no doubt that embedding technology enriches forms of expression and is also conducive to speeding up dissemination. However, just stopping here is unimaginative and lacks verve.

On Halloween in November 2017, when searching for the word "Halloween" on Baidu Baike, the first thing that popped up in the search box was not text, but various animations and symbols with distinctive Halloween symbols; When searching for "Halloween" on Google, what popped up was not text either, but a short video about Halloween. Although these ideas are quite entertaining and for the occasion only, they are also enlightening: embedding is not only a technical means, but also has special narrative significance, such as a sense of implicitness and transition. In the online narrative, how to explore new narrative methods and motivate users to participate and socialize needs to be explored urgently.

(3) Reconfigurable with New Meaning Created

With the popularization of relevant software applications, everyone can supplement, modify, forward, or add tags and titles to video texts with almost no technical barriers, to reconstruct the meaning. The impact of this reconfigurable technical function on narrative is multi-fold. On the one hand, it makes it easy for videos to be ridiculed and spoofed, leading to arbitrary tampering with the truth, and under the "seeing is believing" mindset, the reconstructed video is even more deceptive. On the other hand, it constitutes a process of social collaboration. Netizens' comments, replies, adaptations, imitations, and creation of sequels are like a relay race. In this process, viewpoints tend to become more diverse, and forms tend to be richer, and increasingly illogical methods, scene representations, and related factors enter the social communication system, making the "stream" of images a non-linear stream of meanings.

In a word, the textualization mechanism that videos are breakable, embeddable, and reconfigurable is not only the structural basis of the new audiovisual language, but also the precondition for individuals to freely use video, which implies the transfer of production rights and dissemination rights. Through textualization, video has become a new way of connection among people, and between people and society. Whether we are good at using video to expand communication power, and whether we are good at configuring various ways of expression and encouraging message forwarding, all depend on our understanding and grasp of the new structure and mechanism of video.

3. How to Grow: The Development Direction of New Audiovisual Communication

What will happen to the future audio-visual communication landscape, and how will it develop? There are multiple perspectives to answer this question. As far as the specific pattern is concerned, its development will be affected by factors such as Internet technology empowerment, capital game, policy rules, and other factors. For example, China's three major Internet giants (Baidu, Alibaba, Tencent, BAT for short) completed the acquisition or expansion of video websites in 2015 and early 2016, thus becoming the big three in the industry, while another Internet giant LeTV was defeated in the capital game; in just a few years, it staged a big show of "seeing it rise and seeing it collapse". Also, with the boost of capital, in-house shows, online movies, online live broadcasts, and short videos have become the next big things one wave after another.

This paper attempts to return to the general sense in investigating the development direction that new video communication should take. Combined with the previous discussion, I think there are two basic premises for judging the future direction: one is to pursue the expansion of communication activities and the richness of bodily sensations in communication, which are the two internal needs of human development and social development. Communication is the basis of human activities and exchanges, two needs that must be accompanied by technical support and go hand in hand with it; second, behind the various breakthroughs of new audio-visual communication against TV communication, is the shattering of traditional communication relationships and mode of interaction.

Interaction is the essential feature of new audiovisual communication, which combines the dual characteristics of mass communication and interpersonal communication. These two premises determine that the following issues must be considered in the progress of practice.

(1) How to Better Participate?

The "newness" of the new type of audiovisual communication is manifested in the breaking through of the constraints of the mass media and forming a new platform for everyone to participate in. It takes individual empowerment as the internal driving force and forms a new value appeal. In other words, public participation in content production has become the norm in communication. In the era of mass communication, the power of audio-visual information production and dissemination is in the hands of a few people, which can be described as a "representative system" of video; A few people use video to speak for people's lives and dreams. In the Internet age, people can freely use video to express themselves and present themselves. People participate in the production and dissemination of videos in a way that is visible, perceptible, usable, at any time, at random, anywhere, even filming themselves on video. This mode of participation, sharing, and use has a profound impact on social ideas and life needs, because when society becomes used to communicating in a certain way, it is bound to be internalized into people's conceptual structure, enter the field of social re-practice, and collectively in unconscious ways form new social activities. This puts forward new requirements for new audiovisual production and dissemination: how to let more people participate in content production, activate the motivation of users to participate, and make users become new productive forces? And how to give full play to their respective strengths and establish a synergistic mechanism combining professional and social strengths?

(2) How to Interact More Deeply?

Interaction is the essential feature and fundamental advantage of new audiovisual communication that is different from TV communication. From the perspective of technological development, future technology must be about becoming more realistic and more convenient in re-presenting real human interaction situations, that is, to better present the richness and immersiveness of people's face-to-face experience, boosting people's deep experience and participation.

(1) Advancement of Interactive Narratives.

The continuous evolution of technology has created numerous ways of disseminating and consuming information. It is also changing the preferences and expectations of users. People increasingly want to have more control over the way they consume information,[4] so as to obtain richer sensory experience.[5] The discussion area in early online live broadcasts, "shake", "like", bullet chat, patronizing, and even the appearance of gamified news works, all see direct connections between people and content with the intervention of human behavior. In the future, in addition to the development of technologies such as VR that can create a strong sense of immersion, the narrative art of interactive video will become more and more important. How to better create a "sense of presence" and a sense of being the "protagonist" and enhance the connection and dialogue between users and content will become an important starting point for enhancing interactive narratives.

(2) The Expansion of Interactive Situations.

Communication does not just carry information; it also creates scenes for interactions for members of society. The formation of such interaction scenes is based on the common experience of the members. In many cases, people repost videos not because of how well-made the video is and how rich the information is, but because it has become a way to maintain social relations, interactions, and affections. Video creates a new life-like coexistence and interaction field in a "visible" form. It should be pointed out that the new audio-visual interactive narrative is not only manifested in the creation of external interaction scenes, but more in

---

4 《New York Times 2016 Annual Report》 p. 28
5 Wang Xiaohong. [J]. "Essential Interaction" of Online Video Communication and its Significance 王晓红. [J]. 论网络视频传播的 "本质性互动 "及意义. 中国网络视频年度案例研究[M].北京:中国传媒大学出版社

promoting interactions in terms of emotions which happen internally. Take YouTube's globally-popular "unboxing video" videos and "blind box unboxing" videos on Douyin (Chinese TikTok) with tens of thousands of hits as examples: these videos show people taking toys out of boxes in the simplest way of recording, showing various creative "unboxing scenes". Such seemingly simple unboxing videos have made many users addicted, and toy companies have changed their packaging strategies to attract more people to show toys "unboxed". The reason is that short videos transcend the notion of "information" and create a relational interactive situation of shared unboxing. In this situation, the function of video has gone "beyond viewing", and becomes deeply linked to people's consumption behavior and use situations (including relational activities).

In addition, how to better serve should also be a key topic for future audio-visual communication. Today's content dissemination is no longer broadcast on a single screen. Content is placed in a multi-channel dissemination environment as a kind of information flow, life flow, and even commodity flow, into considerations of how content production, consumption, platforms, and environments can form an organic interactive relationship, so as to achieve the maximum value of the content by relying on each other. Therefore, precise service is becoming more and more important, which pinpoints users' needs, emotions, and experiences. Today, the advancement of video interaction technology provides the possibility to meet and develop all the "micro" needs in life, such as content, emotion, and market. However, no matter how technology evolves, even in the age of intelligent media and the popularization of machine writing, one thing should be fundamental: the future development of audio-visual communication must rely on the power of technology to better serve the needs of people.

(Wang Xiaohong, Professor, Faculty of Journalism and Communication, Communication University of China)

NEWS GAME: CONCEPTS, MEANINGS, FUNCTIONS AND PATTERNS OF INTERACTIVE NARRATIVES

Zeng Xiangmin and Fang Xueyue

Abstract: With the deepening of media convergence, its forms and methods are becoming more and more diverse, and news games are produced against the background of such content innovation and reorganization. The fusion of news and games has also made news games the focus of attention and controversy. Focusing on the concept, meaning, and function of news games, the principle of text deconstruction from the perspective of interactive narrative rules, and corresponding research in different respects etc., this paper analyzes news games, sorts out the dissemination phenomenon of some news games and the underlying principles, and further clarifies that news games are a new way of news narrative. Through case analysis of news games' narrative patterns, this paper provides constructive recommendations for future planning, design, and innovation, etc., of news games.

Keywords: news game, media convergence, interactive narrative

At the current time of media technology reform, traditional news reporting has also developed from one-way story consumption and information dissemination to interactive construction of user participation and control. The combination of news and games has become an important direction of news report product innovation. Like many new integrated products and new roles in this era, such as infotainment, pro-am, and prosumer, news and games also collide and intersect with each other.

What is "News Game"

Here, we must clarify the periphery and the core of news games. News games are not a simple cross-border combination, but a new structure and deep integration of content and narrative. So, what kind of innovations and changes can be produced in the interaction of these two industries?

News Games Are Not Simple Pastimes and Recreation

When it comes to games, some people will naturally think of pastimes and entertainment. Therefore, when news encounters games, many people will have such preconceptions that the rationality and neutrality of news seem to be deconstructed by the pastimes and entertainment brought by games. Socrates said that there is no description of the original elements from which all things are composed.[1] Therefore, for news games, its definition is not created simply by combining the definitions of news and games, but we can understand news games with the help of the meanings of news and games themselves. For its own right, news is a report of recent or ongoing facts, but in the concept of news games, people pay more attention to the identification and analysis of the concept of "game" than the discussion of the meaning of "news". Therefore, it is necessary for us to return to the original meaning of games to understand the changes it brings to news. Here, many game designers, game historians, and even philosophers have discussed the definition of a game. The famous game theorist Brian Sutton-Smith considered a game to be the realization of a voluntary control system.[2] Clark C. Abt said in his famous *Serious Games* that a game is context with

---

[1] Gui Yuhui, Zheng Da, Zhao Kui, Tan Min. Principles of Game Design, Tsinghua University Press, 2011, p. 89. 桂宇晖、郑达、赵奎、谭敏:《游戏设计原理》, 清华大学出版社

[2] Avedon E, Sutton-Smith B. The Study of Games. New York: John Wiley & Sons, 1971.p.405.

rules, and he even directly pointed out that every election, international relations, and private disputes can also be called games.[3] Therefore, we cannot understand games as purely recreational pastimes.

In fact, the academic world has long distinguished the game itself from toys and play designs, and the distinguishing elements are divided into two opposite parts: play and game, whole and part,[4] as shown in Figure 1. There are differences between game and play in the purpose and process of production, and the key to expanding their differences is gamification design. Sometimes it is difficult for us to distinguish whether a news product is a good news game, and we may even question its attributes for being a news game. The most fundamental reason is that it is difficult for people to judge the degree of gamification of news products and the value of gamification. In the theory of game design, all good games are gamified learning tools, whether they are labeled educational or not.[5] We believe that the same applies to news game products. A good news game must have the values of learning, education, and dissemination.

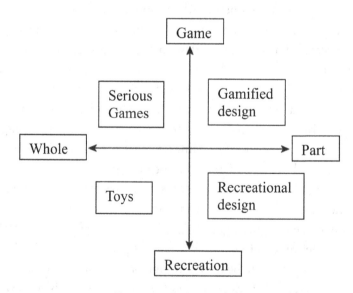

Figure 1 Game and Play

[3] Abt C C. Serious Games. New York: Viking Press, 1970.p.6.
[4] Chen Jingwei. Game Psychology. Communication University of China Press, 2015, p. 82. 陈京炜:《游戏心理学》，中国传媒大学出版社
[5] Ibid.

News Games Are the Product of News Gamification

Going back to its origins, many believe that the concept of "news games" was first proposed by Uruguayan game designer Gonzalo Frasca when he founded Newsgaming.com in 2003. As a type of interactive news, news games are distinguished from other types of news products mainly by their game characteristics. Since 2003, news games have gone through 15 years of development. During this period, many researchers in academia and industry have tried to define news games. To sum up, there are mainly two kinds, one is a rather general concept, that is, a news game is a serious game closely related to news reports.[6] The other is a specific explanation in terms of its form and function, that is, news games refer to the integration of news reports and video games, and on the basis of ensuring the authenticity of facts under the principles of journalism, using games to carry out media communication, with the purpose to provide a virtual experience of real news events to the user community.[7] In both of the above two statements, the relationship between news and games is mentioned. The former pays more attention to game elements, while the latter pays more attention to the characteristics of news.

Obviously, when we use the concept of news game, we are interpreting a new form of news from the perspective of news communication. In the concept of news games, both "news" and "games" play an important complementary role. As the most basic content support for news game products, facts are the driving force behind the production of news games, and the addition of game elements gives news facts a beautiful coat, making the latter more attractive. And this "dressing" process is not a simple superposition process, but an evolutionary one, a process of gamification. Gamification is the use of game design elements in a non-game context,[8] and news games are actually the product of news gamification. Therefore,

---

[6] Zhang Jianzhong, Wang Tianding. Towards New Media Convergence: When News Meets Games. Modern Communication, No. 11, 2016. 张建中、王天定:《迈向新的媒体融合:当新闻遭遇游戏》, 《现代传播》

[7] Wu Xiaoli. When News Meets Games - On the Current Situation and Development Strategies of News Games. Journal of News Research, No. 21, 2016. 武晓立:《当新闻遇上游戏---浅谈新闻游戏的现状和发展策略》, 《新闻研究导刊》

[8] Chen Jingwei. "Game Psychology", Communication University of China Press, 2015, p. 82. 陈京炜:《游戏心理学》, 中国传媒大学出版社2015年版

we believe that news games are the gamification of news information, which promotes the dissemination and understanding of information through the interactive participation and control of users.

News games are essentially a form of promoting information dissemination, through infusing entertainment into education. For news games, facts are the core, and game elements are supporting structures and forms, in which news facts are more tangible, more experience-friendly and interactive, and more communicable.

News Games Mine Value and Promote Content

News games are a multi-layer processing of content based on information collection, data research, and traditional reporting. The process of news gamification is also a process of value mining and promotion of content, and it is also a cross-media narrative in the context of media convergence. The traditional reporting forms using text, sound, and pictures as media can be transformed into integrated interactive games, thus forming products which are multi-layered and diverse.

The Significance of News Games

Improve News Visibility and Readability

The inherent interactive and participatory nature of games makes it a very dynamic information carrier, which in turn becomes an important guarantee for the vitality of news. It seems that any news related to gamification has a certain dissemination power, for example, Al Jazeera's "Pirate Fishing"[9]: 80% of the game users logged on to the Al Jazeera website for the first time[10]. Additionally, a video of the game "7 Ways to Defy Death"[11] was viewed 260,400 times, bringing considerable traffic

[9] Pirate Fishing. Al Jazeera. http://interactive.aljazeera.com/aje/2014/piratefishingdoc/

[10] Zhang Jianzhong, Wang Tianding. Towards New Media Convergence: When News Meets Games. Modern Communication, No. 11, 2016. 张建中、王天定：《迈向新的媒体融合：当新闻遭遇游戏》，《现代传播》

[11] Gaming Review: 7 Ways to Defy Death by The Washington Post. https://www.washingtonpost.com/graphics/health/defy-death/

to the publisher, The Washington Post. News games piggybacked on games, putting themselves under the limelight of gamification. Against the meta background of the trend of news gamification, its style has brought innovation to the original traditional news form. This is also the crucial reason why news games have sprung up in recent years. Simultaneously, the interactivity, entertainment brought by games, and various media attributes given by new media make news games an important means of information optimization, turning the simple one-way communication in the past to a multi-directional one, and turning boring reading into an educational experience infused with fun, while pure text information turns into a media fusion product with both visuals and texts.

Transparency in Information Dissemination

Compared with traditional news, the lack of authenticity of online news has always been criticized by people. Therefore, how to give full play to the rapid dissemination ability of online news, but at the same time ensure its authenticity, has become a problem that all media people need to think about.

We have found that many media organizations have made attempts in this field. As early as 2012, through CNN Ecosphere Project[12], CNN began to experimentally share the data of users' discussions on the ecological topic on its special online forum, for more users to access. The most striking aspect of this project is that user behavior can affect more people through group communication. The information that users pay key attention to on the platform is not the information actively pushed by an artificial intelligence algorithm by recording user behavior, but the information matrix generated by other users' independent behaviors. Therefore, the information the user is paying attention to may not be what he or she desires but is surely what he or she needs and finds important. In this process, users can see the communication changes caused by all the information interactions. In fact, this also makes the information communication process transparent, and visualizes the editing process which is behind the scenes for traditional media. At the same time, this also de-facto makes the news production process transparent; information

---

[12] Ecosphere, CNN, http://edition.cnn.com/2012/06/15/tech/cnn-ecosphere-rio/.

generation, content production, and communication paths are all clear at a glance, which not only satisfies users' demands for information traceability, but also provides users with a channel for information verification.

Predict the Future

The collaboration between the news and gaming industries has changed the meaning of information communication. The core of news games is "program rhetoric", which restores and simulates events by constructing data models.[13] Therefore, constructing an open deconstruction system in a fixed user group can not only communicate information, but also harvest new data analysis problems and use them as the basis for decision-making. In the case of CNN's Political Prediction Market[14], the conclusions drawn from game data served as predictions of election results. Ability to obtain future results through news dissemination makes news games even more valuable compared with news that simply disseminates information. News is no longer a form of transmitting information, but a way of generating new information and predicting the future.

Textual Deconstruction of News Games: A New Way of News Narrative

The news game is an integrated product of the of information dissemination and interactive experience brought about by the combination of news and games with technological progress. It is a new product form that allows users to obtain news information through the experience of interactive games. In other words, news is the core in news game communication, and game is its communication method. In news games, games play important roles in bringing about a change in the narrative strategy of news, which we call "deconstruction". The reason why news games break away from traditional news and general interactive news and form a new school is that they have a unique ability to deconstruct text. News games decompose information elements in traditional news and

---

[13] Yue Liancheng. "News Game: A New Attempt to Integrate News---Concept, Features and Functions. Modern Audio-Video Arts, No. 9, 2016. 悦连城:《新闻游戏:融合新闻的新尝试---概念、特征与功能》，《现代视听》

[14] Political Prediction Market. CNN. http://edition.cnn.com/2015/12/01/politics/cnn-politics-debate-sweepstakes-rules/index.html.

reassemble them into gamification thinking. According to the different orientations of news games, we divide them into the following two categories.

Closed Deconstruction

The news game producers of this deconstruction method have formulated a detailed and thorough deconstruction strategy for the news text. The user's path to receive and use information is within the framework specified by the producer. In essence, the content producer dominates the deconstruction. For example, "Pirate Fishing" (picture 2) released by Al Jazeera in 2014 is a news game with fixed deconstruction built on the traditional news documentary format. The whole report mainly revolves around the reporter's in-depth investigation into the waters of Sierra Leone with the leading of local law enforcement officers, and the process of collecting evidence of illegal fishing of Korean sailors there. In this case, news games become an alternative form of news content. The product adopts an interface design similar to a task-based game, allowing users to intervene in the game from the perspective of an investigator, and connecting the dots in the entire operation through various visual links. At the same time, in addition to adding the visuals from the documentary, the environment and space are also cleverly designed, such as the office space, mail sending and receiving interface, etc. All kinds of items in the scene have hyperlinks, providing users with rich detailed information, greatly enhancing the richness of interaction and participation. The atmosphere of exploration and decryption also attract users to continuously try to understand the news content, optimizing news communication. Content producers divide the full documentary into multiple short videos according to the design ideas of situational games, and then imitate situations such as email sending and receiving, indoor inspections, etc., making information communication more engaging and interactive. With the evolution from a close-looped documentary to an interactive news game, "Pirate Fishing" can be said to have completed the deconstruction of news content by gamification, turning the linear information flow into points of information based on the clues of journalistic investigation. Thus, users take the initiative of accessing information, which enhances the interactivity of the news. However, the entire content arrangement is still based on the editor's presupposition. Therefore, the deconstruction leader of the entire news game is still the content producer.

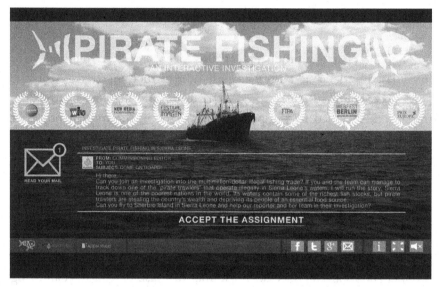

Figure 2 News Game "Pirate Fishing"

Open Deconstruction

The text dissemination of news games deconstructed in an open way has an open pattern. The participation of users is the driving force of news text deconstruction, whose leader is essentially the user under the guidance of the producer. Compared with "Pirate Fishing", Political Prediction Market, a news game launched by CNN during the 2016 U.S. election, has obvious characteristics of open deconstruction. It imitates the operation mode of the stock market and allows users to vote for or against. If the user's position prevails, which resembles the bullish expectations of prices of owned stocks, then the user's promotion index will increase, and the user with a higher promotion index may have the opportunity to participate in the final election. The process by which users acquire news has itself become news and a narrative driving force. Thus, news games move beyond the scope of deconstruction set by the content producer, and users become an important catalyst for deconstructing news.

From this perspective, news games have two different strengths in the deconstruction of news texts. Compared with the former, the latter has a deeper degree of deconstruction, and the result of the deconstruction is unknown.

Gamified Narrative Strategy Based on Classification of Text Deconstruction Methods

Viewing from the development of news games, the initial stage can be called "editing games", and its main purpose is to use the interactivity of new media to make boring text information more attractive; then with the continuous development of society, the performance of news games on political issues is particularly prominent, so "political games" have become an important sub-category of news games; in addition, from the perspective of news production demands, "documentary games" also play an important role, which is usually based on the presentation of history, and can have some influence on current society.

The above three game types are classified according to two aspects: form and theme. These classifications are not on the same dimension, and there are limitations of the news games each category can include, which has caused some difficulties for systematic research on news games. Therefore, by evaluating the degree of gamification and gamification strategies of news game products, we divide them into the following types: text editing games, virtual experiential games, and social investigation games. Among them, text editing and virtual experiential games belong to the larger category of closed deconstruction, while news game products of open deconstruction usually have the characteristics of social investigation, so they can also be called social investigation games. In general, the degrees of gamification of the above three types are different, and the degrees of deconstruction of text information are shown in Table 1. In addition to the characteristics of their types, these news games can also be compatible with the characteristics and functions of other types, but nevertheless showcase the characteristics and functions of their own type.

Name of News Games	Degree of Gamification	Degree of Text Deconstruction	Types of Text Deconstruction

Text Editing Games	Low	Low	Closed
Virtual Experiential Games	Medium	High	Open
Social Investigation Games	High	Medium	Closed

Table 1 Comparisons of Degrees of Gamification and Text Deconstruction of Different Types of News Games

Narrative Strategy of Text Editing News Games: Combining Linear and Non-linear, Expanding Multi-Dimensional Integration Experience

This kind of news game uses basic interactive functions to deconstruct and gamify, and realizes preliminary gamification by combining traditional news narrative arrangement and basic game design. Therefore, it has the lowest degree of gamification and the most direct deconstruction of traditional text information. Usually, this type of news game is mainly text, and supplemented by pictures or videos depending on the situation. Its operability is very strong, and it can to a certain extent avoid some problems caused by a lack of timeliness due to the long production cycle.

Sid Meier, the legendary designer of the "Civilization" series of games, believes that "A game is a series of interesting choices."[15] Compared with traditional print media that controls the order of information and the size and position of the text to control readers' attention, games are more varied according to this statement. In the process of producing text editing news games, news producers will change the text form according to the content of news topics, communication purposes, channels, etc., and deconstruct texts by utilizing the nonlinear narrative characteristics of online media. The time, place, events and other major elements in the news event will have various possibilities such as ones that are chronological, flashbacks, and interludes with different choices made by users, which makes the

---

[15] Kevin Werbach, Dan Hunter. How Game Thinking Can Revolutionize Your Business. Zhejiang People's Publishing House, 2014.p.32.

narration of the whole event change from a single linear narration to one that combines both the linear and nonlinear. Thus, the gamified narrative structure can become more complex.

For example, "1000 Days of Syria"[16], released in 2011, is a text editing game in its simplest form. Users enter the game scene through a third perspective and news facts are narrated using a diary-like form. There are also many hyperlinks embedded in the text so that users can click to drill down into a key piece of information whenever they want while reading. Such a combination of linear and non-linear narrative allows hyperlinks with interactive properties to connect more news details into the news itself, thus forming an information network around news events, and event details are presented more elaborately. It not only avoids the overly lengthy background description in traditional news, but also increases the information load of the entire news event multifold. At the same time, this tree-like text structure also builds a customized version of news for users. Clicking on different options will present different news content to users, which is more in line with the trend that users actively and selectively receive news in the Internet age. The news event itself is the trunk of the tree, and the branches of different thicknesses are information elements with different levels of importance and details, decomposing the text into information points such as time, place, event, etc., and then a news element is used as the narrative trunk that connects it all. In this way, information points can be attached to the truck according to a certain logic, with links either direct or indirect, and users can either search for information details upwards, or explore information sources downwards.

However, "1000 Days in Syria", when compared with "Syrian Journey"[17] which appeared four years later, is a little too monotonous in form. The latter adds illustrations and supplementary explanations on top of text narration, and the content is more concise, the deconstruction pattern clearer, and the main theme of the news appears more prominent. What's worth mentioning is that "Syrian Journey" adopts the first-person perspective in the narrative process, placing users in the news events, and using immersive narrative methods to make news texts interact more

---

[16] Simon Parkin. 1000 Days of Syria-turning War Journalism in to A Game. http://www.1000daysofsyria.com/about/.

[17] Syrian Journey. BBC. http://www.bbc.com/news/world-middle-east-32057601.

closely with users. This realizes the transformation from simple textual narrative to experiential narrative. This transformation is an important direction for the future development of text-editing narrative, and it is also a direct manifestation of this type of news games transitioning to one with deep text deconstruction.

In addition, when some news does not have obvious time and space concepts but does have content points, the non-linear narrative of game is more practical for text deconstruction. For example, "Factitious"[18], a fake news testing game launched by the fact-checking agency Politifact, moves beyond the narrative of factual elaboration, and uses question-and-answer to interact with users, converting information points into questions, and using option settings and questions sorting to restructure the text. This gives a stronger sense of game and allows users to access more information in the game.

In the process of this type of gamification, content producers use one line as the narrative trunk, and at the same time decompose many information points with different perspectives and central event objects, and then connect all the information with the trunk, forming a closed loop for users to receive information by making their own independent choices. The user's choice in reading is autonomous and random, but because the scope of deconstruction is relatively fixed, it is difficult for users to stray outside this scope. In this type of news game with a relatively low level of gamification, game elements are mainly reflected in the fact that it gives users the right to choose the order and focus of information, and the user's choices deconstruct the news text. Meanwhile, with non-liner narrative, the amount of news information has become greater, which is in line with the consumption needs of people in the Internet environment. From another point of view, the narrative of such news games has many similarities with the narrative arrangement of traditional news. For example, each independent text also retains time, place, characters, events and other elements of information, and the language of the text is relatively calm and objective. Therefore, this genre has not completely gotten rid of traditional news narrative, which is why we call it the most basic news game.

---

[18] Zhou Yujia. How to Fight Fake News? Americans Say: "Play Games!". https://mp.weixin.qq.com/s/w3qA7J45Ss4u34OulDtu1g. 周羽佳:《如何打击假新闻?美国人说:"玩游戏呗!"》

Narrative Strategy of Virtual Experiential News Games: Applying
Game Sessions to Achieve Immersive User Experience

Virtual experiential games are news games that imitate pure game
design and use the arrangement of game sessions. With the continuous
advancement of technology, the gradual deepening of design concepts,
and the continuous integration of different industries, news practitioners
are no longer satisfied with the simple combination of graphics and text,
but are moving towards more design-and-experience-oriented all-media
news products. News games that imitate experiential games are the most
detached from the characteristics of news forms, and are also the most
game-like compared to the other two types of news games. They usually rely
on or imitate the framework of existing games to arrange the distribution
of news information. In the early stage of planning, content producers
need to select one or more game templates to be imitated according to
the goals of communication and prepare for decomposing news texts
by listing the game elements available in the templates. There are many
ways of decomposition, either directly or indirectly, such as using game
session settings to insert news information into different game junctures,
or converting information points into images, sounds, videos, etc.,
integrating more into the game. Usually, the closer the integration between
the two is, that is, the higher the degree of infusion of deconstructed
information points into various sessions of the game, the better the effect
of the game. At the same time, by comparing different cases, we find that
the design angles and user experience of different experiential news games
are not homogenous. For example, also on the topic of US election, The
Washington Post made a news game that is different from the CNN one.
The game is a mobile device game called "Floppy Candidate"[19]. Its design
prototype is the highly-reputed "Flappy Bird", and the highly topical news
events of the candidates are used boldly as design elements in game sessions.
The combination of sound and picture is fitting and proper. Gamification
and deconstruction are achieved through integrating each element in news
events with each existing game element. In the game's character setting,
the birds in the original game correspond to the presidential candidates,

---

[19] "Whoever Passes the Test Will Be Elected: Floppy Candidate Spoofs the US Presidential
Election," http://www.18touch.com/shuiguoguanliaoj.html, December 15, 2015.

and the background elements correspond to elements related to the general election, such as the obelisk, the White House, mailbox servers, the walls between Mexico and the United States, etc. In the setting of sessions, during the game or after the mission fails, the screen will pop up with multiple choice questions on hot news about the corresponding candidates. If the player answers incorrectly, they can click the link to enter the news page for more details. After the user fails the game, the most topical quote of the chosen candidate is played. For example, if Hillary Clinton is the chosen candidate, and she fails, her line "I suppose I could have stayed home, baked cookies, and had teas" will be played. Such a series of designs combines game design with news narratives well, which is both interesting and has certain values for communication. The reason why content designers choose such a game prototype for adaptation is not only about considering the operability of production, but also the influence of the prototype game on the adapted products. Therefore, when producing such products, producers usually choose games that are well-known or already have large user resources as prototypes, in order to expand the dissemination and influence of products. The "Uber Game"[20] theme interactive game by the Financial Times also falls into this category.

Narrative Strategy of Social Investigative News Games: Strong Interaction and Strong Data

This type of news game mainly guides users through open deconstruction, and in a form similar to social surveys, obtains user information through gamified interactions, thereby gaining added news value. Therefore, this type of news game is usually highly interactive, a category that maximizes the interactive function of new media. Generally, this type of news work has a complete platform design, and the settings of questionnaires, role-playing, dialogue and other situations are its main way of content arrangement. In the past, we measured the quality and communication effects of traditional news production through data such

[20] "'Media Industry x Games' Case Packaging: Reporting/Interaction/IP Development, Directing Attention with Novelty", Tencent Media, https://mp.weixin.qq.com/s/pzXBeux0p1LU4Fs3ZJUVzw, October 19, 2017.《"传媒业x游戏"案例打包:报道/交互/IP开发，用脑洞指挥注意力》，腾讯传媒

as reading volume, audience ratings, and forwarding volume. However, for news games in the new media environment, background data collection is more valuable than the simple download volume for assessment. Because the rich background data can not only reflect the quality of the game, but also become the basis for its operation strategy. In this way, the large amount of data received in the background of the news game can also help journalists to find valuable content from it, and even create more meaningful information to predict and influence the future.

We divide the process of deconstructing news texts with this type of news game into three stages: the first stage is semi-deconstructing news. That is, the content producer lists the points of news facts. The form of listing is varied, but the purpose is to disseminate independent information points to users, while there is no direct or necessary connection between each point. In this process, the thinking of content producers has changed from the pre-setting mode with text editing to one about open guidance. The second stage sees in-depth interaction between users and news, laying the foundation for the subsequent generation of updated news points, with the user's choices and feedback endowing news with new content. The third stage is to reorganize information points, that is, content producers recombine the deconstructed information to generate new news texts. In this stage, the new information and the original news are integrated to form a richer information circle, and content producers can capture the newsworthy information points and recombine them to form new news texts. The capture of new information usually serves the purpose of the first stage: open guidance.

Usually, in the first stage, content producers with top-level design thinking abilities already assess and plan in detail for the content production of the third stage, so that the news text of the third stage can echo the semi-deconstructed news text in the first stage, forming a complete news narrative system. This is also in line with the agenda setting theory in news communication, that is, by providing information and arranging relevant topics, it is possible to effectively sway which facts and opinions people pay attention to and the order in which they talk about them.[21] Therefore, in multimedia interactive news games, the deconstruction of

---

[21] Wei Lingfang. "Agenda Setting" in the Internet Age, News World, No. 2, 2009. 魏玲芳: 《网络时代的"议程设置"》，《新闻世界》

news texts has also become a tool to achieve agenda setting. The essence of deconstruction is to analyze users' feedback on news events and to visualize public opinion. Therefore, this type of news game is usually used in large-scale news events with strong influence on public opinion. In the operation of the "Political Prediction Market" game mentioned above, the first stage of deconstruction of the game uses the form of a questionnaire. The set questions include various news hotspots scattered during the general election, and the users' votes reflect the underlying public opinion direction behind many news points. Pushed by that direction, the content producers list, analyze the information and draw conclusions, creating final content for the third stage of deconstructing. After the news game went online, it received a large amount of user data through the answering session, including users' personal information, views on hot issues of the general election, and even political inclinations. For the candidate team running for the election, it is one thing to attract more people to vote, moreover, on the other hand, tens of thousands of users have disclosed their political inclinations through the news game platform, which offers certain reference for the formulation of election strategies of each candidate. This news game's data showed that Clinton's chance of winning the Democratic race was 82% on May 8,[22] and the result was confirmed two months later.

From this point of view, the interactivity of the multimedia interactive platform helps the deconstruction of text in news games move beyond the external user interface to in-depth information mining. Google has also used an open-style new media interactive platform to obtain data and produced a large number of data visualization works with significant visual impact. For example, The WebGL Globe[23] is a browser data visualization of public data around the world associated with geographic information. It can show data on our planet in 3D, which includes the search volume of keywords such as world population and earthquake distribution. From this point of view, news games with open-style deconstruction have found a new added value - news value on the basis of past big data analysis, which is the reinterpretation of news information by game interactions. In this

[22] Yue Liancheng. "News Game: A New Attempt to Integrate News---Concept, Features and Functions. Modern Audio-Video Arts, No. 9, 2016. 悦连城：《新闻游戏:融合新闻的新尝试---概念、特征与功能》，《现代视听》
[23] The Web GL Globe, Google, http://globe.chromeexperiments.com.

process, interactions in the game become an open narrative, allowing users to participate and create new information. The integration of OGC, UGC, and PGC forms new narratives and content. Such added value has also become the most important reason of existence for this genre of news games.

The Essence of Gamification: The Transfer of Choice

To sum up, on the basis of adhering to the principles of news, different types of news games have different gamification strategies. In essence, they have different angles and methods when it comes to the structure and deconstruction of news texts. From the blending of linear and non-linear narratives in text editing, to the disassembly and integration of news content and the game itself in virtual experiential games, to the re-creation of news content in new media interactive games, all are new ways of deconstructing text. At the same time, the news function caused by deconstruction will change, thus producing interesting communication effects. From the user's perspective, the three types of games above provide users with the opportunity to choose, and the transfer of information selection rights has become the most critical point of news games in deconstructing news texts, which is why news games can stand out from the vast ocean of interactive news to form its own field. This also confirms the validity of the above-mentioned "a game is a series of interesting choices." Therefore, we believe that all interactive news or interactive products containing news information that can provide users with content selection rights within a specific range can be discussed in the theoretical category of news games.

In addition, the transfer of selection rights manifests differently in different deconstruction methods. In the fixed deconstruction, the transfer of the right of choice has a limited scope, it can only determine the order in which the user receives the information and the scope of reception, while open deconstruction gives room to the scope of the influence stemmed from the right of choice – users' choices which can become another booster to news production.

News Elements That Can Be Used
in News Game Design

News topics used in news games usually have strong influence in a certain period or field, so the news elements will be very rich, including the six major ones - person, time, place, event, cause, and the occurrence process. Which elements are most suitable for the design of news games has become the main problem to overcome in production. In other words, the question is what kind of elements in the news are those that when producers see them, they will immediately think of turning them into gamified elements and key points? We will analyze the elements worthy of use in news texts from the following aspects.

Characters: Game Roles

Every good news story needs a talking "face", and the game world is no exception. This "face" is the driving force to promote the use of the entire news game and leads users into the game scene. In the news game, there are two orientations in the settings of characters. One is the setting of the role of the news event that goes deep into the game, that is, the protagonist of the news event and related character settings, which makes the content of game richer. It is the foundation for the composition of the game plot. The other is the role that the news game gives to the user, that is, the role setting that leads the user into the game. In any type of news games, users are given roles. Some are the protagonists of news stories, and some are observers of events, such as in "Pirate Fishing" when users act as investigators, and "Uber Game" where users take on the role of an Uber driver, etc. Therefore, whether it is the role setting internal to the game or the user role setting external to the game, the purpose is to closely link users with news events.

Location: Game Scene

A game is a system with set rules, in which the user must be in some specific environment. For news games, the scene comes from one or multiple locations described by the news event itself. Location has many advantages for news visualization. Whether it is its own image information or the sense of space, it provides a broader information bearing space for network media which is in two-dimensional space. In addition, with the continuous development of technologies such as augmented reality and VR technology, the scenes of news games have surpassed the space we normally understand, and gradually extended to a three-dimensional space similar to reality. In a wider space, people's perspective changes and behavior changes may lead to contact with richer information dimensions. Therefore, using news locations for scene planning can create more information space for news games. Concatenation of multiple scenes can form the prototype of a news game. For example, NetEase's VR report "Don't Panic, There is No Radiation" launched on the 30th anniversary of the Chernobyl accident using technology to present the real news scene of 30 years ago to users. Most news games simulate reality by extracting representative scenes in news events, creating a game atmosphere for users. Therefore, this is also one of the most commonly used design elements for the immersive narrative technique that news games are good at.

Process: Game Session

The occurring process of news can be understood as the concept of plot in the game, that is, the story-based situations that users will encounter in the game. Many excellent news games rely on the experiential narrative through session settings, excelling ahead of traditional news forms. Often news events worth making into news games are of multifaceted or conflicting events. Conflict is the most attractive and essential part of a story, and it still holds true in news games. The transfer of the right of choice presents news results not in the way of descriptive text but through effects of user experience. Content producers convert the praise and criticism of news results into the ups and downs of user emotions, which makes the news more appealing and communicable. Therefore, the most fascinating part of news games is that users experience the contradictions in news through choices, which conflict with each other. For example, "Thinking Like a Mayor" produced by Caixin converts the impact of pollution on the urban environment into the result of different choices, and the content of the news is incorporated into the game, with the user's emotions controlled through game sessions; in "Syrian Journey", users hesitate in choosing a comfortable but expensive retreat route, or an economical but dangerous one; in another example - "Daily Life of the Emergency Room"[24], users get lost in a variety of emergency and non-emergency cases.

The Truth of News Games

When discussing the meaning of the existence of news games, we can't get around the problems caused by the conflict between the principle of news authenticity and the inherent subjectivity and virtuality of games. As far as the meaning of "news facts" is concerned, for the authenticity of news reports the "reality" is the foundation, "possibilities" are realistically present, and "interpretability" is the "truth" understood through interpretation. The news truth that people can obtain actually lies in the description of "news events" based on facts and the degree of understanding of realistic "possibilities".[25] And this "level of understanding" depends on people's subjective way of thinking. The subjective thinking of both producers and users has a subtle influence on the authenticity of news in the process of news production and dissemination, that is, the process of news production and dissemination is a process established on top of news facts by the subjective thinking of people in line with news ethics and rules. The same is true for news games. In our opinion, there is not a simple conflict between the objectivity, authenticity of news, and the subjectivity, virtuality of games, but rather it is a kind of organic fusion.

The Fusion of Reality and Virtuality

The news game always cuts into the news event by simulation or imitation, through which users obtain news information during the interactive experience. Regardless of the kind of news game, they organically integrate virtuality and reality, build virtual environments and plots, etc., based on content from reality, and use virtual or hypothetical subjective

---

[24] Emergency Life. Zero Media. https://0media.tw/p/ergame/. 急诊人生, 零传媒. https://0media.tw/p/ergame/

[25] Yao Junjia. Interpretation of the Significance of News Authenticity. Journal of Social Sciences, No. 6, 2007. 姚君嘉:《新闻真实性的意义阐释》, 《社会科学》

settings to create a platform for users to better receive information. This lets users either indirectly or directly become the first person to intervene in the news practice, thus greatly optimizing the news reading experience and improving the efficiency of news communication. Therefore, the news game is not another new "architecture" on the opposite side of reality and fact, but a new "banner" built on the foundation of facts. Its combination of virtuality and reality makes the entire news system more stable and news products more recognizable.

The Fusion of Journalism and Art

News games provides us with an artistic way of seeing things. Since ancient times, there have been many definitions of art. From the perspective of functionality, art can be used to express emotions and induce aesthetic experience, etc.[26] In addition, since ancient Greece the theories of imitation, expression, formalism, reception, etc. - some of them are centered on the external world, some are centered on the author, some are centered on the work, and some are centered on the reader - all hold that art has a recognizable inner unity.[27] We argue that the gamification element in news games is actually an emotional expression based on objective facts. We might as well regard it as an artistic expression tool; the reproduction of news by content producers is actually narrating the facts of the news in an artistic way. It has been demonstrated above that news games are a new form of narrative of news, so this narrative can also be regarded as an artistic narrative strategy. Whether it is visual optimization of news games, multimedia use, or text deconstruction methods, games are an artistic expression of journalism. From this point of view, news games have become fusion products of news and art. To sum up, the news game is a normative mechanism for obtaining information; it is serious, careful and conforms to the values of news. At the same time, news games provide us with a broader and optimized narrative space, allowing users to obtain real information in the virtual world and understand objective facts from

---

[26] Zhou Jian. How to Define Art - Re-understanding Danto's Philosophy of Art. Doctoral Dissertation of East China Normal University, 2013, pp. 54, 7. 周建:《如何定义艺术---丹托艺术哲学再认识》，华东师范大学博士学位论文
[27] Ibid.

a subjective perspective. It is a product of intense collision and effective fusion between highly subjective art and highly objective news. Art and news are fused in the collision, and a new understanding of reality is born in the progress.

Conclusion

In news games, the game adds new content to the form and function of the news text. Through the games' deconstructing of news text, the news industry finds a breakthrough to re-create itself in a new field. The increase of attention, readability, visibility, and the added value of predicting outcomes are the most valuable things of news games. Most of the current news games are still extensions of traditional news, and their production is usually based on traditional news content. However, as seen in our research and analysis of news games' deconstruction of text, the focus of news games on the content of news texts is different from that of traditional news. Whether it is the choice of tasks, the design of voice, the arrangement of perspectives, or the arrangement of clues, all show the uniqueness of games. Therefore, we believe that the production of news games should be in the top-level design of planning for news event reporting, and become part of a joint force of communication together with other diverse products.

We have already entered the Web 3.0 society, which gives us a more effective and more optimal mode for network information exchanges, which can promote knowledge more effectively and timely, and make more audiences feel the joy of knowledge.[28] Therefore, the information acquisition environment created by news games for users through interesting and open narrative modes is in line with the characteristics of Web 3.0. Fundamentally speaking, news games are actually a way of deconstructing news texts. "Games" are its shells, and what really brings us meaning is the experience of receiving information hidden under the shells. In the future, we will usher in the era of Web 4.0, Web 5.0 and

---

[28] Ma Zhenping, Yang Shanyuan. Mode for Network Information Exchanges Based on Web3.0. Information and Documentation Services, No.1, 2011. 马振萍、杨姗媛:《基于Web3.0的网络信息交流模式》, 《情报资料工作》

eras of even richer information exchanges. News games may only be a way of information deconstruction in this era. The popularity of VR technology, the deepening of the notion of intellectual property, and the fusion of different industries has made us see that there will be more forms of information deconstruction and reorganization that are more effective in the future. The future of news games has far too many possibilities. Perhaps, news in the future will no longer be limited to "games", but the deconstruction of news texts by gamification is already on the way, and research on its narrative patterns will continue.

(Zeng Xiangmin, Professor, Doctoral Supervisor at the School of Television, Communication University of China; Fang Xueyue, Editor of China Daily.com)

NARRATIVE STRATEGY OF THE CO-TEXT OF ONLINE SPRING FESTIVAL GALA—AN ANALYSIS ON TEN YEARS OF CCTV ONLINE SPRING FESTIVAL GALA

Zhao Shuping, Wu Hao, and Wang Yueru

Abstract: Due to attributes of it being a traditional TV variety show, the narrative strategy of the CCTV Online Spring Festival Gala presents a pronounced mainstream value orientation and cultivation effect. In terms of its archi-text, the narrative theme of the Gala embodies remarkable patriotism. Influenced by the pre-text, the Gala selectively absorbs grass-roots discourse and presents a unique grass-roots image. Turning to the main text, the stage design directly participates in the presentation of the main text style. Through the transformation from para-text to link-text, the live audience, hosts, and netizens of the Gala jointly form a virtual interactive field, which continuously generates emotional energy and connection. Looking forward to the future, the optimization of the narrative strategy of the Gala should adhere to its own characteristics, form continuous archi-text by fixed program forms, and improve the flexibility of co-text through appropriate absorption.

Keywords: CCTV Online Spring Festival Gala, narrative technique, co-text

Introduction

Since its launch in 2011, the CCTV Online Spring Festival Gala has completed its first decade. The Gala, being in nature a TV variety show, recreates various artistic programs through technology, giving the audience comprehensive aesthetic enjoyment. In addition, in order to fit the Internet communication environment, the CCTV Online Spring Festival Gala has continuously improved its "sense of the Internet". Compared with other types of TV variety programs, the Gala has created a more enthusiastic on-site atmosphere and interactive effect for netizens.

The theory of co-text was put forward by Professor Zhao Yiheng in the book "Semiotics: Principles and Problems". It refers to the factors carried by the text, hidden behind the text, outside the text, or at the edge of the text – factors that actively participate in the composition of the meaning of the text, and affect the interpretation of meanings.[1] Professor Zhao systematically and in detail divides co-texts into six categories: pre-text, which is the general term for other texts that have had an impact on the text before it is generated; para-text, which is the accompanying factors that are completely exposed on the surface of the text; archi-text, which is the text clusters that the text belongs to; meta-text, i.e., "text about the text"; link-text, i.e., the "linking factor" of the text, that is, other texts that the recipient interprets actively, or passively links with so that they are received together; preceding or ensuing text, that is, the special relationship that exists between the two texts. Based on the classification of co-texts by Professor Zhao, this paper divides the co-texts of the ten years of CCTV Online Spring Festival Gala and focuses on its narrative strategies, in order to define and analyze the show in a more normative and rigorous manner.

Generative co-text	Pre-text	The ceremonial concept established by CCTV Spring Festival Gala; the multicultural context formed by traditional culture, Internet culture, grass-roots culture, etc.

---

[1] Zhao Yiheng. Semiotics: Principles and Problems [M]. Nanjing University Press. 2016. 赵毅衡. 符号学原理与推演[M]. 南京大学出版社

Explicit co-text	Para-text	Program broadcast time, space scene design; short promotional videos; hosts, guests; production units, stage design team, etc.
	Archi-text	TV variety shows are a traditional TV program genre; online shows, as a relatively new genre compared to TV, have certain Internet characteristics in terms of program category, language type, theme setting, narrative mode, and session setting.
Interpretive co-text	Preceding text	The use and innovation of the regular mode of TV variety shows and the narrative strategy of CCTV Spring Festival Gala; the inheritance of CCTV Spring Festival Gala's media ritual; the replication of video websites' New Year's Eve galas; the reference and collage of internet cultures, grass-roots cultures, subcultures, etc.
	Meta-text	Media reports; netizen discussions.
	Link-text	Weibo hot search keywords; "homing stations" and various interviews, pop-up activities, etc.; discussions in other fields.
	Ensuing text	Spring Festival galas held by provincial TV stations; New Year's Eve galas created by online platforms.

Table 1 Co-text of CCTV Online Spring Festival Gala

From the perspective of the co-text theory, the genre of CCTV's Online Spring Festival Gala is a manifestation of archi-text, and it is also in the most obvious and largest category of archi-text. As an index sign, it instructs the recipient how to interpret the symbolic text in front of them, while attracting his or her attention. Focusing on the narrative strategy of the CCTV Online Spring Festival Gala, this article deduces the intertextual relationships between the co-text and the main text of the Gala, as well as within the co-text.

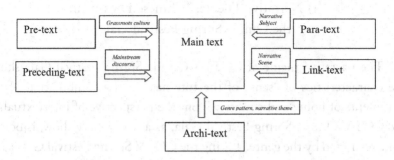

Figure 1 Intertextual Relationships

By analyzing the characteristics of the archi-text and para-text of the CCTV Online Spring Festival Gala, as well as the intertextual relationships between other texts and these two types of texts, this paper argues that in the mainstream discourse system, the narrative strategy of the CCTV Online Spring Festival Gala is still in the framework of a traditional TV variety show, showing an obvious mainstream value orientation and cultivation effects. In terms of intertextuality, the archi-text and para-text of the Gala are also influenced by pre-text and preceding-text.

1. Family and Country Sentiments in Archi-Texts and Narrative Theme

The narrative theme affects the audience's overall judgment of the text, and also defines the boundaries of the audience's expectations to a certain extent. Narrative themes are divided into narrow and broad senses. In a broad sense, the narrative theme of TV works refers to the reproduction of a certain person or type of people and things. In a narrow sense, it refers to the central idea or main content. As a type of archi-text, the theme participates in the generation of the main symbol system and affects the interpretation of the meaning of symbols. In the same way, the narrative theme of CCTV's Online Spring Festival Gala also affects its grasp of the goal of the Gala to a certain extent.

(1) Narrative Theme: "Chinese Dream" in the Online Spring Festival Gala

The narrative theme of CCTV's Online Spring Festival Gala shows the characteristics of "sense of the Internet" in the combination of the sentiments of home and country. From the perspective of intertextuality, the CCTV Online Spring Festival Gala, as a TV variety show, is bound to be restricted by the genre. Taking the CCTV Spring Festival Gala as an example, singing and dancing, language and opera are the main types of its programs. Due to the requirements for the atmosphere at the time of the Spring Festival Gala - New Year's Eve needs to create a nationally festive, warm and harmonious festive atmosphere - among these three main types of programs, the song and dance programs that can best embody this atmosphere have become the type of program with the highest proportion.

Era	Theme of CCTV Spring Festival Gala
1983-1992	Unity, Forging ahead, Joy, Patriotism, Unification
1993-2002	Reunion, Striving forward, New century
2003-2012	Harmony, Joy, Good life, Reunion
2013-2020	Chinese dream, Building a well-off society, New era, Joy, Better life

Table 1 Summary of CCTV Spring Festival Gala Themes Over the Years

Year	Theme of CCTV Online Spring Festival Gala
2011	Hundreds of millions of netizens celebrate the New Year; Chinese people across the globe send New Year's Greetings; Click on happiness; Download joy; Upload creativity; Share the fruit of hard work; Celebrity carnival (celebration, striving forward, happiness, creativity)
2012	Reunion Online; Hold happiness; Dream Upload (Reunion, Happiness, Dream)
2013	N reasons why I love China
2014	Gather up positive energy; Pass on the Chinese dream.
2015	Abundant blessings to millions of homes; Sharing Chinese New Year together.
2016	Internet life of the Chinese
2017	China, joy, live
2018	Strengthen the country with connections; Technological hub of the new era

2019	Bring love home
2020	New year's new wish; my youth carnival
2021	My youth carnival

Table 2 Summary of CCTV Online Spring
Festival Gala Themes from 2011 to 2021

The CCTV Online Spring Festival Gala has formed a program category similar to the CCTV Spring Festival Gala with such archi-text, that is, the genre patterns of a TV variety show. The first CCTV Online Spring Festival Gala in 2011, with the theme of " Hundreds of millions of netizens celebrate the New Year", brought global netizens into the audience of the party, echoing the word of the "network" nature of the Online Gala. It can be seen that, unlike the CCTV Spring Festival Gala, the online Gala has a relatively high degree of freedom in artistic creation. In addition to the keywords of "dream" and "country", there are also a certain number of popular songs and original songs of Internet celebrities.

In terms of the theme of the gala, as the representative of the official discourse, the CCTV Spring Festival Gala carries important national ceremonial significance. As shown in Table 1, the theme of the CCTV Spring Festival Gala basically revolves around national mainstream themes to meet the audience's expectations for the festive atmosphere and their prayers for fullness, unity, joy, auspiciousness, and hope. The CCTV Online Spring Festival Gala, which is also in the official discourse system, also needs to have a lofty spirit of the times and a broad cultural outlook, and flexibly use Internet buzz words with mainstream discourse orientation to highlight the "sense of Internet" and youthfulness of the Online Gala.

In 2013, "Chinese Dream" became the hot word of the year across the whole country, and CCTV Online Spring Festival Gala also used it in its theme script. The definition of the "sense of Internet" has also changed from simple "Internet users' participation" to the communication of socialist core values such as the "Chinese Dream", "Chinese Power", and "Chinese Beauty" in cyberspace. From 2015 to 2018, although "sharing", "Internet life" and "live broadcast" in the theme words of the CCTV Online Spring Festival Gala reflected a certain "sense of Internet", the retention of the word "country" still confirmed the Online Gala's "Family-country oneness" narrative strategy. In 2020 and 2021, the themes of the Online Gala were both "My Youth Carnival", replacing "Internet" with "youth", and the positioning of the Online Gala has gradually been determined, that is, one that is more youthful and more recognized by the Internet, a TV variety show with young people as its core audience.

(2) The Expression of "Sense of Internet" with Mainstream Value Orientation

Since the first CCTV Online Spring Festival Gala in 2011, the theme "Hundreds of millions of netizens celebrate the New Year" has brought global netizens into the audience of the party, echoing the word "network" nature of the Online Gala. In the second session, the theme "Click on happiness; Download joy; Upload creativity; Share the fruit of hard work", in the way of parallelism, connected the theme of "happiness, joy, creativity, hard work". The group of verbs "click, download, upload, share" not only increases the sense of internet, but also emphasizes the subjectivity of the audience, reflecting the importance the Online Gala attaches to audience participation. In 2012, the use of the annual buzz word "Hold Zhu" in the theme words showed the traditional media's insight into the online world. In general, in 2011 and 2012, the Online Gala defined "Sense of Internet" as netizens relying on the Internet to participate in the Gala remotely and sharing their online life.

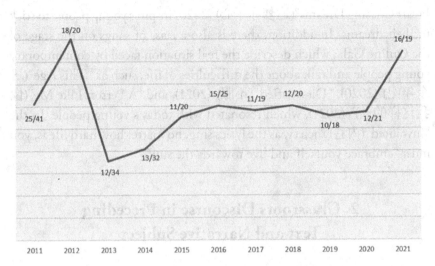

Figure 2 Proportion of Song Programs in CCTV
Online Spring Festival Gala over the Years[2]

Since 2013, the proportion of song programs in CCTV Online Spring Festival Gala has increased year by year. The theme of the song programs reflects the narrative theme of the Online Gala to a certain extent. As can be seen from Figure 2, singing and dancing programs occupy about half of the Online Gala. Different from the CCTV Spring Festival Gala, the song programs in the Online Gala are mainly solo or small-scale chorus, and there are fewer large-scale song and dance shows. In terms of song types, Internet songs and popular songs are the main ones. Especially in the first Online Gala, hot Internet songs represented by "Mouse Loves Rice" (老鼠爱大米), "Old Boy"(老男孩) and "Free Flying"(自由飞翔)all appeared together.

Among the 19 shows of the 2021 Online Gala, there are 16 song shows. It can be seen that song programs are playing an increasingly important role in the Online Gala. In terms of the themes of the songs, "home and country" and "dream" are the two keywords. "Coming Home Often"(常回家看看) (2016) was sung by the voices of countless people who are away from their hometowns, expressing the desire of the whole country to "go home and reunite" during the Spring Festival; "Red Flag Fluttering"(红旗飘飘) (2013) and others more directly expressed patriotism. "Innocent

---

[2] In 2011 and 2012, the first sessions of the galas were selected as the research object.

Heart Chasing Dreams"(追梦赤子心) (2020) inspires young people to stick to their dreams. In addition, there is also a class of songs on the stage of the Online Gala, which describe the real situation faced by contemporary young people and talk about the difficulties of life, such as "This Age"(这个年纪) (2020), "Dissatisfied"(不服) (2021), and "A Person Like Me"(像我这样的人)" (2021), which resonated with today's young people. In the "involuted"(内卷) society, as the lyrics sing, no matter how hard life is, you must "embrace yourself and live towards the sun".

2. Grassroots Discourse in Preceding Text and Narrative Subject

The narrative subject, or the teller of the story, is also the direct expressor of meanings. On the stage of the Online Gala, there is a grassroots group, most of which come from ordinary backgrounds, or even from the fringes of society, but rely on a unique skill or mainstream value appeal to enter the mainstream discourse, with a "straightforward" way of discourse, and participated in the expression of the meanings of the symbols of the Online Gala.

The word "caogen" (草根) is a literal translation of the English word "grassroots", which was originally coined in the United States in the 19th century. In China, "grassroots" was first used by people of Hong Kong and Taiwan, calling the civilian class "grassroots class"; between the start of the Reform and Opening Up and 2000, "grassroots" mainly referred to the "ordinary, civilian, mass, and folk"; after 2000, the meanings of "humble origin, low social status, maverick, different from official discourse" were added to "grassroots".[3] The "grassroots class" refers to those who are politically and economically weak, have limited discourse power, as well as distinct regional characteristics. Their demographic is relatively complex, and both urban and rural dwellers may be categorized into them. With the continuous refinement of daily life by this class, the characteristics of "grassroots culture" have gradually become clear.

[3] Yuan Xiujie. Staring at "Grassroots" in "Focus"——Exploring the Etymology and Meaning of "Grassroots"[J]. Beauty and Times, 2007(04):29-30. 苑秀杰.凝视"焦点"中的"草根"——探寻"草根"的词源、词义[J].美与时代

(1) Narrative Subject: Selective Absorption of Grassroots Discourse

Grassroots groups did not originally belong to the mainstream discourse system. They were on the fringes of society and were not valued sufficiently. Thanks to the rapid development of Internet media, "grassroots" found discourse fertile soil for "rooting and sprouting". From the perspective of intertextuality, the narrative subject and narrative theme presented in the Online Gala are directly related to the selective absorption strategy of the grass-roots discourse in the preceding text, that is, the CCTV Spring Festival Gala. This strategy mainly covers two layers of meanings: the preservation of part of the original meaning of the grassroots and the extension of the meaning of the grassroots culture.

After grassroots culture entered the mainstream discourse, although some individual, rebellious, and confrontational elements have also been eliminated, there are still many shows that can reflect the original meaning of "grassroots", that is, independent and innovative shows that are good at using entertainment to resolve serious topics. Grassroots, as the narrative subject of the Online Gala, can be divided into three categories: Internet celebrities or folk talents who can bring joy to the audience, heroes from ordinary backgrounds worthy of praise, and working people at the social bottom who need to be given attention to. And these three types of people happen to be able to convey the core values that CCTV Spring Festival Gala or the Online Gala hope to deliver: joy, happiness; dedication, patriotism, enduring hardship, and striving forward.

There are two main forms of such shows. One is folk arts and skills, such as the folk acrobatics "Fancy God Face" (2013) by Song Xiaodong from Shandong, and the full-of-energy anime song "Nine Nine Eighty-One" (2021), performed by the inheritor of Huayin Old Tune, aka "the originator of Chinese rock and roll", etc. All these shows reinvented folk acrobatics and traditional culture in a novel and interesting way. The second is talent show. The Online Gala has broken the fixed pattern of traditional song and dance performances. The types of talent include works with independent and innovative thinking, impersonator shows with a "sense of copycat", and unique skills that ordinary people do not have. In addition, CCTV does not limit its attention to the bottom of the society. It is a grassroots show as long as it is of the masses and the common people, shows through which people can tell, express, and release their emotions and visions.

In the CCTV Spring Festival Gala, the grassroots people did not directly participate in the narrative at first but achieved presence of the discourse subject in a way of "representation". For example, in language programs, comedians, among the prominent are Zhao Benshan and Huang Hong, who represent the grassroots, have risen in the Spring Festival Gala. Later, some grassroots people who became popular on the Internet got the opportunity to independently appear on the Gala, breaking the confines of professional actors interpreting grassroots life. In 2002, the Internet singer Xue Cun, who became popular with "People from Northeast China are Living Lei Feng"(东北人都是活雷锋), appeared on the stage of the Spring Festival Gala with musical Pingshu "Away from Home"(出门在外), symbolizing that the grassroots discourse subject represented by netizens could also express the "grassroots voice" in a "straightforward" way. After 2006, grassroots made a breakthrough on the stage of CCTV Spring Festival Gala: in 2008, a group of grassroots construction migrant workers led by Wang Baoqiang, sang a song "The Song of Migrant Workers"(农民工之歌), leaving a deep impression on people; in 2009, singer Ma Guangfu and others from a rural area sang "Beyond the Dream"(超越梦想) on the same stage with professional singers, which won wide acclaim; in 2011, the Rising Sun band(旭日阳刚组合), Xidan Girl Ren Yueli(西单女孩), and "Coat Brother" Zhu Zhiwen(大衣哥) in 2012 became the collective Gala memory for a generation.

For the grassroots people, whether it's "acted by others" or "talking about oneself" on the stage independently, they are all signs that CCTV's Spring Festival Gala attaches great importance to folk discourse. In terms of discourse content, even if it comes from common people, the "grassroots spirit" of CCTV Spring Festival Gala is still presented in the praise of the pure and frugal qualities of the people, the emphasis on striving forward and dreams, and the concern for the disadvantaged groups, and any rebellious and maverick elements quietly disappear in the process of being absorbed into the mainstream discourse. As a result, the CCTV Spring Festival Gala has gradually formed a media landscape in which mainstream discourse and grassroots discourse are presented on the same stage and intermingle with each other, which also provides a reference for the discourse of the grassroots narrative subject in the Online Gala.

(2) "Grassroots Heroes" in the Narrative of Family and Country Sentiments

Humankind is emotionally attached to the two words "home" and "country", which to some extent also belong to an "imagined community". As a media ritual, the CCTV Online Spring Festival Gala cannot completely get rid of the narrative framework established by its pre-text: the CCTV Spring Festival Gala, which is a national ceremony. From the concept exchange of "ordinary hero" and "grassroots", we can clearly see that the Online Gala caters to the mainstream discourse. Although postmodernism and the mass discourse system have the nature of dispelling the discourse of power, they do not dispel socially accepted values and moral standards. In other words, even if grassroots discourse is "incorporated" by mainstream discourse, it still has the ability to reflect the everyday feelings of the grassroots people and create collective memory and a sense of collective identity, thereby causing the audience to affirm national identity, social achievements, major policies, and the pride of being Chinese.

There is such a group of people in the Online Gala: most of them come from the bottom of the society, and their education level is not high, but they are hailed as heroes. In news clips and interviews, when the host asked the Great Wall sanitation worker Chang Shitou, they had the following dialogue:

"This is such hard work, why not consider another job?"

"We use our own hard work to guard the beauty of the Great Wall. The Great Wall is the pride of China, and the Great Wall is our home, so we don't change jobs."

From this, we can see that the concepts of "home" and "country" have been exchanged invisibly. "Loving one's home" is equivalent to "loving one's country", and thus ideology has penetrated into grassroots programs. Scholar Wu Yan believes that the social ideological significance of grassroots as a group is gradually weakening. However, in the mainstream discourse system and "home and country" narrative framework of the Online Gala, the grassroots people still undertake the important task of expressing a sense of social mission and conveying the ideals and values of society, even if this should belong to the elite culture.

On the stage of the Online Gala, grassroots shows not only show joyful talent performances, popular Internet celebrities of the year, and grassroots heroes, but also focus on real grassroots lives. In 2012, musician Min Qun created a musical story "Beijing Brothers"(北京兄弟) for migrant workers, and invited 61 migrant workers to chorus about the thousands of ordinary people who work hard for their children and families.

"Do it if you have work, find it if you don't"

"I see that he always has endless energy, and sweat often soaks his shirt."

"Full of strength to work hard for children and family"

The simple lyrics show the fine character of the working people at the grassroots level of China since ancient times. In addition, the Online Gala has also focused on some grassroots families with special labels, such as the "civilized family" in northern Shaanxi, the four-generation family of art, and the aerospace family in Inner Mongolia on the Online Gala in 2017, which are models of excellent grassroots families.

In general, on the stage of the Online Gala, the grassroots group, as one of the narrative subjects, have assumed the enormous responsibility of spreading core social values. After being absorbed by mainstream discourse, the meaning of "grassroots" has been extended. The style of grassroots, being one of the narrative subjects of the Online Gala, is the result of the interactions of various texts, including the pre-texts represented by grassroots culture, and the CCTV Spring Festival Gala's practical experience of absorbing the grassroots discourse.

3. Effects and Emotional Connections of Para-Text and Narrative Scenes

The scholar Wang Changcai argues that the para-text may also be converted into main text under certain conditions.[4] The stage space design

---

[4] Wang Changcai. Pan-text and Explicit Text: Two Understandings of "Co-text"[J]. Research in Chinese Language and Literature, 2018,24(02):9-16. 王长才.泛文本、显文本: "伴随文本" 的两种理解[J].中国语言文学研究

in the narrative scenes, on the one hand, enters the audience's sight as a para-text along with the main text, and plays the role of embellishing the atmosphere, but when called upon by the show narrative or stage scheduling, stage design directly participates in the display of the main text, turning itself into part of the main text.

(1) Narrative Scene: Rich Sensory Experience Empowered by Technology

The narrative scene of a TV variety show refers to the stage space and special symbols presented by the development of internet technology and the iterations of artificial intelligence. The Online Gala differs from the fixed "tea-table style" space design of CCTV Spring Festival Gala, by making full use of internet elements and technological achievements to create a youthful, lively, techy narrative scene. In the Online Gala, the stage space appears in front of the audience as a symbol in the para-text of the program, directly affecting the audience's reception of the program text. Through technological empowerment, the stage space design of the Online Gala has continuously gone through multiple iterations and has experienced the following three stages:

The first stage saw the use of lighting and physical stage sets to show program effects. For example, the first Online Gala was recorded at the Water Cube. The studio covered a very large area, and the brilliant lights made it look like a "big production" concert scene. A large LED screen was placed behind the stage, but its function was relatively monotonous and only existed as the stage background and a tool for video links.

In the second stage, with the development of the Internet culture and media convergence, richer and more diverse Internet elements have been added to show. For example, in 2012, at the top of the Online Gala stage hung the "@" symbol in LED lights representing the Internet; in 2013, a large ring screen was used to create a party atmosphere themed "Chinese + friends + private"; in 2014, the "tree-table style"[5] design mimicking the

---

[5] It comes from traditional Chinese culture. Specifically, it is a kind of theater tradition: in the studio, the audience sits in a circle around a round table, facing the stage. The round table is usually decorated with flowers, tea, and various snacks such as sunflower seeds and peanuts. Viewers can interact with each other while watching the show. Since its establishment in 1983, the CCTV Spring Festival Gala has maintained the form of a "tea house".

CCTV Spring Festival Gala was replaced by a more relaxed and free area where the audience can stand at will and can sing and dance with the show. In addition, in terms of space scheduling, the 2014 Online Gala had the main stage and the left and right side stages and added elements such as containers and graffiti walls to cater to the preferences of young netizens.

The third stage is to enhance the sense of reality and immersion of the performance by means such as projection, virtual implantation, hologram, and virtual reality. For example, in 2019, the Online Gala debuted the painting "Twelve Beauties" from Forbidden City with naked eye 3D technology; in 2020, the robot "CCTV Xiaoyang" appeared on the stage by holographic projection; and in 2021 the "Real Persons+CG" dance which put real persons and animated figures on the same stage wowed the audience with powerful visual effects and was widely praised by netizens. On the stage of the 2021 Online Gala, stage design and lighting design were the two highlights. Lighting combined with stage design and the background screen achieved the unique visual effects of 19 shows. The stage design was a bold concept of "Magic Cube", with the keywords of Internet, technology, modernity, magic and simplicity. The outside of the Cube was a huge ring and changed its inclination with angles controlled by digital devices, forming a visual contrast with the cube, thereby bringing a variety of visual experiences. There are two huge screen matrices made of smaller screens on both sides of the stage, and a high-definition glass screen on the ground. Together they created a "three-dimensional" space and displayed rich creativity working together with each specific show.

(2) Interactive Space Expanded by Cloud Technology

Scholar Li Wei revises the theory of "co-text" and argues that almost all co-texts can be transformed into link-texts to participate in the process of receiving, understanding and interpreting, that is, the conversion of para-texts into link-texts.[6] The large LED screen that originally belonged to para-text in the stage space, with the blessing of Internet cloud technology, achieved real-time interaction with Chinese people around the world. The

---

[6] Li Wei, Jiang Xiaoli. Attempts to Revise and Expand the Theory of "Co-text" - Discussing with Professor Zhao Yiheng[J]. Gansu Social Sciences, 2012(04):251-255. 李玮, 蒋晓丽. 试对 "伴随文本" 理论进行修正与扩展——与赵毅衡教授商榷[J]. 甘肃社会科学

families or transportation hubs connected at the other end affected the transformation of the stage space from para-text to link-text. By forming a virtual field with the live audience, the hosts, and the audience using all kinds of Internet terminals, emotional energy and relational connections were continuously generated.

Using Internet technology to connect with netizens through video, real-time interaction or even more joyfully: real-time singing activities, is another iconic program of the Online Gala following the "Internet Affairs" series. In 2011, the first Online Gala launched a video connection after the song "Old Boy"(老男孩). Two young netizens discussed the heavy but warm family issue of "paternal love" with Chopsticks Brothers; in 2016's Online Gala, Phoenix Legend (凤凰传奇), Jeff Chang (张信哲), and ordinary families from northern Shaanxi, Heilongjiang, Shandong, Jiangsu and other regions sang "The Most Dazzling National Style"(最炫民族风) and "Love, Just One Word"(爱，就一个字). In the "virtual" sphere constructed by the Online Gala, the emotional energy related to "Spring Festival Reunion" has been continuously accumulated, enriching the happy festive atmosphere of Spring Festival celebrations and family reunions across the whole country.

If the above-mentioned real-time singing activities are Spring Festival carnivals that belong to the common people, then the video connections that started in 2017 and are of more national significance, have integrated the sentiments of "family and country", achieving deeper cultural identity and ideological unity. For example, in 2017, the National Supercomputer Center in Wuxi, members of the Tiangong No. 2 laboratory, members of the Jiaolong deep-ocean submarine team, the Tianyan telescope team, the "Wukong" dark matter satellite team, and the C919 airliner research team demonstrated China's high scientific and technological development levels; The Libyan peacekeeping police riot squad, video linked with in 2018, and the 30th Chinese navy escort team that returned from the Somali waters in the Gulf of Aden, video connected with in 2019, showed the values of dedicating one's youth to the motherland, through singing songs such as "Sing to the Motherland"(歌唱祖国) and "My Motherland and Me"(我和我的祖国).

4. Optimization of the Narrative Strategy of CCTV Online Spring Festival Gala

As a new genre that is relatively different from traditional TV texts, the Online Gala has its special manifestations in program content and session settings. With the wave of reform in traditional TV shows, the fixed shows and sessions formed in the early years of the Online Gala, as well as even MC announcing, have been cancelled one by one, and the integrity of symbols has been damaged to a certain extent, which also triggered the authors of this paper to think about ways to improve the Gala's future narrative strategies. In the reform of traditional mainstream media that emphasizes innovation and integration, how can a show brand be formed? How can the core advantage of the various Spring Festival galas that spring up on the Little New Year's Eve be maintained?

(1) The Stability of the Form of the Gala and the Continuity of Archi-text

As a "framing factor", the archi-text regulates the text and also serves as an index sign to indicate how the recipient of the text should interpret the symbols in the text. In the ten-year development of the Online Gala, the "Internet Affairs" series and "Hot List" series have successfully established the style of "officiality, celebration, Internet, and youth subculture". With the development of the times, these "new" programs in the early years were gradually replaced by updated content, so the integrity of the content was affected. Innovation is indeed important, but as an official discourse-led festival activity that reflects the reality of online life, how to form and consolidate media rituals is still a "required course" for the Online Gala.

From 2014 to 2018, "Internet Affairs" series by the Journey to the West Band (西游乐队) was active in the Online Gala, and formed a youth subculture in early Online Galas with the intertextual creation method of collaging social facts, Internet hot events, and jokes, becoming an iconic show. Take the show "Internet Affairs 2013" as an example, on the one hand, the program uses playful Internet language to appeal to the identity and group resonance of netizens. On the other hand, by going through relevant social facts and national events, the show successfully connected with the higher-level sense of national belonging and identity.

The "Hot List" series was also once an iconic session of the Online Gala. The releases of lists such as "N Reasons I Love China", "China Internet Hot List" and "Annual Popular Portraits of Chinese Youth" interprets the core values of the official discourse in the form of media celebrations. Taking the 2013 Online Gala as an example, the "N Reasons I Love China" online selection activity finally came down with three "most popular" reasons, which are not only convincing but demonstrate a solemn and authoritative national image.

The reason I love China	Award speech script
China is Beautiful	Chinese cuisine is tasty, but what is more beautiful is the laborers who make the taste; Chinese art is beautiful, but what is more beautiful is the wise heart that creates art; Chinese landscapes are beautiful, but what is even more beautiful is the loyalty of those to protect the homeland. Tens of thousands of beauties have jointly achieved the far-reaching and incomparable Chinese beauty.
Chinese Power	Not all power is all-powerful. In our country, some power is expressed as beauty, like a trickling stream, and some power is expressed as love, moisturizing things silently, and some power manifests itself as resilience and sacrifice, ordinary but great. These beauty and love, kind thoughts and actions have created the simple but mighty Chinese power.
Chinese Dream	There are three kinds of dreams in the world; one is the individual dream, big or small, which enriches our life; the second is the collective dream, which is like a flag, allowing us to move forward together; the last is the union of the collective dream and the individual. Like a sail and a ship, they power each other. In China, all three kinds of dreams can be realized. I love China.

Table 3 Award Speech Script of 2013 "N Reasons
I Love China" Award Ceremony

In contrast to the unspoken meaning of everyday life, ritual is a collective and public "statement".[7] Fixed shows represented by the "Internet Affairs" series and the "Hot List" series constitute the integrity of the Online Gala symbols in the way of content continuity, time continuity, and character continuity, forming a media ritual. However, judging from the 2021 Online Gala, the "decentralized" arrangement emphasized visuals but weakened the public participation and the integrity of symbols being a media ritual. In this regard, this paper argues that even "dramatic" transition of traditional media needs to adhere to some "unchanged" things. Only by shaping the Online Gala into a set of more distinctive ceremonial symbols, is it possible to continue to exert the influence of the brand and be a champion of core social values.

2) Innovation of the Gala and the Flexibility of Co-texts

The co-text of the Online Gala affects the generation of the symbolic meaning of the text and the interpretation of the receiver. But if the role of the co-text is overemphasized, it becomes an obsession. For example, the Online Gala in 2021 saw a lot of elements of Bilibili.com, such as the hot contestant Laziness (懒惰) from the Bilibili variety show "Rap New Generation"(说唱新世代), Bilibili influencer Party Girl (党妹), virtual game characters "Gongsun Li"(公孙离) and "Rainbow Rhythm" (彩虹节拍) with the characteristics of "Bilibili Otaku Dancing" (B站宅舞)[8], etc. While many young audiences were attracted, this also caused netizens to "almost think they were watching the Spring Festival gala at Bilibili.com" and other complaints.

It is true that young and sub-cultural participating guests and program forms, as the para-text of the Online Gala, can quickly and accurately evoke group identity. However, as a gala of official discourse, the CCTV Online Spring Festival Gala still needs to be distinguished from the New Year Eve gala held by Bilibili, which only has purely entertainment functions. The concept of "weak symbols" mentioned by scholar Zhao Yiheng in the book

---

[7] Peng Zhaorong. Theory and Practice of Anthropological Ritual [M]. The Ethnic Publishing House, 2007. 彭兆荣.人类学仪式的理论与实践[M].民族出版社

[8] Otaku Dance is a dance activity related to ACGN culture. It originated from the trial dance area of NicoNico animation in Japan. ACGN is the combined abbreviation of the English words of Animation, Comic, Game, and Novel. It is a new word stemming from ACG and is popular in the Chinese cultural circle. (from Baidu Baike)

"Semiotics: Principles and Problems " says that if the meaning can only be understood completely or mostly by context, then it is a "weak symbol". For the CCTV Online Spring Festival Gala, if its para-text and archi-text are all generated under the influence of ensuing text such as the New Year's Eve gala at Bilibili, then over time, the co-text will likely steal the thunder, and the CCTV Online Spring Festival Gala will also fall into the passive status of being a "weak symbol".

In general, the CCTV Online Spring Festival Gala, as a type of TV variety show, has continued the genre norms, and uses the "home and country" narrative strategy in the mainstream discourse system, and highlights its important role in championing core social values. In terms of narrative strategy, the selective absorption of grassroots culture has become its main narrative feature in the past ten years, gradually forming a narrative style that is different from CCTV's Spring Festival Gala. In addition, the echoing of national scientific and technological breakthroughs and the application of stage presentation technology help it become a special media spectacle. Facing the future, the CCTV Online Spring Festival Gala should continue to embrace technology, explore new forms, and integrate internet culture and traditional culture, so as to break down the barriers between different circles of culture, embody the lofty spirit of the times, while also being acutely empathetic to real everyday life.

(Zhao Shuping, Professor, School of Television, Communication University of China; Wu Hao, PhD student, School of Television, Communication University of China; Wang Yueru, Master's student, School of Television, Communication University of China)

KNOWLEDGE COMMUNICATION IN AUDIO PUBLISHING FROM THE PERSPECTIVE OF ORAL COMMUNICATION

Liu Hong and Teng Cheng

Abstract: Audio publishing in the new media environment is an important supplement to traditional print publishing. Most of the content of audio publishing is based on print publishing, and on this basis, secondary creations are carried out. As we all know, the essence of publishing lies in the communication of knowledge, and audio publishing gives words sound. The research focus of this paper is to analyze the oral feature of knowledge dissemination in audio publishing from the perspective of oral communication, and interpret it from the lenses of knowledge scene, community sharing, knowledge environment, knowledge thinking, etc. As information technology continues to advance, we explore and analyze the secondary dissemination of knowledge with audio publishing, and probe on a case-by-case basis the information time knowledge conversion, the reshaping of learning ability, the guidance for returning to print reading, and the planning of knowledge dissemination, so that audio publishing can revive human oral culture at a higher level in the future.

Keywords: Oral Communication, New Media Environment, Audio Publishing, Knowledge Communication

Oral language plays a pivotal role in the history of human knowledge communication. Canadian scholar Harold Innis even argued that Greek civilization is a reflection of the power of oral language.[1] Oral communication can be said to be the oldest form of communication for human beings, while audio publishing can be called the most modern form of communication. The bridge between the two is print publishing. In a sense, from oral communication to print publication is a process of establishing the status of knowledge communication. The words themselves are silent, but the words record the human voice. It can be said that so far, the vast majority of human knowledge inheritance has been completed through communication by print, which belongs to the vertical transmission of print. Meanwhile, the horizontal transmission of print had to wait for the invention of the printing press. Although the foundation of today's audio publishing is Internet broadcasting, audio publishing is not the same as broadcasting, because the former is based on print publishing. The difference between audio publishing and print dissemination is that audio publishing is a new type of publishing using the form of the Internet. It can be said to be a kind of secondary publishing. By way of "oral" communication, audio publishing reorganizes and adapts traditional print publishing. In other words, it is a process of screening and steering of print knowledge.

1. Theoretical Description of Oral Communication and Audio Publishing

The research on oral communication can be traced back to the era of Plato. Now, oral communication also occupies an extremely important position in communication studies in the United States of America. As of today, the US National Communication Association has changed its name five times. In 1997, it completed the "final" de-oralization when it renamed itself from the Speech Communication Association. In fact, oral communication has a longer history and deeper academic accumulation than mass communication. It started from public persuasion and debate

---

[1] Harold Innis, translated by He Daokuan. Empire and Communications. Beijing: Renmin University of China Press, 2003: 3. 哈罗德·伊尼斯.帝国与传播[M].何道宽, 译. 北京: 中国人民大学出版社

in ancient Greece, and it is closely related to philosophy, political science, logic, etc., and is an important part of Western humanities.[2] "De-oralization" does not follow that tradition. As early as in the beginning stage of human development, oral language was the first medium for knowledge dissemination. It is too hasty to deny oral dissemination. Therefore, as we trace oral dissemination it becomes clear at a glance that oral communication is the main medium of knowledge dissemination, which is an established fact and also a focus of scholars' research. Therefore, scholarly research on oral communication has not ended because of "de-oralization". In 2004, American scholars Michael Dues and Mary Brown's book *Boxing Plato's Shadow: An Introduction to the Study of Human Communication*'s writing on resistance and re-recognition of rhetoric of Plato and Aristotle, and its historical treatment of oral communication, is completely different from the overview of communication studies by American scholars Wilbur Schramm and E.M. Rogers. Scholar Harold Innis's emphasis on oral tradition in *The Bias of Communication* was stated above, and Innis further focused on the adaptation of the written language to oral tradition, oral tradition in the Homeric epics, and the discovery of its role in the development of nations, etc. Walter J. Ong, an American scholar of the same Media Ecology school, also carried out a systematic study of oral culture in his book *Orality and Literacy: The Technologizing of the Word*. Although there are still many problems to be solved in the research, the combing and dialectical demonstration of primary oral culture, secondary oral culture, and written culture are enough to show the scholar's strong emphasis on oral communication. In addition, in French scholar Michel Foucault's *The Order of Discourse*, he relied on discourse to discuss order, power, etiquette, etc... Whether it is oral tradition, primary oral culture, secondary oral culture, or the order of discourse, or the interpretation of spoken language itself and the relationship between spoken language and its actors, they all pay consistent attention to the time, context, and cognition of "oral language".

The core concept of oral communication is "spoken language/speech",

---

[2] Xu Shengquan. Who Was the First Doctor Of Communication? - The "Oral Communication Department" Ignored by Chinese Academic Circles and its History [J]. Press Circles, 2019(8):35-44,87. 徐生权.谁是第一位传播学博士？——被中国学术界所忽略的"口语传播系"及其变迁[J].新闻界

and thus it is a study of speech or "talk studies". If it is a "talk study", then the sub-disciplines of oral communication are self-talk studies, relational talk studies, group talk studies, and public talk studies.[3] The communication of information in the early days of human beings was undoubtedly carried out by oral means, which of course also included the communication of knowledge in ancient times. According to Walter J. Ong, a scholar of the Media Ecology, the so-called native oral culture is a culture that does not know what print words are. Before the appearance of print words, the communication of knowledge had always been through oral language, According to Ong, people learned by teachers passing down knowledge to students; the apprentices listened and then repeated what they heard; they mastered proverbs, learned to reorganize various aphorisms, and other 'formula'-style material; they learned through collective recall, not through rigorous research.[4] In the native oral culture, if conceptualized knowledge is not repeated orally, it will soon die out. Therefore, people in oral culture must spend a lot of energy to recite the things that have been learned painstakingly for generations.[5] In other words, knowledge, like information, has obvious uncertainty. This uncertainty is a double-edged sword. On the one hand, it exaggerates the sanctity of knowledge, giving knowledge a mysterious color, which crucially manifests in some festive rituals through which the replication of knowledge is possible; on the other hand, this uncertainty makes knowledge a privilege of a small number of people, who can not only monopolize the interpretation of knowledge, but may even resist invention of writing words, which make knowledge certain.

If we can deeply understand original or native oral culture, we can better understand the new world constructed by written words and understand its

---

[3] You Zixiang. Oral Communication in the Digital Age: An Analysis of Discipline Name, Core Concepts and Core Competencies [G]//Li Zhan. Oral Communication in the Digital Age: Theory, Methods and Practice – Conference Proceedings of the First Academic Seminar on Oral Communication across the Taiwan Straits. Xiamen: Xiamen University Press, 2014 (12): 1-14游梓翔.数字时代的口语传播学：一个学科名称、核心概念与核心能力的分析 [G]//李展.数字化时代的口语传播：理论、方法与实践——第一届海峡两岸口语传播学术研讨会论文集.厦门：厦门大学出版社

[4] Walter J. Ong, translated by He Daokuan. Orality and Literacy: The Technologizing of the Word. Beijing: Peking University Press, 2008: 4-5. 沃尔特·翁.口语文化与书面文化：语词的技术化[M].何道宽，译.北京：北京大学出版社

[5] Ibid. 31.

essence; we can also better functionally understand the kind of people who were literate: their thought process was not just born out of natural forces, but directly or indirectly constructed by the technical force of writing. Without the written language, the minds of literate people would not have the ability to think as they do now, and they would not be able to express their thoughts in spoken language to the level they can today. The power of written words in changing human consciousness surpasses all other inventions.[6] We can say that the written words have created knowledge, or we can say that the writing of language has solidified knowledge. Because words can record knowledge, and this record can reduce the uncertainty of knowledge. There is an example to explain this issue. In the era of no writing, human beings also had history. However, the most difficult period for us to figure out so far is the history of the pre-literary era. Not only is there no written record, but more importantly, we can only rely on a small number of the remanent oral legends. Whether these oral histories are recited by folk artists or passed down from generation to generation through oral epics, they all have one thing in common, that is, they are full of mysterious exaggeration. Part of this kind of exaggeration has to do with what they recorded, and part of it has to do with how they were distributed. In this sense, written words not only have the function of recording, but also have the ability to verify facts. That is why, to this day, we still reckon that we should look at history through written words.

The invention of written words and the application of printing made publishing an important medium for knowledge communication. Some scholars also call writing words "technology"[7] - knowledge began to be expressed and spread through the "technology" of the written word. After the advent of printing (the era of "new media" was ushered in), oral communication has been neglected to a certain extent, and written publishing has become the main form of knowledge transmission. We can think of writing words as a space medium, while oral language in the traditional sense is a time medium. Therefore, what we see more in ancient folk artists is their repeated recitations, not only for memory, but also for vertical transmission. Until today, the new media environment has brought about the fusion of audiovisual media: listening and seeing

---

[6] Ibid. 59.

[7] Ibid. 62.

are no longer separated reception channels as they were traditionally. The way we receive knowledge changed from hearing to seeing, and then from seeing and hearing. The audio publishing platform of new media makes "hearing" once again one of the important ways to receive knowledge. Today's "hearing" is different from hearing in the era of primitive oral culture. The original oral communication of human beings can be said to be based on pure oral culture. Today's auditory communication is based on text communication.

Audio publishing is a new type of publishing, which has gradually become the focus of users' attention with the evolution of the mobile Internet era. Compared with large-scale and professional mass communication, multimedia communication can truly be realized in the process of oral communication. People can rely on one or more communication channels for exchanges and can adjust and switch the channels in time according to the changes in communication situations.[8] Recently, the mobile platform "Cloud Listening" of the "National Team" was launched, and content dissemination of the category of "pan-knowledge" resonates with it. The content published by the audio platform is not all for the mass market, but also for the niche market. They all have the element of knowledge dissemination. Throughout audiobook portals, mobile audio platforms, etc., knowledge-based content is an important part of most audio publishing platforms, such as the mobile audio platforms "Get"(得到) and "Zhongdu"(中读), which are mainly knowledge-oriented. At its root, the essence of publishing lies in the supply and storage of knowledge. Some scholars have pointed out that audio publishing is different from paper publishing and electronic publishing, in that it has the special property of an audio medium, with audio language as its main production. Therefore, audio publishing is the production, editing, and transmission of knowledge and information, with content creation using audio language as the main carrier.[9] Although audio publishing is publishing, it is based on sound transmission. To be precise, it is based on Internet broadcasting. Therefore,

[8] Li Yaming, Wang Qun. Oral Communication: A New Discipline Urgently Needed to be Constructed [J]. Editorial Friend, 2014(7): 65-69. 李亚铭，王群.口语传播学：一个亟待建构的新学科[J].编辑之友

[9] Tong Yun, Zhou Rongting. The Landscape of Audio Publishing with the Technological Innovations of 40 Years of Reform and Opening up [J]. View on Publishing, 2018 (9): 20-33. 童云，周荣庭.改革开放40年技术革新下的有声出版图景[J].出版广角

audio publishing does not turn sound into text, but converts text into sound. This is a test for the dissemination of human knowledge. After all, before this, what we were good at was converting sounds into written words. Think about the written compilation and publication of CCTV's "Hundred Schools Forum"(百家讲坛) program and you will understand this point. Interestingly, it is easier to turn words into sounds than to turn words into images. It stands to reason that the relationship between words and pictures is closer, because both belong to visual communication. However, written words can be said to be a kind of differentiated visual to human beings, because there is a threshold for written words (you need to be literate), but there is no threshold for pictures, and almost everyone can understand pictures. Written words use indirect vision, while pictures use direct vision. Therefore, when we say that today is the age of visual communication, we are referring to image communication, not written text communication. Although pictures are older than written words, the communication of written words has a longer history than the transmission of images. Chinese people like to say that seeing things once is better than hearing about them a hundred things. The "seeing" here is not seeing in the sense of seeing written words, but in the visual sense. It refers to seeing before the visual communication era; it is about seeing it one time; it is seeing to witness. Judging from the history of film, even though there was an era of silent films, sound films soon appeared, and picture and sound have been almost perfectly combined. In the age of television, we can see that written words and pictures are still in conflict. Many people like to read quietly, reflecting a contradiction between written words and sounds. However, audio publishing allows us to see the conciliation of written words and sounds. It is not a recitation of poetry and prose, but a sound interpretation of written works.

At present, the content production process of most audio publishing platforms is a process of "secondary selection". The so-called secondary selection can also be understood as secondary creation, or secondary publishing, which is making audio products based on text content.[10] However, seeing audiobooks as an appendage of text publications is a

---

[10] Cui Yuke, Zhang Cong, Huang Qiuqiu. A Preliminary Study of China's Audio Publishing Industry [J]. Modern Audiovisual, 2018(5): 74-77.崔玉可，张聪，黄秋秋.我国有声出版行业初探[J].现代视听

manifestation of the lack of a comprehensive view of audiobooks.[11] Audio publishing is built on the basis of written texts, that is, on the basis of written publishing. In terms of dissemination of knowledge, although there are many differences between audio publishing and the original oral language era, there are still overlaps, and legacy inheritance. Our understanding of spoken and written culture begins with, not before, the digital age.[12] The digital age or the current new media age has given us a new understanding of the "secondary oral culture".[13] Looking back at the source, written culture was established on the basis of oral culture. Later, in the early days since the advent of publishing, the traces of oral culture in written texts were still visible. But with the continuous maturation of written culture, the traces of oral culture have become less and less seen. It is undeniable that written culture has always been affected by oral culture until today. And in the era of secondary oral culture, audio publishing as a new mode of oral cultural expression has been echoing the written culture, and the interaction and feedback between the two have never ended, especially in knowledge communication. The words that are truly spoken are always present in the whole environment of human existence. The meanings of words continue to emerge from the context of the present times. And, of course, past meanings shape present meanings in various ways, but they are no longer identifiable.[14] Secondary publishing of audio publishing is both a challenge to and an opportunity of traditional text publishing.

---

[11] Tong Yun, Zhou Rongting. The Landscape of Audio Publishing with the Technological Innovations of 40 Years of Reform and Opening up [J]. View on Publishing, 2018 (9): 20-33. 童云，周荣庭．改革开放40年技术革新下的有声出版图景[J].出版广角

[12] Walter J. Ong, translated by He Daokuan. Orality and Literacy: The Technologizing of the Word. Beijing: Peking University Press, 2008: 2. 沃尔特·翁. 口语文化与书面文化: 语词的技术化[M].何道宽，译. 北京: 北京大学出版社

[13] Ibid. 2.

[14] Ibid. 35.

2. Knowledge Communication Through Audio Publishing

Audio publishing is considered to be a new type of publishing, but from a historical point of view, knowledge communication by audio publishing can be traced back to the initial form of communication. In today's secondary oral culture, knowledge communication by audio publishing is mirroring that by the original oral culture. "Poetry chanting" and "speech making" in the era of native oral culture are instant interactions and exchanges among the audience and between the audience and speakers in a given scene; in the new media environment (secondary oral culture era), knowledge communication by audio publishing extends the scene, so that the limited audience interactions develop into sharing in a community.

(1) The Extension of Scene

Yu Guoming argues that the scene is a kind of stipulation based on the time and space environment when the user uses the communication. This kind of stipulation has certain restrictions on people's access to the choice and use of a product, and also provides a direct possibility for certain information that meets the needs of the "scene ".[15] In the era of native oral culture, knowledge communication integrated time and space: the disseminator and the recipient can interact at any time. In the era of written culture with the advent of written publishing, the scene of on-site interactive knowledge dissemination was replaced by an independent knowledge reading scene, and the dissemination has always been one-way. During this stage, knowledge dissemination showed an elitist tendency, gradually fading away from the influence of oral traditions, and fully deriving from written publications. Sun Wei believes that mobile media removes "scene" from the framework of physical space, and media breaks through the shackles of binary opposition, intertwining the two incompatible concepts of "mobile" and "scene", creating an unprecedented new "mobile scene"

---

[15] Guo Ying. The Return of the Audio Sense in the Era of Mobile Communication [D]. Wuhan: Huazhong University of Science and Technology, 2018. 郭缨. 移动传播时代听觉回归研究[D].武汉：华中科技大学

in human society.[16] In the era of mobile Internet, audio publishing in the new media environment has once again reproduced the interactive scene in the era of native oral culture. Mobile broadcasting has created multiple interactive scenes for audio publishing. The knowledge interaction scene of audio publishing is both fixed and fluid: every fixed scene may move at any time, and every moving scene may also freeze at any time. The knowledge dissemination scene of audio publishing can be switched by users at any time, and the dissemination of knowledge traverses through time and space.

(2) Sharing in the Community

As with the native oral culture in the era of oral communication, the secondary oral culture also produces a strong sense of community, because the process of listening to people is the process of forming a group of listeners; the process of reading texts makes the individual turn to his or her inner being. The groups produced by the secondary oral culture are much larger than those produced by the primary oral culture, too large to even be calculable - this is what the Canadian scholar Marshall McLuhan calls the "global village".[17] From the era of native oral culture to the era of secondary oral culture in the new media environment, knowledge communication has returned to the communities and to some extent achieved group sharing. In the new media environment, knowledge communication of audio publishing organically combines interaction and sharing. If the native oral communication era emphasized interaction, then today's new oral communication era emphasizes sharing. This is very important for knowledge communication, because interaction is not equal to sharing. Interaction has a vertical connotation in the traditional sense. In other words, interaction can also be said to be the product of vertical communication. Sharing, on the other hand, has the characteristics of horizontal communication. From this, we can also find that the vertical and horizontal movements of knowledge communication are different.

---

[16] Ibid.

[17] Walter J. Ong, translated by He Daokuan. Orality and Literacy: The Technologizing of the Word. Beijing: Peking University Press, 2008: 104. 沃尔特・翁.口语文化与书面文化: 语词的技术化[M].何道宽，译.北京: 北京大学出版社

Vertical communication is more about being authoritative and classic, while horizontal communication emphasizes interest and popularity. Most audio publishing platforms mobilize users through knowledge content, encourage the sharing experience, combine the online and the offline, build interaction in circles, and explore appealing knowledge distribution models. For example, most platforms will set up a mutual encouragement mechanism during the sharing process, in which not only the shared person will get free knowledge experience, the sharer himself will also get the corresponding knowledge gift, sharing knowledge orally in the process of interpersonal communication; other platforms will establish a sharing circle, combining online and offline knowledge communication activities to carry out the sharing process. What we discussed above are basically sharing situations in a relatively passive state, and there are many users who actively share on these platforms, further distributing knowledge to users with the same interests, obtaining a whole new experience.

(3) Comparison of Two Ways of Oral Communication

Complex, abstract categories rely on writing words to provide structure to knowledge and distance it from actual life experience. There is no such category in oral culture, so in conceptualizing knowledge and expressing all knowledge in oral language, it has to be more or less close to life in order to make the unfamiliar objective world approximate to the more immediate, familiar, interpersonal, interactive world.[18] We can simplify human information communication into two types. One is sound communication, which is the combination of oral communication and auditory communication. Words are spoken to people. That is to say, without hearing communication, there is no oral dissemination. The other is visual communication, including written communication and visual communication. Although these two kinds of human communication can be summarized as organ communication, that is, they are all transmitted through human organs, the mouth and ears are used for sound communication, and the eyes are used for visual communication. However, among them, written communication is special, because writing is an indirect medium. Humans are born with eyes. However, without

---

[18] Ibid. 32.

learning, humans cannot read written words. In other words, the written word is a medium with a threshold. It sets a threshold for human eyes, and it is this threshold that brought the communication of human writings on the road of knowledge communication. The characteristic of knowledge communication in native oral culture is "memory"; the purpose is to keep knowledge alive and communicate it. In written publishing, which is mainly about knowledge communication, such characteristic is no longer the core. It is worth noting that with current audio publishing, human visual communication and sound communication have come together. It should be said that this fusion is different from the integration of sound and picture on TV. TV communication is still a kind of visual communication after all, and TV is not based on written communication. In other words, TV actually conflicts with written texts to a certain extent. This can be seen from the dislocation of narration and pictures. The debate about which is more important - words or pictures – does not stop in the TV industry. When we discuss media convergence today, we find that this fusion does not only appear in the connection area of traditional media and new media. Greater media fusion may occur in the way of human communication, that is, the fusion of visual communication and sound communication. For example, auditory communication is based on written communication; it can also be said that today's new oral communication itself is based on written communication. Therefore, this also improves auditory communication's level of knowledge communication.

(4) The Communication of Ideas

In native oral culture, thinking and expression tend to take on the following characteristics: additive rather than subordinate.[19] In oral culture, long-time thinking and communication with others are closely linked.[20] By the age of written culture, thinking is often independent and introspective. After the emergence of electronic media, media content turned to "entertainment". So the scholar Neil Postman proposed the purpose of "Amusing Ourselves to Death" of electronic media, and the media of sound or picture or a combination of the two no longer produce

---

[19] Ibid. 27.
[20] Ibid. 25.

thought-provoking "knowledge", which is a rejection of knowledge communication in the era of the native oral culture. The written word ("written publishing") once again presents itself in the image of "technology", trying to awaken people's thirst for knowledge through written words. Although written words can unleash the power of lexicons in an unprecedented way, the written or visual representations of words are not real words, but "secondary imitation systems" of words. Thoughts inhabit words, not written texts. Written texts can acquire meaning because visual symbols point to the world of spoken words.[21] Compared with "the world of audio words", written words suffer losses in the interpretation of thoughts. The lack of thoughts in the world of electronic media is temporary, because such a state is opposed to a real habitation of thoughts. Audio publishing builds a path for the knowledge of "thoughts", and its knowledge communication sometimes is even superior to written symbols. Although oral communication in the new media era is based on written symbols, it has been constructed through the oral language of the speaker and ideas can spread on the basis of texts. Take for example author Liu Cixin's award-winning work *Three-Body Problem*. An "oral communicator" (speaker) of the "Get"(得到) app divided the book into "fifteen thought experiments" and expanded the text through speeches. I believe that everyone has a new thinking and re-cognition in the subconscious level of *Three-Body Problem* once again. In audio publishing, knowledge no longer appears with a condescending and difficult face. The "text publishing" "heard" in many mobile audio platforms presents the other side of these published texts. "Audio publishing" turned these texts from just a "reading through" experience into interpreted knowledge and the spread of ideas.

3. Secondary Dissemination of Knowledge with Audio Publishing

The emergence of new media and the popularization of mobile broadcasting have promoted the secondary knowledge dissemination of audio publishing, which not only formed a new form of knowledge popularization, but also had a certain impact on the in-depth dissemination

---

[21] Ibid. 57.

of knowledge. In the era of fragmented communication, audio publishing adapts to fragmented reading sessions more easily than text publishing. It can convert information time into knowledge time, thereby further reshaping learning abilities. Audio publishing based on text publishing leads the return of text reading, and focuses on human initiative, de-elitization through planned knowledge dissemination, and breaks down the barriers of oral "writing".

(1) Information Time Transformed into Knowledge Time

The biggest feature of the new media environment is fragmented communication. Viewing from the diachrony of knowledge communication, knowledge time and information time alternate during the time of mobile Internet mediation. According to the latest 17th National Reading Survey Report released in April 2020, the average adult Chinese national uses the mobile phone 100.41 minutes every day. These times are scattered across rest, before going to bed, work commute, physical activities such as exercise and housework, driving, eating, and other situations. Although overall, the average daily contact time with the phone is relatively long, but considering how diverse the situations are, the constant switching of space breaks up the time and causes many obstacles to knowledge acquisition. People basically cannot create a continuous and in-depth knowledge reading scene in these fragmented times, but can only obtain information or knowledge in scenes where time and space overlap. However, audio publishing provides such an overlapping scene. In the above scenes, oral communication of audio publishing has no effect on the activities of the subject, and in these "same" scenes, two parallel but extremely close timelines are generated. We may be lost in thought in the "time scene" where the sound is received, but the other timeline, the main scene of the event, is mostly unchanged.

The new media environment continues to extend the time limit of audio publishing. Knowledge communication in the era of native oral culture is likely to be lost in a second if there is no strong control over time junctures. Audio publishing has brought a large amount of content to people, but not all information is knowledge.[22] A lot is information,

---

[22] Wu Yun, Yan Wei. Generation, Evolution, Challenges, and Re-cognition of Publishing Concepts: Research from Perspective of Concept History [J]. Chinese Editors Journal,

but not knowledge. "Knowledge is a collection of information that was extracted and transformed from an ocean of information, and which then was recognized, selected, sorted, deepened, and systematized".[23] And while people's requirement for utilizing time is constantly improving, they are also not able to spend more energy on the extraction and selection of the "ocean of information". The emergence of audio publishing platforms just meets the current group need, mediating in terms of information selection and matching usage time. By examining the knowledge content carried by the current audio publishing platforms ("Get"(得到), "Himalaya"(喜马拉雅), etc.), we found that the average duration of audio is mostly about 21 minutes to 30 minutes. Such a length is relatively suitable for fragmented times such as eating, walking, riding vehicles, and before going to bed. Through the effective use of these fragmented times, information time can be converted into knowledge time.

(2) Reshaping of Learning Abilities

In the era of native oral culture, knowledge was less traced in the process of dissemination and reception, and even when traced, the process used was mechanical duplication and recalling, because "knowledge" might fleet away in a moment. Audio publishing, on the other hand, has a huge knowledge base, which allows us to continuously trace it. Today's audio publishing platforms are providing more convenient ways to trace knowledge. For example, the co-founder of "Get"(得到) Tuo Buhua(脱不花) pointed out in a speech that among the questions raised by its 30 million users, the most common question seen in the background is: I am engaged in a certain job in a certain enterprise, and I have taken the "Organizational Behavior" course taught by Mr. Li Yuhui. What courses should I take next? In view of this situation, they carried out work of research and development known as "Get Brain"(得到大脑), whose artificial intelligence technology enables the traceability of knowledge and realizes network communication of knowledge tracing. The audio

---

2018(10): 21-27. 吴赟，闫薇.出版概念的生成、演进、挑战与再认知：基于概念史视角的考论[J].中国编辑

[23] Tian Hongmei. Library's Transition from Information Service to Knowledge Service [J]. Information Studies: Theory and Application, 2003 (4): 312-314.田红梅.试论图书馆从信息服务走向知识服务[J].情报理论与实践

publishing platforms' tracing of knowledge is intelligently answering the question of "what else can I learn?" from user groups. There will also be more and more online audio platforms tracing knowledge through algorithms and other artificial intelligence methods, and there will be "tutor"-guided knowledge communication to bring users quick, thorough, interpretative reading of knowledge. Knowledge tracing is flexibly extended in these ways beyond the linear flow of time.

(3) The Return of Reading

All written texts are inextricably linked with the world of speech and natural language habitats, both indirect and direct. Only by virtue of such links can written texts produce meaning. Written words cannot escape oral culture in any way.[24] However, the native oral culture no longer exists. As far as words cannot escape from oral culture, the "secondary imitation system" (written words) has given birth to the development of the secondary oral culture. Going with the closed cycle of knowledge communication, audio publishing will also lead people back to written publishing, or written texts again. In-depth communication of knowledge is no longer just at the level of spoken words, but is internalized through existing written publications, going deeper both logically and with in-depth knowledge cognition. There will be such a phenomenon in life: some people will buy the original novel to read after watching some movies and TV series. This shows that the impact of original works exists when it comes to reading, and this impact is usually prominently reflected in written publications. In this sense, we can also regard audio publishing as an interpretation of the original work, which is not only a popularization of knowledge of the original work, but also an interpretation of the original work from different angles. Since knowledge communication of audio publishing is established on the basis of written publishing, its leading of the return to reading is not only the driving force for the reciprocal relationship between the written and spoken language but is also conducive

---

[24] Walter J. Ong, translated by He Daokuan. Orality and Literacy: The Technologizing of the Word. Beijing: Peking University Press, 2008: 4. 沃尔特·翁.口语文化与书面文化: 语词的技术化[M].何道宽，译.北京: 北京大学出版社

for the cycle of speech and written words, forming an effective knowledge communication process.

(4) Planning of Knowledge Communication

In the era of native oral culture, knowledge communication has a strong "live broadcast" feature due to its live nature and on-site presence of participants, and there was little overall pre-planning of knowledge communication. However, audio publishing in the new media environment can carry out planned and intelligent knowledge communication. Viewing from the way of knowledge expression, knowledge communication in native oral culture was basically unplanned, which is closely related to the characteristics of "pre-text" technology itself of the oral tradition. Nonetheless, as early as Pericles' time, Athens was already filled with the voices of reading books nationwide, while Herodotus was a genius of speech, who was keen on arousing the interest of readers,[25] At that time, Herodotus was well aware of how to be a "well-spoken person". Knowledge communication in the new media environment can be aimed at one's own target group and make use of the characteristics of one's own media. For example, in an audio program on the interpretation of music, the broadcaster can talk in a way that combines fully the ways of listening to music, so that the audience can experience a full sense of presence. Not to mention that music has been an important part of oral communication since as early as the oral era. The planning of knowledge communication in audio publishing is prominent in the setting of many courses, including the determining of speakers and topics.

Knowledge barriers are broken down with "well-spoken persons". Tuo Buhua said: "I have a very important identity in our company, which is called to represent the 'uncultured people'. Liu Songbo and Li Yuhui, professors at the School of Labor and Human Resources of Renmin University, both have set up courses on 'Get'. But in our conversation, I said 'Teacher, it is no problem for you to talk to your doctoral students like this - their level is very high. But I'm sorry, we people can't understand

---

[25] Harold Innis, translated by He Daokuan. Empire and Communications. Beijing: Renmin University of China Press, 2003: 73. 哈罗德·伊尼斯.帝国与传播[M].何道宽, 译.北京: 中国人民大学出版社

it'. The knowledge content of 'Get' becomes the 'speech" that gets to be communicated on a basic level only after the simplification process."

4. Conclusion

Although Plato's thoughts were presented in dialogue form, the refinement of his thoughts was produced by the influence of written words on intellectual activities, since Plato's dialogues were actually written texts. These ideas were written in words, and the form of expression is dialogue. So from a dialectical point of view, Plato's dialogues tend to use analytical methods to clarify issues; on the other hand, the dialogue form was inherited by Socrates and Plato from the more "integrative", non-analytical, narrative spoken form.[26] The native spoken language culture has ceased to exist due to the appearance of words, but because written words and spoken language cannot be separated from each other, the "secondary oral culture" was born. Although the communication of knowledge in the oral language culture was once interrupted, the knowledge feature of written publishing has been revived in the secondary oral culture. Written publishing is helping knowledge communication in audio publishing, which in turn is also revising the native oral culture.

(Liu Hong, School of Television, Communication University of China; Teng Cheng, School of Television, Communication University of China, and School of Media, Guizhou Minzu University)

---

[26] Walter J. Ong, translated by He Daokuan. Orality and Literacy: The Technologizing of the Word. Beijing: Peking University Press, 2008: 80. 沃尔特·翁.口语文化与书面文化: 语词的技术化[M].何道宽, 译.北京: 北京大学出版社

BEHAVIORAL LADDER FOR INFORMATION-BASED INCOME GROWTH: A STUDY BASED ON INFORMATION USE OF URBAN POPULATIONS WITH RELATIVE DEPRIVATION

Ye Mingrui and Jiang Wenxi

Abstract: Groups in "relative poverty" have become an important concern in the field of social research since China's complete victory in eradicating absolute poverty. It is therefore of great economic and social significance to safeguard the development interests of this group of people in the wave of industry transformation driven by digital economy. From the perspectives of the digital divide and relative poverty, this study investigates the constraining influence resulting from the existing bottlenecks in information literacy on information-based income growth for this group. Textual data was collected through fieldwork investigation for adoption of a qualitative research method, and this group's income growth path is categorized into four stages, namely: perception, planning, action, and evaluation. Based on the above, this study finds that the constraining effects of information literacy and existing bottlenecks in information-based income growth mainly include bias in the construction of mimetic environments, lack of systematic structure of cognition, the "coupling dilemma" in commercial realization of social capital, and emotional attributions in self-evaluation. Apart from this, the corresponding information literacy support system has provided limited assistance for individuals in terms of skills support and professional evaluation. This study suggests that the constraints such as information capacity and social capital form a ripple effect, resulting in the restraining effect of income growth behavior.

Keywords: Information-Based Income Growth, Low-Income Population, Information Literacy, Digital Divide, Post Poverty Era

After China eliminated absolute poverty[1], the issue of relative poverty should continue to be the focus of poverty reduction, and the issue of increasing the income of middle-and-low-income groups with income above the poverty line becomes particularly important. At the same time, on the one hand, the rapid development of the Internet-based digital economy pushed by the pressure of current circumstances has also spawned the emergence of many new social economic sectors. On the other hand, middle-and-low-income urban dwellers have for some time faced the plight of income decline or even unemployment as a result of the huge shock brought by the pandemic to the real economy, which has prompted many of them to try to move towards the digital economy to expand revenue channels.

However, the existing research shows that the individual's information skills and application levels have a direct impact on the individual's income level. To a large extent, the population with low income levels has a great overlap with the population with weak positions in terms of information skills and information possession. In the wave of digital transformation of the entire national economy, the "relatively poor" urban population in a disadvantaged position in information will inevitably be subject to an income-growth bottleneck due to their lack of information skills, and thus may not be able to fully enjoy the benefits of industrial transformation. The concept of "relative poverty" itself also confirms this logic from another aspect. It includes not only the evaluation of income and wealth, but also the evaluation of the individual's social cognition and perception. It refers

---

[1] Information Office of State Council of the People's Republic of China. China's Practice of Human Poverty Reduction. People's Daily, April 7, 2021中华人民共和国国务院新闻办公室：《人类减贫的中国实践》，《人民日报》

to a "relative sense of deprivation" at the social level pointing to a sense of vulnerability, lack of voice, and social exclusion, etc. Its connotations include income, skills, rights, and self-identity.[2] Therefore, with the realization of the poverty alleviation goal and the improvement of overall social income levels, from the dual perspectives of the information gap and relative poverty, we need to turn our attention from the impoverished population in the past to the low-income "relatively poor" population, studying how this group will use information technology to achieve individual income increase, and the problems faced in the process of realizing income increase under this path.

1. Research Questions and Methods

In a general sense, "information-based income" refers to the means of increasing income through and relying on information and Internet communication technology. In this kind of income increase actions, Internet information, Internet technology means, individual information literacy, and social capital built through the information network are all involved as key elements. A review of the existing literature found that the effect of the ability to obtain and use effective information on the income increase of rural households has been confirmed by research[3], while the research on urban residents using the Internet and other information means to achieve income growth through the supply of products and services has been little researched. At present, most of the related studies on farmers' information-based income increase focus on how information technology is organically embedded in the whole process of agricultural production and sales. However, due to the huge differences between production and revenue paths, many factors affecting information-based income growth

[2] Zhang Chuanzhou. Connotations, Measurement and Governance Policies of Relative Poverty. Journal of Northwest Minzu University (Philosophy and Social Sciences Edition), No. 2, 2020. 张传洲：《相对贫困的内涵、测度及其治理对策》,《西北民族大学学报》(哲学社会科学版）

[3] Zhang Li, Huang Teng, and Liu Tianjun. Can the Internet Bridge the Digital Divide in Agricultural Products Market? - Micro Data Analysis of Apple Growers in Shaanxi Province. Journal of Agro-Forestry Economics and Management, 2018, No. 6. 张丽、黄腾、刘天军：《互联网能弥合农产品销售市场的数字鸿沟吗?——基于陕西省苹果种植户的微观数据分析》,《农林经济管理学报》

in the agricultural production environment cannot effectively align one-on-one with those in the production and operation scenarios of urban low-income people for the purpose of increasing income – many factors even do not exist in cities at all. Such differences in circumstances between urban and rural areas of information-based income growth activities constitute the necessity of choosing the urban space for research in this study. In addition, with the advancement of urbanization and the continuous enhancement of mobility between urban and rural areas, the deepening of urban-rural integration, the urbanization of the local rural population, and the migration to cities have also necessitated that this study should be completed in the urban context.

Combined with China's institutional characteristics and the aforementioned policy background, the concept of "information-based income growth" in the local context is not simply the general income growth of all classes of people. Viewing from macro income demographics, with the elimination of absolute poverty, the lower-middle income groups will become an important focus group in China to improve people's livelihood and promote economic development in the next step. With the advent of the "post-poverty era", the "relative poverty" faced by low-income groups will gradually become pronounced and persist for a long time.[4] It is foreseeable that the political and social system with Chinese characteristics determines that "information-based income growth" will inevitably carry more social and political significance in addition to economic implications, and that this action will also be significantly skewed and emphasized towards "low-income groups" in the future.

In cities, the two characteristics of "low income" and "information poverty" interplay among the relatively poor groups, who are particularly prone to the hardships in growing information-based income because their information needs cannot be met. Compared with the general group, they have the characteristics of a typical information vulnerable group, these are, "in the information society, due to the limitations of subjective and objective conditions, in the process of information accessing, acquisition, storage, application and communication, compared with mainstream social

---

[4] Yu Shaoxiang. Long-term Mechanism Construction of Poverty Governance in the Post-Poverty Alleviation Era. Jiang Huai Forum, No. 4, 2020. 余少祥：《后脱贫时代贫困治理的长效机制建设》,《江淮论坛》

groups, the groups that are disadvantaged and in need of corresponding support".[5] The huge overlap between information disadvantaged groups and those with barriers to information-based income reasonably promoted this study to focus on information-based income increasing behaviors for information disadvantaged groups.

Therefore, the research object of this paper is limited to the urban low-income group, and the behavior of "information-based income growth" is focused on the reality that individuals in this urban group, aside from the limited fixed income, use Internet-based information technology means to participate in labor production, services, or investment, so as to obtain additional income growth, achieving an overall increase in individual income. Different from digital labor, the information-based income growth behavior of information disadvantaged groups discussed in this paper mainly uses digital knowledge, information, and skills as the carrier of labor participation rather than the main means of production.[6] The forms of labor participation include not only the hiring economy based on information matching platforms, but also product production, distribution, investment, etc. The forms of employment are part-time and entrepreneurship.

In 1999, the US National Telecommunications and Information Administration (NTIA) defined the digital divide as "the divide between those with access to new technologies and those without"[7]. The advancement and popularization of Internet technology has driven research on the digital divide from physical access to information literacy. Jan Van Dijk pointed out that the physical access gap of the digital divide is gradually narrowing, while the skills and use gap is increasing.[8] Specifically, the analysis of the use gap pays more attention to "examining the gaps in people's use, skills, interest, and motivation, etc., with regard

[5] Xie Xiao. Information Vulnerable Groups. Information Rights, Information Consumption and Information Poverty Alleviation. Journal of Academic Library and Information Science, 2015, No.3. 谢笑：《信息弱势群体：信息权利、信息消费和信息扶贫》,《大学图书情报学刊》

[6] Han Wenlong, Liu Lu. Digital Labor Process and Its Four Forms. Finance and Economics, No.1, 2020. 韩文龙、刘璐：《数字劳动过程及其四种表现形式》,《财经科学》

[7] Telecommunications, N.and I., Administration, Falling Through the Net: Defining the Digital Divide, 1999, NTIA Washington DC.

[8] van Dijk, J., K. Hacker. The Digital Divide as a Complex and Dynamic Phenomenon. The Information Society, Vol. 19, No.4, 2003, pp. 315-326.

to the Internet"[9], finding and arguing that the differences in use time, type, and content of media users will lead to the digital divide.[10] More educated Internet users make more use of the Internet for activities "enhancing capital"[11], and the advantaged classes have made full use of digital resources to solidify their class advantages in the process of information empowerment, widening the gap between them and the disadvantaged.[12] In his local research on skills and use gap, Ding Jianjun found in his fieldwork on farmers in Wuling Mountains that "low ability to utilize information is one of the main factors causing poverty". Ding interprets information needs not being met as information poverty, which plays a catalytic role in the vicious cycle of poverty.[13] and Qiu Zeqi's research conclusion also supports this view, arguing that "the differences in their benefits from the Internet have replaced the early access gap and become a new form of digital divide".[14] Therefore, based on the above analysis and considerations, this study bases itself on the digital divide theory, and use the existing information ability discriminating indicators to specifically investigate the process of using information technology to increase the income among the relatively poor urban population who are in the information disadvantaged position, probing the main reasons for restricting information-based income growth behaviors and their potential impact.

---

[9] Li Xiaojing. New Changes in the Digital Divide: Diverse Use, Intrinsic Motivation and Digital Skills: A Field Survey of School-aged Children in Henan and Shanghai. Modern Communication (Journal of Communication University of China), 2019, No. 8. 李晓静：《数字鸿沟的新变：多元使用、内在动机与数字技能——基于豫沪学龄儿童的田野调查》,《现代传播》(中国传媒大学学报)

[10] van Deursen, Alexander JAM, and Jan AGM van Dijk. The Digital Divide Shifts to Differences in Usage. New Media & Society, Vol. 16, No. 3, 2014, pp. 507–526.

[11] Hargittai, E. & A. Hinnant. Digital inequality: Differences in young adults' use of the Internet. Communication Research, Vol. 35, No. 5, 2008, pp. 602-621.

[12] Xie Jungui. The Wealth and Poverty of Information: A Study of Information Differentiation in Contemporary China. SDX Joint Publishing, 2004. 谢俊贵：《信息的富有与贫乏：当代中国信息分化问题研究》,三联书店

[13] Ding Jianjun, Zhao Qizhao. The Causes of Information Poverty in Rural Areas and Measures for Poverty Alleviation: Taking the Wuling Mountain Area as an Example. Library and Information Service, No. 2, 2014. 丁建军、赵奇钊：《农村信息贫困的成因与减贫对策——以武陵山片区为例》,《图书情报工作》

[14] Qiu Zeqi et al. From the Digital Divide to Dividend Gap: The Perspective of Internet Capital. Social Sciences in China, 2016, No. 10. 邱泽奇等：《从数字鸿沟到红利差异——互联网资本的视角》,《中国社会科学》

This study has selected low-income people in Beijing as the research sample. The annual per capita disposable income of the respondents was about 15,000-25,000 yuan (about 2,400-4,000 US dollars). According to the national quintile income group data, the target group is comprised of the lower-middle income group (per capita disposable income of about 16,000 yuan, or about $2,500) and the middle-income group (per capita disposable income of about 25,000 yuan, or about $4,000).[15] From the perspective of individual living environment, the actual purchasing power of low-income people living in first-tier cities like Beijing has been squeezed by the high local price index and consumption level, and their income level is far behind the annual per capita disposable income of local residents in Beijing, which is about 68,000 yuan (about 10,700 US dollars).[16] The group's relatively poor status is prominent, and there is a more realistic and urgent need to increase income. And therefore, there is a relatively strong willingness to expand revenue channels. Supporting the information abilities of this group will help improve their social integration and quality of life, further revitalize the labor force and the market, and strengthen social stability and development factors.

The data collection was mainly obtained through semi-structured interviews. We selected samples from five Beijing areas, urban and suburban, namely, Dongcheng District, Chaoyang District, Miyun District, Shunyi District and Fengtai District. We interviewed 23 respondents which resulted in documentation of about 140,000 Chinese characters. In addition to interviews, the respondents' family situation and Internet usage habits were investigated, and the WeChat marketing groups and Moments created by the respondents were observed. The respondents are in industries including delivery, housekeeping, logistics and others. They are aged between 28 and 56 years old, with mainly junior high school as their highest education. The content of the semi-open questionnaire mainly covers basic information capabilities, the actual situation of income increase, relevant information needs, information

[15] National Bureau of Statistics. 2019 Statistical Bulletin of the People's Republic of China on National Economic and Social Development. China Information News, March 2, 2020. 国家统计局：《中华人民共和国2019年国民经济和社会发展统计公报》,《中国信息报》
[16] Beijing Municipal Bureau of Statistics. Beijing 2019 Statistical Bulletin of National Economic and Social Development. China Information News, March 2, 2020. 北京市统计局：《北京市2019年国民经济和社会发展统计公报》,《中国信息报》

environment and assistance, etc. At present, most of the literature on boosting the development of the digital economy focuses on the macro level, and the existing quantitative research indicators lack attention to the difficulties of information access on the individual level. Based on the foundations of these previous studies, this paper uses the NVivo software to conduct the three-level coding of the Grounded Theory pertaining to the interview text. Through the analysis of the interview text and the observation of the respondents' online behavior, first the representative descriptive text is extracted to form 54 open codes to present the weakened information abilities of individuals. Then, 13 main axis codes are obtained according to the organic association extraction category of open coding to obtain observation indicators. After further sorting and supplementary interviews around the main axis code, five theoretical codes are identified, namely, the construction of mimetic environment, systematic cognition, capital reality transformation, information circulation integration, and the individual and social dilemma. In the research, the theoretical code is compiled into four behavioral stages and one action assistance theme. The weakening causes and hindering mechanisms are explained along the main body's behavior pattern.

The respondents in this survey all live in urbanized areas in Beijing, with income levels above the poverty line, with relatively complete wireless Internet physical access conditions or affordability of network traffic costs and are equipped with smartphones and other network equipment. Therefore, physical access is not included in this discussion.

2. Information-based Income Increase: Insights from the Perspective of the Behavioral Ladder

In Jens Rasmussen's analysis of cognitive work, he proposes a conceptual framework called "decision ladder" to articulate the basic path structure through which decisions are formed.[17] This behavioral decision-making framework mainly includes three phases: situational analysis, evaluation, and planning. The starting point of its decision-making behavior begins

---

[17] Rasmussen, J. Information Processing and Human-machine Interaction: An Approach to Cognitive Engineering, North-Holland,1986.

when the actor is "activated" (activation), and which then triggers the action awareness (alert). In this study, information-based income increase is regarded as an action decision made by low-income individuals. In addition to the fact that their actual economic situations prompt the original income increase willingness, the factors that motivate this group to decide to use the Internet and other information technology paths to achieve income increase are to a great extent affected by their own information environments. Drawing on the conceptual framework of Rasmussen, combined with the findings and analysis of the field survey, this paper proposes a four-stage ladder division (as shown in Figure 1) for the information income increase behavior of the relatively poor urban populations. The initial stage is the perception of information path in the information environment, which then evolves towards the ultimate goal of increasing income. In this process the individual's demand for and utilization of information is also deepening. After going through the two specific behavior stages of planning and action, individuals enter into the evaluation of the continuous behavior process, and then make the choice of suspending or continuing the behavior, forming a spiral structure with openings, and entering the next behavior ladder cycle. The control and internal strength of that control formed by individual actors over information and information technology constitute the key to the continuation of information-based income-increasing behaviors. The relationship breakpoints with different characteristics presented on each step that directly hinder the income-increasing behavior from continuing to advance to a higher level.

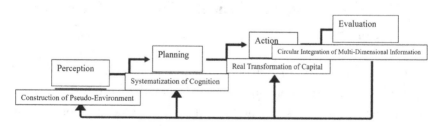

Figure 1 Income-increasing Behavior Ladder

(1) Perception Stage: Construction of Pseudo-Environment

This is the initial stage for the information disadvantaged group to start the attempt to increase income. Individuals actively or passively receive relevant information to achieve income increase in the path of information technology and form a basic perception of the income increase scenario based on the relevant information they have already possessed. Part of the information in this stage becomes the triggering factor for the information income-increasing behavior to be initiated, and then enter the planning stage. For low-income people in the information disadvantaged position, the quantity and quality of information required to trigger the behavior are relatively low. This has laid a fundamental hidden danger for the continuation of the subsequent income-increasing behavior and the realization of the income-increasing effect.

First of all, insufficient information possession is the main source of the risk of blind income increasing behavior. As information disadvantaged groups, the lack of sufficient information has become an obvious constraint for these relatively poor groups to access a new industry. This insufficiency is mainly manifested in two aspects: insufficient cognition of general information in society and the lack of knowledge in specific fields. For example, some respondents suffered income losses due to lack of legal knowledge, and when some respondents directly participated in stock market investment, they were blindly optimistic: "basically, short-term investments can all make money." Insufficiency of information possession may not only lead to immediate decision-making mistakes, but in the long run, the incompleteness of knowledge clusters restricts the functioning of schema. This means when in the future mobilizing and organizing the pre-existing information for processing new information, the information disadvantaged groups still lack the support of knowledge and experiences.[18] The macro-positive trend of successful income growth and individual inspirational cases have been incorporated into the media agenda in large numbers, and the narrative of digital economic participation presents

---

[18] Hao Yonghua, Lu Heqiu. Framework Competition and Meaning Construction of Risk Events: A Study Based on "Poison Capsule Incident" Sina Weibo Data. Journalism & Communication, No.3, 2014. 郝永华、芦何秋：《风险事件的框架竞争与意义建构——基于"毒胶囊事件"新浪微博数据的研究》,《新闻与传播研究》

a "mirage of participation".[19] Thus, it is easy for the general audience including the low-income groups to form one-sided subjective cognition, which also increases the risk of blind income increasing behaviors in the subsequent stages.

Secondly, there is a lack of diversity in information sources, and the awareness of information identification is inhibited by strong ties. Some respondents who tried to increase their information-based income decided to enter the industry for too simple reasons, such as "recommended by friends", "someone else around me is doing it", "(the superior of the e-commerce marketing network) said this is pretty good", showing that they are significantly influenced by their strong ties in the social network. In an environment of insufficient information, they face information inequality between senders and receivers, and close contacts in the three-dimensional space of social networks are the main components of information sources. Compared with people with higher media literacy, information disadvantaged groups have lower frequency of media contact or activities outside their own social circles, with insignificant differences in social strata, and are rarely in the cross sections of multi-angle sources. Therefore, their cognition of the same object lacks dialectics and objectivity. The main communicator who guides respondents into the industry may have their own interests, and the credibility of information has been restricted from the beginning of communication. For example, some respondents follow their friends who are senior e-commerce agents to become junior agents, and their friends can get commissions for developing lower-level agents. The lack of diverse sources inevitably leads to limitations of the angles and levels of information acquisition. It will also strengthen the individual's cognitive bias to a certain extent; due to the lack of sources that form a negative skeptical attitude, the perception of blind optimism in the decision-making process is aggravated. The limited sources of the information disadvantaged groups have brought relatively strong and concentrated information contact stimuli, resulting in their high degree of trust in the sources. In addition, there is a certain information echo chamber effect within the circles of strong ties, leading to even greater lack of critical questioning, thereby gradually moving people away from

---

[19] Chen, J.Y. The Mirage and Politics of Participation in China's Platform Economy. Javnost-The Public, Vol.27, No.2, pp.154-170.

objective cognition, forming an early cause of industry selection errors and inefficient business behavior.

Thirdly, information value judgment affects perception construction and causes the distortion of the mimetic environment. People with strong information abilities, in the face of complex content in the process of media exposure, display relatively good "appropriation" media literacy skills, that is, the ability to meaningfully sample and remix media content.[20] When some interviewees talked about using online platforms to participate in domestic work, they felt insecure about this attempt to increase income because the media reported a lot of vicious crimes involving domestic service workers at the time. Comparatively, information disadvantaged groups are more likely to over-amplify the sample when they mix the acquired information into the overall cognitive system. The reason for such perception construction of this negative tendency may be due to the higher individual economic vulnerability of people with low income and employment levels, or the difficulties they face in life. For the needs of risk avoidance and psychological burden transfer, some individuals tend to form negative social cognition when selecting information. When rational information value judgment and perceptual bias coexist, it is easier for them to lose self-awareness in the information vortex and form a distorted pseudo-environment in the self-centered information network, eventually overestimating and misestimating the business risks, and give up opportunities to increase income prematurely.

(2) Planning Stage: Systematization of Cognition

Compared with the previous stage, the planning stage is the beginning of the implementation of the income-increasing behavior. The individual actor has a clearer demand for the quantity and direction of information, as well as the depth of technology utilization. Its purpose is to serve the next stage of specific income-increasing actions. At this stage, the ability to integrate information and the planning of action paths have become bottlenecks that individuals need to break through in the process

---

[20] Jenkins, H., M. Ito, and D. Boyd. Participatory Culture in a Networked Era: A Conversation on Youth, Learning, Commerce, and Politics. Wiley, 2015.

of increasing information-based income, which directly impact the effectiveness of next-stage actions.

In terms of information integration capabilities, the realization of information-based income requires actors to have a certain degree of systematic cognition, especially when they participate in online business models by means of information technology. However, due to the lack of awareness of information architecture, most individuals engaged in information-based income increase have a systematic lack of focus on "people, goods, and fields" at the meso-level in practice, which directly limits the realization of subsequent income increase actions. The survey finds that manual laborers or people engaged in repetitive labor tend to lean towards income increase practices with low physical requirements and certain flexibility. However, the number of sessions and social network coverage involved in their practices are far larger than their own highly subdivided jobs. The practice of increasing their income on information platforms has put forward a test to their comprehensive abilities and information resources. However, compared with people with higher information literacy, information disadvantaged people often have no willingness and are basically unable to systematically think about income-increasing models and then fill in the required information or skill gaps according to a framework, before starting income-increasing behaviors.

However, the construction of cognitive frameworks provides a must-have support for systematic cognition. Erving Goffman's Framing Theory holds that framing is the joint participation of the micro individual experience and the macro social cultural influence.[21] In terms of individual experience, most of the information disadvantaged groups have low levels of education, and they have insufficient training in the ability to search, screen, and integrate complex information on a large scale. Under the vertical subdivision work system in the real society, most work in grass-roots positions mainly entailing simple labor, and they also lack the opportunity to structure information in a systematic way in their jobs. In terms of thinking mode, information disadvantaged people mostly passively receive

---

[21] Zhu Tian, Zhang Cheng. Cognition of Communication Structure in Internet Circles from the Perspective of Framing Theory. Modern Communication (Journal of Communication University of China), No. 10, 2015. 朱天、张诚:《框架理论视域下互联网圈子的传播结构认知》,《现代传播》(中国传媒大学学报)

information, instead of actively thinking about the information needs for income growth and then searching for information accordingly.

As far as action paths and vision are concerned, the limitations of the individual's vision and distance also squeeze the possibility of path optimization, and make the problem-solving process fall into a cycle of short-term effectiveness, raising the cost of increasing information-based income. When information vulnerable people encounter new problems, the lack of systemic cognition affects their insight into problems and solutions. During the interviews, it was found that many information disadvantaged people not only have a large information gap when they began to grow their income, but generally only act when the obstacles are directly related to the information gap. Faced with obstacles, they seldom deduce the problems that may lie in between business sessions. For example, when some respondents found price disadvantage of the product they resell, they would search for relevant information of the purchase price but would not think about the reliability of the individual distributor, in addition to the price disadvantage in the marketing process. In such cases, what they face is not to find needs and solve multiple needs at once, but to experience the short-term effectiveness cycle of "problem encountered - problem solved" many times, which greatly increases the cost of information processing and reduces individual information utilization efficiency.

(3) Action Stage: Real Transformation of Capital

This stage is one that sees the most significant behavioral externalization in the income-increasing behavioral ladder, where the individual starts his or her own income-increasing practice on a relatively fixed online information platform. The individual income increase behavior at this stage will be subject to clear regulatory requirements and constraints of the participating information platform. It will require the individual to invest a certain amount of money, relatively fixed time, more intellectual resources and other participation costs. They will also face the risk of being punished or direct loss for inadequate operations. The amount of information capital and social capital supported by an individual also has a more significant impact on behavioral outcome at this stage.

1. *The "Coupling Dilemma" Between Information Skill Shortcomings and Network Social Capital.* Insufficient internet skills affect income-increasing actions mainly in older information disadvantaged people, which are mainly divided into two situations: lack of use of Internet platforms and lack of internet skills. In the interviews, the older respondents have basic abilities to operate WeChat, but they have partial difficulties in using food delivery apps and shopping apps which are more complex, or have little knowledge about them, due to reasons such as physical functions, media literacy and usage habits, etc. They master Internet skills more slowly and have a fear of difficulties; at the same time, because they are less involved in the cybersphere, their scope of knowledge of internet applications is limited, leading to insufficient awareness of online channels that may be beneficial to their income-increasing behavior. Meanwhile, compared with the general population, their abilities in actively searching for information, extending the internal functions of software, and the desires of trying new applications are weaker, which further compresses the space for them to expand Internet applications.

The shortcomings of information skills among relatively young information disadvantaged people are more reflected in the lack of efficiency when using information tools to participate in specific industries. Many studies have shown that Internet platforms have a positive role in constructing and promoting the formation and proliferation of individual social capital,[22] however, for information disadvantaged individuals who try to increase their income through the information path, due to the lack of support of necessary skills in a certain field, the value of social capital is often difficult to be effectively converted, so that the income increase effect cannot be achieved. In the research on information-based income increase of information disadvantaged people, we define this phenomenon as a "coupling dilemma" of network social capital in the process of real value transformation. The meaning of the word "coupling" in physics refers to the transfer or conversion of energy from one circuit to other circuits in a

---

[22] Cattell, V. Poor People, Poor Places, and Poor Health: The Mediating Role of Social Networks and Social Capital. Social Science & Medicine, Vol.52, No.10, 2001, pp. 1501-1516.

circuit system, thereby causing similar changes. The "coupling dilemma" proposed here by borrowing this concept of physics shows that in the action of increasing information-based income, even after having a certain scale of Internet social capital on the information platform used and participated in, due to a lack of necessary industry skills or insufficient knowledge of the industry, this advantage cannot achieve a "coupling" relationship with the income increase action itself, and capital advantages cannot be effectively transmitted, thereby restricting the growth of economic income.

For young information disadvantaged people, due to the lack of skill training in e-commerce and other related industries, they have not been able to efficiently use the Internet to increase their income. Many respondents engage in reselling and as agents lack the awareness and ability in online marketing speak and persuasion needed in this industry. They are only able to rely mainly on manufacturers' promotional graphics and online templates, and their effectiveness in maintaining customer relationships is limited. WeChat Moments and peer-to-peer content in the group chats are their main marketing means, and there is a lack of follow-up infiltration and precise connections. In contrast, an agent with high information literacy was observed in the study, whose persuasive speech is situational, dramatic, and personalized, conducts effective customer management on past buyers, and retroactively shares user experiences to increase the agent's own credibility. The difference of communicated content in in the process of increasing income directly affects the communication results and user behavioral desires. Although cyberspace strengthens and increases the social capital of individuals and the possibility of using it to increase information income, the lack of basic skills for information disadvantaged people may still become a breakpoint for establishing effective connections with potential markets. With the same accumulated amount of private domain traffic, information disadvantaged people have limited abilities to revitalize this traffic and fail to form a value-adding cycle of "purchase - feedback - promotion - new purchase".

2. *Short-Term Income Increase: A Conservative Choice Due to Risk Avoidance and Realistic Psychological Compensation.* A significant trend in the survey is that information disadvantaged people have high enthusiasm for activities that can make cash in the

short-term, while relatively less willing to try methods that require a certain amount of up-front investment with long return periods and greater returns. This is similar to the attitude and tendencies of rural residents when facing whether to invest in information technology for agricultural production.[23] On the surface, this can be understood as their lack of ability to vertically integrate and rationally handle income-increasing information, that is, the lack of systematic understanding and planning of the time dimension for other necessary investments, operations and return cycles other than themselves in the early stage of income-increasing, making them prone to stagnation or rushed advances in the action phase. However, from a more in-depth perspective, a long cycle in the action phase means that more information is required to participate and support, richer knowledge supply, and the judgment and processing of larger-scale related factors. Although the investment of such enhanced capital theoretically has the opportunity to bring about a greater effect of increasing income, for low-income people who are disadvantaged in information, the realization of these investments is another realistic information processing skill barrier.

Looking further, even if individuals aspiring to increase income fully master the knowledge reserves and information skills for long-term income increase, the investment of early capital, time and energy is still an obstacle that cannot be ignored when information disadvantaged people cross the digital gap of information-based income increase. The main reason why most respondents are reluctant to invest a lot of time or energy is mainly the potential risk of losses with income-enhancing actions. For ordinary rural residents, even if the income increase action fails, they still retain basic living materials such as land, house, and small-scale family farming as a guarantee, but most urban low-income people do not have such fallbacks. Therefore, when they face potential risks and possible accidents,

---

23 Ye Mingrui. Research on Internet Innovation Diffusion in Rural Areas from the Perspective of User's Subjective Perception. Modern Communication (Journal of Communication University of China), 2013, No. 4. 叶明睿：《用户主观感知视点下的农村地区互联网创新扩散研究》，《现代传播》(中国传媒大学学报)

the characteristics of a "rational economic person" will be more prominent, and their relatively fragile anti-risk ability determines that they pay more attention to risk prevention against economic losses as they try to increase income, which in turn lean more towards being conservative in action.

(4) Evaluation Stage: Circular Integration of Multi-Dimensional Information

Information disadvantaged people evaluate their own income increase behaviors at each stage as well as after a complete income increase process, and make decisions on subsequent behaviors. It needs to be clarified that since the four stages of the entire behavioral ladder are a continuous cycle, the evaluation of the behavior itself does not only happen after the specific income-increasing action is launched, income-enhancing individuals also evaluate ongoing income-enhancing attempts during the perception and planning stages.

In the evaluation process, the main factors that affect the individual's judgment and decision on his own actions include the individual's own knowledge state, predicted consequence, actual operation, and behavioral goal.[24] The individual's consideration of these four elements sequentially forms a relatively independent closed loop, and the subsequent behavior is decided according to the final evaluation result. Through the investigation of these four elements in the evaluation process of the information-based income actors, it is found that the knowledge state achieved by the actor during evaluation and the attribution analysis of the actual income increase operation exert the most restrictive influence on evaluation results and the realization of subsequent income growth.

1. *Cognitive Formation: Structural Deficiencies and Problem Infiltration.* At each stage of income-increasing behavior, whether the cognitive state that affects the assessment results can be formed correctly and completely depends on the individual's comprehensive processing ability for existing information and action feedback in the stage where the individual is, which also

---

[24] Fidel, R. Human Information Interaction: An Ecological Approach to Information Behavior. Cambridge, Massachusetts, MIT Press, 2012.

determines when one stage ends, if the individual can improve, adjust, or still be stuck in income growth. In reality, due to the lack or insufficiency of this processing ability, what often ensues is an irrational, extreme tendency in the next action plan. When observing the entire income-increasing behavior as a continuous and complete process, it can be found that the problems affecting and restricting the formation of correct and effective knowledge states in the income-increasing behavior of low-income people present a structural feature, which affect and restrict each other:

First, information disadvantaged people lack the awareness to compare information sources, whose level of authority, objectivity and participation experience can be used as criteria for information screening. It should be pointed out that although information disadvantaged people by and large maintain a high trust in official media in judging rumors, the penetration of official institutions is limited on sharing information about income increasing on the micro level. And few respondents rely on official sources primarily for information-based income.

Second, information disadvantaged people seldom use more professional information and communication platforms when searching for information, which leads to their contact with less professional and less in-depth information. The presentation of information is simple and lacks order, which increases information noise and weakens reference values.

Third, information disadvantaged people have insufficient knowledge reserves, which suffer in providing assistance for information screening and judgment. And it is easier for this group to follow the guidance of the coders in the process of information decoding.

Fourth, information disadvantaged people lack the shaping of a systematic information structure. Therefore, in the face of information from different aspects and standpoints, they fail to subdivide, categorize, and incorporate it into their own cognitive framework. They are prone to oscillate between complete denial or wholesale acceptance, resulting in unsatisfactory acquisition of required information.

It can be seen that the evaluation stage is the decisive one that promotes the continuation of each behavioral stage. But in this seemingly continuous cycle, the restrictive factors for each stage to continue are not purely from the previous stage. In the perception stage, the distortions of information possession, the number of information sources, and the perceptual construction of the pseudo-environment will be gradually amplified in the planning stage, highlighted in the action stage, and will eventually penetrate the final result evaluation behavior, affecting the individual's attribution analysis of their revenue-generating operations. Similarly, the limitations of information integration abilities in the middle and later phases of the evaluation stage will affect the ability and effectiveness of individuals to prevent and solve problems, which will in turn penetrate later behavioral stages and throughout the whole income-increasing process.

2. *Attribution Analysis: Self-Serving and Emotional Tendencies during Introspection.* After a complete income-increasing process, the specific income-increasing operations in the action stage constitute the most significant evaluation objects for this round of income-increasing practice by income-increasing attempters. However, directly due to deviations in the results of the introspective attribution process, the attribution validity is low. And the group's disadvantages in information also to a certain extent weakens the rational value of the evaluation, so that the evaluation often fails to improve the income-growth scene or bring more rational decision-making, which also cause their misjudgments at the micro and meso levels in the early participation stage to eventually lead in different directions for different respondents.

Due to cognitive biases, some respondents showed a significant tendency of self-serving attribution in their evaluation.[25] For example, with unsatisfactory sales, a respondent who is a reseller on Wechat invested a lot of money to upgrade to a high-level agent. Upon evaluation, the person tended to attribute the main cause of poor sales to the external business environment. Although the respondent was aware of the high price of the product, the person simply blamed it on the low agent level that limited the room for price bargaining, while ignoring the mismatch

[25] Guo Jing et al. Research Status and Prospects of Self-Serving Bias. Advances in Psychological Science, No. 7, 2011郭婧等:《自我服务偏向研究现状与展望》,《心理科学进展》

between product quality, brand premium and the objective needs of target groups or institutions during the attribution process. This led to overly optimistic expectations and blind re-investment. Another direction after the evaluation is the suspension of income-increasing behavior. When objective factors bring extremely obvious and tangible setbacks, they may also lead to excessive pessimism of information disadvantaged people. At the same time, they have insufficient knowledge of the deep rules and hidden opportunities of the industry they are in, under the influence of emotions, their increased investment and the uncertainties of income-increasing results greatly inhibit the possibility of continuing income-increasing behaviors.

Viewing the two options together, information disadvantaged people have a sense of introspective thinking, but there are obvious limitations in the depth of retrospection into their own behavior and the breadth of thinking about external social interactions. On the one hand, such limitations lead to them ignoring many important factors, and even misjudging the main reasons for the success or failure of income increase activities, laying a hidden danger for the information disadvantaged to invest in income increasing activities again before the problem is solved; on the other hand, the limitations also cause them to miss opportunities for adjustment and potential benefits. However, whether it is information possession or information abilities that compromises the value of evaluation, information disadvantaged people need more professional and diverse information support from outside in order to break the current cognitive barriers and achieve a breakthrough in the path of increasing information-based income.

4. Action Assistance: Individual Difficulties and Social Shortcomings

Based on the above investigation, it can be seen that in the practice of information-based income increase for low-income people, the lack of information abilities and the basic support of social capital have become practical obstacles that jointly restrict income increase. As a countermeasure, at the moment when basic level resources are temporarily weak, in view of the constraints existing at different stages, if an effective systematic assistance supply can be formed, it will provide assistance in areas such as information platform construction, information service supply, information skills assistance, and professional support in income-increasing actions, etc., thus forming an upward pulling effect, theoretically a positive effect for the relatively poor people in increasing information-based income (as shown in Figure 2). However, for relatively poor people with lower incomes, although some of the problems in actual situations have been addressed in existing literature on information poverty alleviation with general strategies, combined with the data of the fieldwork looking into existing assistance system, however, it was found that under the existing assistance system, the difficulties of individuals and the shortcomings of social factors make it difficult for potential assistance measures to really work. With neither high-level pull nor bottom-level support, the income increasing behavioral ladder of low-income people lacks a strong upward fulcrum, and it is easy to become a castle in the air. Participants are trapped in difficulties and even breakpoints at each stage, and the income increasing process cannot be continued vigorously.

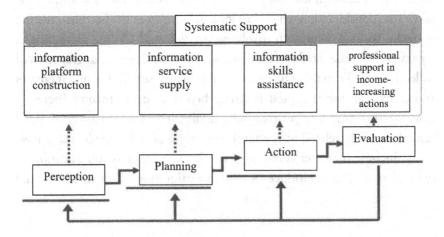

Figure 2 Assistance Factors in Each Stage on the
Income-Increasing Behavioral Ladder

At the individual level, the level of information security awareness of low-income people has become a real hidden danger. Some information disadvantaged people encountered false cash-outs, Ponzi schemes, and bad commercial insurances, etc. For example, a respondent engaged in manual labor used most of his disposable income to purchase a commercial insurance plan with strict cash-back conditions. During the interviews, it was found that most of the information vulnerable people did not clearly declare relevant information needs even after encountering difficulties due to lack of legal and security common sense.

In addition to human capital, class solidification and difficulties in making breakthroughs reflected by observing their social capital also constitutes an inhibitory factor in the income-increasing behavior of information disadvantaged people. A number of respondents showed shortcomings in the three-dimensional criteria which include range, upper reachability, and extensity.[26] The social network of information disadvantaged people with lower levels of occupation and income lacks high-quality nodes and structural holes,[27] and is relatively strongly repetitive and closed. The mismatch between the existing social relations of people with lower occupational levels and the target consumer group could become a breaking point in the supply and demand chain. And the divide of cultural interest given the social stratifications would not be taken into consideration when they look upward from the bottom, creating obstacles to income growth involving marketing.[28] Online marketing is separated from the fixed service place, and also weakens the aggregation of collective social capital. The correlation between service income increases and individual social capital is strengthened, and the income increaser is required to play a larger role individually. The accumulation of social capital is closely related to the family of origin and the employment level of the income increaser is closely related, so social class solidification in the real society also produces a negative migration effect in the virtual

---

[26] Lin, N., Social Capital: A Theory of Social Structure and Action, Cambridge: Cambridge University Press, 2002.

[27] Burt, R., Structural Holes: The Social Structure of Competition, Boston, MA: Harvard Press, 1992.

[28] Swartz, D., Culture and Power: The Sociology of Pierre Bourdieu, Chicago: University of Chicago Press, 2012.

class, limiting the possibility of upward mobility of the relatively poor and information disadvantaged people.[29]

From a social perspective, there are also obvious shortcomings in public social support that individual income increasing actions need to rely on. In terms of public information assistance, about half of the respondents did not know that their community or library provided public information services. Most of the respondents who did know were unable to participate because of conflicts between training hours and working hours, and only learned about the events after they had finished. Learning outcomes are difficult to solidify due to lack of practical feedback and guidance. At present, public information service training suffers from low frequency, low intensity, and lack of pertinence, and it is difficult for some information disadvantaged people to improve their basic Internet operation skills through public services. In addition to the skill level, public assistances such as more professional network application technology training, income increase feasibility assistance assessment, and practical information guidance still need to be strengthened.

In terms of assistance at the social circle level, the limitation of information disadvantaged people's access to assistance is reflected in the diversity of social networks. Social network is an exogenous variable of social capital.[30] Its lack of quality, density,[31] and strength is often another manifestation of the lack of valuable social resources for information disadvantaged people. For example, some respondents had too strong of a social network homogeneity, and people in their vicinity also had limited Internet using abilities. So, these respondents lack people to turn to when they encounter complex obstacles. Among the helpers, young and skilled relatives and friends may not be their optimal choice: the gap in knowledge of network applications often gives information disadvantaged people a sense of fear of difficulties and makes them return to their original

---

[29] Peng Lan. The Stratification of Network Society: The Interweaving of Real and Virtual Hierarchies. Modern Communication (Journal of Communication University of China), No. 3, 2020. 彭兰：《网络社会的层级化：现实阶层与虚拟层级的交织》,《现代传播》(中国传媒大学学报)

[30] Zhang Wenhong. Social Capital: Theoretical Debate and Empirical Research. Sociological Research, 2003, No. 4. 张文宏：《社会资本：理论争辩与经验研究》,《社会学研究》

[31] Lin, N. Building a Network Theory of Social Capital. Connections, Vol. 22, No. 1, 1999, pp. 28-51.

patterns. The most obvious manifestation of this phenomenon is digital back-feeding.

In terms of digital back-feeding, the differences of behavioral patterns between the parent and child generation, and the reality of living separately limit the effectiveness of digital back-feeding. When a mother and son were interviewed separately, the son said that whenever parents encountered difficulties, they would help them until parents learned how to do it themselves. However, the mother said that the assistance provided by the son was very limited, and that she "often can't do it after learning just once". The lack of continuity in digital back-feeding also causes the parents' information application abilities to be insufficient to empower themselves.

In terms of information products, most of the respondents did not expand information acquisition channels in addition to daily information channels within the income-increasing scene. Most of them have almost never relied on professional information platforms or paid for online knowledge content, and showed limitations of accuracy, validity, and systematicity when acquiring important information. In the personalized media ecology where information disadvantaged people live, the pothole effect[32] may be more prominent, partially blocking them from media contact with high-quality information and products. Because information disadvantaged people are more sensitive to time and capital investment, their ability to afford and willingness to accept paid information products, skill training, and paid information platforms in the market are also doubtful.

All in all, at this stage, the information-based income increasing behaviors of relatively poor people in cities still mostly appear as inefficient, which is manifested in insufficient effective investment in relevant elements such as time, energy, capital, and skills, and it is difficult to achieve the corresponding value return and income increase. The process of participating in income increasing has also caused the waste of labor resources and social capital in the market to a certain extent. This group's lack of information possession and heterogeneity of information sources

---

[32] Du Junfei. The "Wall Pot Effect": A Hypothesis on Media Ecology. Modern Communication (Journal of Communication University of China), 2018, No. 10. 杜骏飞:
《"瓦釜效应":一个关于媒介生态的假说》,《现代传播》(中国传媒大学学报)

in the perception stage significantly limit the objectivity of their cognitive construction, which in turn affects the validity of the information framework in the planning stage. The lack of planning in the investment return cycle makes information disadvantaged people more inclined to short-term income increase, but the lack of information ability that has not been supplemented leads to the "coupling dilemma" with regards to turning Internet social capital into real value at the action stage. The evaluation stage shares common problems with the first three stages of the ladder and affects the effectiveness of the next income increase behavioral ladder. The negative effects of the four stages accumulate and can even extend into the next cycle of action. Providing legal and institutional security nets for this group of the population in their income-growth attempts, improving the risk protection system for small-and-micro economies, developing a sustainable information skills training system, providing more targeted consultations for information-based income increasing activities and even feasibility studies, and at the same time building shared and mutual assistance platforms with enterprises, allowing market participants of different sizes to share supply and demand information, will help to enhance the vitality of the grassroots digital economy, achieve precise labor attraction and allocation, and optimize the use of resources, thereby expanding income channels for the relatively poor in cities, and providing a realistic path to effectively increase income levels. It is hoped that the analysis in this paper can provide a certain reference for the information behavior research of more types of vulnerable groups in the coming "post-poverty era". Due to the limitation of interview volume, this paper does not further explore the possibilities of restarting after the four stages have completed and thus forming a spiral upward evolution. Respectfully, we leave this research gap for future research.

(Ye Mingrui, Professor, Doctoral Supervisor, School of Television, Communication University of China; Jiang Wenqian, Assistant Researcher, Innovation and Social Service Research Center, Communication University of China)

TOWARDS A PRACTICAL APPROACH IN MEDIA STUDIES: FRAMEWORKS, ROUTES, AND IMPLICATIONS

Gu Jie

Abstract: With the arrival of the mediatization era, media practice is now infiltrating into, as well as impacting every aspect of social life. Based on recent practice shifts in western media studies, this paper first critically reviews practice theories in sociological studies, then establishes a media practice approach based on practice theories of Theodore Schatzki, and finally elaborates on basic frameworks, research questions, outlines, and methods of this new approach. The paper concludes with discussions on the values of the media practice approach as well as implications for media studies in China.

Keywords: Practice Theories, Media Practice, Duality, Mediatization, Localization

"Practice" has always been an important concept carrying many social functions and meanings in Western sociological theory. Sociologists such as Anthony Giddens and Pierre Bourdieu are important representatives of research on practice theory. At the turn of the 21st century, Western sociology once again ushered in a "shift of practice", and a group of new scholars such as Theodore Schatzki, Andrea Reckwitz and Bruno Latour emerged. This shift of practice has profoundly influenced and promoted practice paradigms in consumer sociology (Shove et al. 2012;

Warde, 2005, 2014), media studies (Couldry, 2004; Rivera and Cox, 2016), environmental policy studies (Hargreaves, 2011; Spaargaren, 2011), organizational studies (Feldman and Orlikowski, 2011; Nicolini, 2007) and other research fields.

In recent years, due to the high degree of conformity with the latest changes in the current media world landscape on research perspective, and the continuous exploration and updating of the duality approach in the theoretical framework, the practice paradigm in media research has been formally established in Western academic circles and gradually attached importance to. Relevant empirical research results have gradually increased and achieved a greater academic influence. British scholar Nick Couldry published a paper titled "Theorizing Media as Practice" in 2004, which was the first attempt to introduce practice theory into media studies. In 2010, Brauchler and Postill (2010) co-edited and published *Theorizing Media and Practice*, which for the first time introduced the theory of practice comprehensively and pointed out that media practice research includes three major areas: media and everyday life, media and the body, and media production.

In China, relevant scholars have also begun to notice the potential and value of the media practice paradigm. Huang Dan (2015) proposed in the article "Writing New Press (Media) History: Paradigm Change" that Chinese press history writing should try to change the paradigm with "media practice" as the narrative approach, by describing the media-centered social human practice history to make up for the shortcomings of the "essential theory" of historical writing. In addition, scholars such as Zhou Xiang and Li Jia (2017), Dai Yuchen (2016), and Wang Bin (2011) focused on the concepts of "mediatization" and "spatial shift", which are closely related to media practice, gradually enriching our understanding of the theoretical framework of media practice.

The rise of media practice research in Chinese and Western academic circles to some extent heralds the potential and value of applying social practice theory to open up a new media research paradigm. However, compared with consumer sociology, science and technology research, and other fields, the application of practice theory in media research is still in its infancy, especially in areas such as research paths and research methods, which have not yet formed a mature and systematic framework.

This paper first introduces the rise and basic theoretical identification of media practice paradigm research through a review of relevant literature, and then establishes a theoretical framework of media practice paradigm with Theodore Schatzki's practice theory as the core by critically combing and analyzing social practice theory. The research object, outline, and method of this paradigm are expounded upon respectively. Finally, this paper discusses the theoretical value of the media practice paradigm and its enlightenment for current Chinese communication studies.

1. Basic Theoretical Identification of the Media Practice Paradigm

The basic theoretical identification of the media practice paradigm can be summarized into two core concepts: "decentralization" and "de-dualism". "Decentralization" can be seen as an explicit response of media practice research to the changing development of the media landscape. "De-dualism" is the internal requirement in the theoretical framework of the media practice paradigm to reinterpret the subjectivity of social actors and social order.

(1) Decentralization

Couldry (2004) believes that previous media and communication research can be summarized into five paradigms: American empirical communication research, media political economy, semiotic analysis, critical research, and media anthropology. However, Couldry argues that a common shortcoming of these five paradigms is that they place too much emphasis on media (text, technology, or organization) as the center and focus of the entire media and communication landscape. With the advent of post-modern and Internet society, human media behavior and implications are no longer limited to microscopic and static situations such as newspaper reading or TV viewing in the traditional sense, but are increasingly decentralized, dynamic, and scattered. Therefore, he believes that media studies must shift to practice: "Do not start with media texts or organizations, but focus on practice - not necessarily audience practice, but open, loose, media-oriented, all human social practices" (Couldry, 2004:119). According to Couldry's examples, media practice can include media use in educational practice, media applications in legal practice, etc.

Couldry (2012 / translated by He Daokuan, 2014:39) further pointed out that when media behaviors begin to show a trend of decentralization, the concept of "audience" has significant limitations today: behavior points to media, but does not necessarily regard media as the purpose or objective. Therefore, the "consumer", "audience", or "user" in the traditional sense can already be regarded as the "actor" of social practice today. In this sense, not only is media behavior becoming decentralized, but the understanding and research on the traditional concept of audience should also begin to apply divergent thinking and multiple theoretical perspectives.

When discussing the relationship between media and social practice, Couldry (2012 / translated by He Daokuan, 2014: 47-50) argues that media can either be an integral part of a social practice, or at the core develop into an independent social practice, e.g., the practice of a web search or YouTube video displays. However, in the practice paradigm of media research, it is not important whether media can become the main body of a social practice. Its real value is that it raises some open questions about the relationship between people's behavior and media (Couldry, 2012 / translated by He Daokuan, 2014: 16).

The theoretical orientation of media decentralization also leads to an important research question of the media practice paradigm—the social power relationship of media. Couldry (2012 / translated by He Daokuan, 2014: 58) argues that from the original intention of practice, the paradigm of media practice cannot avoid people's speech and actions in practice. However, the final focus is on the possibilities and constraints of media in the formation of social practice and the realization of social power. Couldry says our understanding of the consequences of media practice cannot stop at the detailed understanding of media habits and that it is important to explore social power form on a large scale. He says the representative habitus in everyday media use involves the social power of media. The focus of this research is essentially to link the micro-level human media behavior with the macro-level social power structure through media-oriented social practice, and finally explore how media practice can actively construct the form and pattern of social power on the one hand, and on the other hand how social, political, economic, and cultural contexts impose constraints on media practice.

(2) De-Dualism

The question of social power relationship of media essentially contains the internal connotation of a dual interaction, which also forms an interdependent relationship with the essential goal of the theory of practice in sociology. In explaining the agency of human subjectivity and the order of social operation, the binary opposition between individualism and holism, as well as subjectivism and objectivism has long existed in sociological theory. Postill (2010: 6) argues that the essential goal of social practice theory is to replace the traditional "dualism" with the "duality" of practice, that is, to find an effective middle way between the social whole and individual actions. Giddens (1984: 2) also argues that, in the face of the basic realm of social life constituted by personal experience and society as a whole, one of the main intentions of the practice theory is to extract the essence of both aspects to solve the basic problems of social life order. Therefore, under the framework of practice theory, social actors are neither dominated by subjective purposes, beliefs, attitudes, or emotions and thus become absolutely rational and autonomous individuals, nor are they purely subject to the external, mandatory, and universal overall norms and structure of society and thus become passive and helpless.

Alan Warde (2005: 146), a consumer sociologist, applies this spirit to the study of consumer subjectivity, and argues that consumers are neither sovereign choosers nor dupes, but social practitioners with learning abilities who are constructing social practice while also being constructed by it. Similarly, in the field of media research, Wang Yiyan (2012: 57) emphasizes that the audience subject is constrained in practice but at the same time has the ability to reverse the structure. Therefore, audience research within the practice paradigm not only helps to make up for the neglect of the structural factors behind audience behavior in the "active audience" research tradition, but also prevents us from falling into the cultural imperialist perspective that ignores audience agency.

Warde (2005: 137) further uses the "duality" of practice to interpret consumers' consumption behavior patterns. He argues that the differentiation and similarization of consumer behavior should be seen as the result of how practices are organized, not entirely the result of individual choice, whether that choice is free or constrained. This principle actually gave birth to another research question in the media practice paradigm: the behavioral pattern in the study of audience and media users. For example, Rivera and Cox (2016) studied how staff in the human resources department of a university in Mexico used internal communication tools. The results show that the fundamental reason for the unpopularity of the newly introduced communication tool lies in the organizational characteristics of human resources as a social practice. For example, the relatively marginal status of human resources practice in the whole education practice leaves staff busy with other tasks all day and no time to learn how to use new media technologies; Human resources practice is work with a high emphasis on interpersonal relationships, so staff are more inclined to use traditional email which is conducive for personal emotional exchanges.

2. Theory of Practice: How to Embody Duality?

All the research questions of the media practice paradigm point to the dualistic connotation of the practice theory. However, social practice theorists have not yet formed a complete consensus on the mechanism of how practice achieves duality. This has also led to many so-called media practice studies that only loosely use the word "practice" to describe the behavior of media use on a surface level, without really touching the dualistic nature of practice theory (Warde, 2005: 132). In fact, in practice theory research, the first-generation theorists such as Giddens and Bourdieu laid an important foundation for the creation of practice theory at the ontological and epistemological levels, while second generation theorists, represented by Theodore Schatzki, led the new practice shift which provided us with a more important reference to make the research of media practice paradigm scientific, specific, and operational.

(1) Practice Theory of Giddens and Bourdieu

British sociologist Anthony Giddens and French sociologist Pierre Bourdieu have always been iconic figures in the field of social practice theory research, and their theoretical framework of practice has been widely cited in media communication research in China for a long time. The core concept of Giddens' theory of practice is Structuration. He defines "structure" as rules and resources, and repeatedly emphasizes that "structure" is not an external restrictive force but a condition and result of an actor's routine practice (Giddens, 1984: 25). Thus, the inherent internal and external tension of dualism is broken by the practice of the actors themselves. Bourdieu, on the other hand, developed Structuralist Constructivism and tried to combine social structure (field) with structured structural disposition (habitus) to develop a dialectic that can walk between the polar opposites of individual and society, subject and object (Bourdieu, 1990: 25). According to Bourdieu (1977, 1990), "habitus" is on the one hand the actor's internalization of the external objective social order, and on the other hand, it has the ability to create and improvise, thus becoming a kink point where duality is realized.

Before the practice paradigm of media studies was formally proposed, important concepts such as "structure", "habitus" and "field" have been involved in many media studies. Borrowing Giddens' theory on the "time-space" structure of modern society, Moores (2005) studied the reception behavior characteristics of British radio and television audience. He pointed out that the daily routine radio and television viewing behavior of British audience on fixed hours and the calendar is only an inevitable result of their daily work and life practice with strong "time-space" characteristics. At the same time, however, this daily work-life practice is "structured" by their own actions. Therefore, in this sense, the reception behavior characteristics of radio and television audience are a result of "duality" rather than "dualism". On the other hand, Bourdieu's "field" theory is more used to study cultural or media production practices. For example, many scholars have pointed out that media production is composed of different fields, such as the field of television and the field of news. The spatial configuration of these fields and the behavioral tendencies of TV and news producers in them are determined by their respective capital and relative power relations (Bourdieu, 1998).

The important contribution of Giddens and Bourdieu's theory of practice is to use the context of practice to turn social sciences back to the ontological basis of "subject-object integration", thus accurately touching the characteristics of social action that is both restrictive and dynamic. However, their theory has been questioned and criticized by academic circles since its inception. Berard (2005: 200) argues that the first-generation practice theory is more of a "reference point" in terms of its value. That is to say, the theoretical framework of Giddens and Bourdieu has its rationality in describing the internal characteristics and external manifestations of social practice, but if it is implemented in specific empirical research, it will often fall into objectivism due to the insufficient explanatory power of the subject's agency. The author further argues that the shortcomings of Giddens and Bourdieu on practice theory research can be summarized as the objectivism tendency in the interpretation of the constraints of practice structure and the mysticism in the interpretation of the agency of practitioners, thus finding it difficult to completely overcome the binary opposition in dualism.

For the "structural" theory, Berard (2005: 200) pointed out that Giddens recreated some essentially binary concepts when explaining the interaction between structure and routinized practice, such as "social integration" and "system integration", as well as "institutional analysis" and "analysis of strategic conduct". Therefore, Berard (2005: 219) argues that Giddens' theory of practice is essentially a "reification of structure". As for Bourdieu, the logical starting point of his theory is the objective condition of social actors, including "class", "group" and "capital". Therefore, "habitus" becomes a "second nature" determined by objective material conditions (Bourdieu, 1977: 79). Although in real life, actors with the same background of material conditions do show a common tendency of action, Bourdieu, with his mechanistic positivist approach, did not convincingly show that there is a necessary causal relationship between the two. Therefore, King (2000: 422) argues that the concept of "habitus" is nothing but a "return" to objectivism.

The objectivist tendencies of Giddens and Bourdieu's theory of practice stem, to a large extent, from their unconvincing, even mystical, account of the individual agency of actors. For example, both Giddens and Bourdieu criticized and avoided the intrinsic and transcendental factors of individual thought and will and turned to "embodied cognitive capacity" as the core in knowing and understanding actors. Bourdieu's "habitus" and Giddens' "practical consciousness" actually point to this embodied cognitive ability. However, Giddens and Bourdieu happened to agree that these two cognitive mechanisms cannot be perceived and articulated by actors, which creates a methodological dilemma in social science research. Bourdieu has tried to base the logic of "habitus" on "opposition", such as male/female, rich/poor, etc. However, Schatzki (1996: 152) argues that in real life and in social research surveys, few people would use this "opposition" logic to reflect and explain their actions. Berard (2005: 216) also believes that the first-generation theory of practice lacked a physical substrate to explain the subjective factors of individual actors. Thus, their theory, while very attractive at the ontological level, lacks a convincing basis at the epistemological and methodological level.

(2) Theodore Schatzki: Practice as a Collection of Subjective and Objective Constituent Elements

The theory of practice represented by Theodore Schatzki, Andrea Reckwitz, and Bruno Latour believes that practice is a collection of subjective and objective elements, and duality is reflected in the coordination and interaction of subjective and objective elements in the process of practice formation. This mechanism provides a new way to solve the existing difficulty of the practice theory (Gu Jie, 2014).

American social philosopher Theodore Schatzki (1996, 2001, 2005) is a key figure in the theoretical shift of practice. He believes that any social practice is a collection of a series of subjective and objective elements, including basic understandings, explicit rules, ends, beliefs, projects, emotions, moods, materials, technology, competence, and institutions. 1 In the formation stage of a certain social practice, the actors will bring their own purpose, basic understanding, explicit rules, etc., together with other necessary physical materials and other objective elements. Then, in a long-term process of socialization and collectivization, these subjective and objective elements will continuously coordinate with each other so that the actors will reach a "consensus" and "tacit agreement" with each other on the operating norms of the practice. Eventually, the constituent elements, operating modes, and actor interactions of the practice become formed and relatively stabilized.

In this formation of practice, we found that Schatzki did not deliberately shy away from the individual subjective factors in the traditional sense such as purpose, beliefs, and emotions. However, according to Schatzki (2005: 480), these subjective elements no longer belong to the individual but to the practice itself after the practice is formed. For individuals who are new to a practice, there is a process of internalization of the elements of the practice: Basic understanding becomes the tacit knowledge of the individual, rules become objects of beliefs, purpose becomes the object of desire. (Schatzki, 2005: 480-481). Therefore, the subjective elements discussed by Schatzki (2005: 481), such as purpose, beliefs, and emotions, are essentially an "objective mind" or media formed based on acausal relationships in the practice (Schatzki, 1996: 50). In response to this idea, Reckwitz (2012: 252) proposes a more vivid metaphor, saying that individuals are actually "carriers" of social practices.

From the results of the formation of practice, the above-mentioned duality mechanism reflects more the structural power of practice, but from the perspective of the formation process, the interaction and coordination of subjective and objective elements reflect the individuality and subjectivity of practice. And this coordination also leads to a certain degree of diversity and tolerance in the final elements of practice. Schatzki (1996) argues that the constituent elements of practice can contain multiple levels or aspects as long as they are normatively "correct" or "acceptable" to each other by actors. For example, the purpose of people engaging in educational practice can include teaching and educating people, fulfilling personal ambitions, and obtaining financial rewards. Therefore, most social practices in real life have various "performances". It is also this mechanism that ultimately contributes to the dialectical unity of the commonality and diversity of social practice, and thus brings order and differentiation to practice behaviors.

The theoretical approach of the aggregate of subjective and objective elements represented by Schatzki has contributed to the further improvement and rationality of practice theory in the following two aspects:

First, Schatzki uses a holistic and diachronic perspective to focus his theory on the process of practice elements coordinating with each other and finally forming a practice, thus skillfully taking into account the two sides of "duality". Schatzki (2001b: 3) believes that the fundamental value of the practice theory lies in revealing the successful internalization process of common knowledge. Rouse (2007: 648) also pointed out that the purpose of the theory of practice is to provide a detailed and in-depth description of how common understanding is transmitted through social interaction". Therefore, the focus of applying the theory of practice should be to reveal how actors are embedded in the processes of formation, development, and changes of a social practice. The fundamental purpose of careful exploration of this process is to reveal the core elements that play a key role in the formation of practice and the interactions between them, so as to gain a more detailed and richer understanding of the dialectical duality relationships between the individual and the whole, the subjective and the objective, and examine the multiple factors and mechanisms that play a key structural or agency role in social action and power order in a broader sense.

As for the exploration of core elements, Schatzki would not make assumptions and judgments about decisive factors (such as class or resource) in advance like Giddens and Bourdieu, but leave the answers to subjective and objective practice constituent elements which are more open, actionable, relatable, so as to avoid congenitally falling into the quagmire of individualism or holism.

Second, Schatzki concretized the duality mechanism of practice into a series of subjective and objective elements, which not only reflects practice more objectively, but also made empirical research operationally feasible with these intelligible and measurable elements. As mentioned earlier, both Bourdieu's "habitus" and Giddens's "practical consciousness" are too abstract. Schatzki boils down practice as a collection of elements such as purpose, attitude, and beliefs. In daily life, people's understanding and knowledge of practice are often reflected in these elements. Thus, in empirical research, people are more accustomed and able to reflect on their own practices in terms of parameters such as purpose and belief.

3. Research Path of Media Practice Paradigm

(1) Research Objects

As mentioned earlier, the "decentralization" and "de-dualism" orientations of the media practice paradigm have led to two major research questions: media social power relations and media behavior patterns. The social power relationship of media is of course realized through people's media behaviors. Therefore, the pattern of media behavior is the logical starting point for the study of the practice paradigm. However, combined with the discussion of the core of practice theory, we will find that if we simply objectively describe or type-analyze user media behavior patterns, we cannot reflect the inherent meaning and requirements of the duality of practice theory. As mentioned above, Warde (2005) argued at first that differentiation in consumption patterns is the result of practice organizational structure rather than individual choices. Later, he revised this principle and pointed out that if the analysis of the formation process of practice is neglected, then the theory of practice is essentially equivalent to the methodology of structuralism (Warde, 2014: 295). From this perspective, Rivera and Cox's (2016) research on the impact of human resource practice on employees' new media technology adoption also suffers from the same shortcomings, because the results of their research are ultimately only a brief description of the relationship of how structural characteristics of the practice and the actors' behavioral patterns determines each other.

Therefore, the research paradigm of media practice should first start with the constituent elements of practice and strive to discover the coordination mechanism of subjective and objective elements in the process of practice formation and development, as well as the core elements that play a key role. With good understanding of the what and the why, one can then form a unique "duality" discovery and understanding of the behavior pattern of media use. For example, Gu Jie (2014)'s research on YouTube user behavior patterns shows that YouTube technology, YouTube management team, and user skills are the three core elements in the formation of the YouTubing practice. The different combination mechanisms of these three core elements also create four different types of behavior patterns for YouTubing practitioners. For another example, Hargreaves (2011) conducted a study on the environmental protection practice initiated internally by a British construction company, and eventually found that the company's hardware conditions and personnel power relations are the core elements that determine the fate of the practice.

The discovery of the core elements of practice should adopt a holistic research perspective, that is to say, the whole of practice should be taken as the logical starting point of research, and then the formation of individual media user behavior patterns should be placed in the birth, development, formation and even the final demise stage of media practice - the entire process is examined. In other words, the subjective actions of any practitioner are the result of the interaction and coordination between the individual and the collective, the subjective and objective elements of practice, and the individual performance of the practitioner and the overall structure of the practice. This approach of taking into account the individual and the whole is actually the embodiment of the dual dialectical requirements of the practice theory. As Shi Boye et al. (2010) said: "The object analyzed by the practice approach should be a collective entity, which is different from individualistic analysis".

The focus on practice elements also responds to Couldry's question about the social power relations of media because the power relations of media are embodied in the interaction mechanism of media and other practice elements. This interaction can take place both within a medium-centric practice and across multiple practices that are intertwined in social living spaces. Furthermore, because the elements of practice can be micro as media-as-texts or media-as-objects (Silverstone, 1994), they can also be macro as complex media organizations, management agencies, or institutions (Bannerman and Haggart, 2014; Schatzki, 2005), so the analytical approach focusing on practice elements enables the paradigm of media practice to have the ability to analyze the social power of media from macro to micro levels, and it also makes practice what Couldry (2012 / translator by He Daokuan, 2014: 58) called the mediator linking media textual analysis and political economy analysis. Warde (2014: 296) also believes that in addition to analyzing the behavioral patterns of consumers, the practice paradigm of consumption also has political economy implications when the focus is turned to the material resources, commercial institutions, or national governments in the rule-forming process of practice structure. Therefore, from the perspective of the second-generation practice theory, the focuses on action patterns and on social power are no longer contradictory to each other, and the media practice paradigm already has the potential to integrate critical and empirical communication research.

Specifically, the media practice paradigm should be able to provide new perspectives and ideas for the following media research fields or questions from the perspective of the operating characteristics and mechanisms of social practice:

Table 1 Research Areas and Questions with Media Practice Paradigm

Research Area/Question	Operational Characteristics and Mechanisms of Practice
Research on Media Use Motivation Media Adoption Research	Participation in Social Practice
Research on Media Use Behavior Patterns	Behavior Patterns and Performance of Practice
Media and Communication History Studies	Changes and Routinization in Social Practice
Media Law, Policy, and Management Studies	Operating Norms of Practice / Organizational Practice
Research on Media Production and Reception	Operational Mechanism of Practice

(2) Research Outline

1. *Identify the Roles and Relationship of Media and Social Practice*

According to the above research questions, researchers first need to clarify the roles and relationship between media (text, entity, etc.) and a social practice. The author believes that in the era of media decentralization, media practice, that is, the way the media intervenes in social practice, can be basically divided into two types:

1) Media core practice: media is the core component of a social practice, such as the YouTubing practice (Gu Jie, 2014), the digital music practice (Werner, 2009), etc.

2) Media participation in practice: media is used as a component to participate in a social practice, such as a media communication tool participating in the human resources practice (Rivera and Cox, 2016), video game use participating in the play practice of adolescents' daily life (Roig, Cornelio and Ardèvol, 2009), media use participating in bodily practice (Postill, 2010: 15).

2. *Identify the Spatial Boundaries of Practice*

In real life, because any media practice is not without exception in the relational network of intertwined practices, and only by examining media practice in the interaction mechanism with other social practices, can we better understand the social power relationship of media practice. Therefore, in the process of media practice paradigm research, it is necessary to consider examining the interweaving and interactive relationship between media practice and other practices in social space from a more macro perspective. However, in daily life, social practices are intertwined with each other, making it difficult for comprehensive social science research. Therefore, it is necessary to establish the spatial boundary of practice research, that is, to clarify which interwoven practices enter the scope of research and investigation.

A more feasible method is to borrow Bourdieu's concept of "field". But we are not trying to completely copy the operating mechanism of "field" but trying to impose a socio-spatial limit on the diverse practices that may be involved in the research. For example, Shove and Pantzar (2007) used Lancaster University as the spatial boundary to study the proliferation and adoption of the floorball practice in the UK and found that the interaction between floorball practice and teaching practice had a significant impact on how staff participated in the floorball practice. Warde (2005: 149) also recommended that researchers try to tap into the influence of diverse practices by asking the following questions: "Which practices are relevant to the practice being studied? How broad is the range of practices that practitioners may be involved in? What are the typical forms of intertwining and interlocking?"

3. *Determining the Time Boundaries of Practice*

The focus of applying the theory of practice is to reveal how actors are embedded in the process of formation, development, and even changes of a social practice. Therefore, the research path must be based on the process of the overall occurrence, formation, development, reproduction, and even demise of a practice. In fact, the process of practice development and changes is a process in which subjective and objective elements coordinate or conflict with each other. That is to say, only in the process of changes and development, those core practice elements that play a leading role become prominent, and the behavior pattern of practitioners is also most likely to become differentiated and change as a result of changes in the practice as a whole. In fact, researchers thus obtain a good opportunity to examine the mutual interaction between the structure and the dynamism in the practice.

In everyday life, however, most of the time practice exhibits an external feature of routinization (Giddens 1984: 50). In this case, the investigation of practice often touches on its structural side, so it is easy to fall into the quagmire of objectivist methodology again. Moreover, in empirical research, due to the constraints of various research conditions, we may not be able to track the process of occurrence, development, and demise of some media practices. Therefore, a more feasible method is to intercept a fragment of the development track of a practice, and conduct accompanying observation and research. The selection of this time segment should preferably cover the process of actors participating in a social practice, because theoretically the initial stage of joining the practice is a key stage for novice practitioners to form a "consensus" on the elements and operating norms of the practice (Schatzki, 1996:76-80). Shove and Pantzar (2007: 164) also believe that peoples' first encounter with a practice essentially contains many seeds for the formation of common understanding in the future. For example, Gu Jie's (2014) research focused on the process of YouTube users joining the YouTubing practice and summarized four modes of motivation for participation.

Second, the time period during which the practice development experiences the most drastic changes should also be the focus of attention, such as when a routinized practice operation mode is broken. According to Giddens (1984: 26), actors tend to have the most reflective ability with regards to a practice during periods of dramatic changes. Therefore, to examine practice in the process of changes is to allow the subject of practice to better reflect on the dual dialectical mechanism of their own actions, thus opening a window for empirical research on the paradigm of media practice. Of course, for some small and short-lived practices, it would be more complete for research to be able to trace the full course of their life. Take the research of Hargreaves (2011) as an example, as an observer, he personally followed the whole process of the environmental protection practice from its initiation, and its development to final termination over a period of nine months.

(3) Research Methods

If the research of positivism focuses on the explanation and prediction of social phenomena, the research of the practice paradigm is to deeply describe and understand the construction and organization process of practice through systematic, detailed, and abstract description. In addition, the theory of practice itself emphasizes the dualistic unity of the subject and object. Therefore, the understanding of the process of practice construction must adopt the methodology of dualistic unity of the subject and object, and a bipolar relationship cannot be formed again between the researcher and the research object. Faced with these methodological challenges, both Schatzki and Giddens believe that actors have the ability to reflect on their own practices. Moreover, as mentioned above, when the elements of practice have been embodied in popularized concepts such as purpose and belief, the practitioner's reflection and expression process will be more direct and easier. In addition, Schatzki (1996: 40-41) also argues that through observation, the outside observer often has a better understanding of the practice than the actor himself. In view of these conditions and taking into account the research standpoint of the integration of the subject and object, a composite research method combining reflexive participant observation and in-depth interview is a relatively suitable method for us to understand practice.

For the participatory observation method, the research of the practice paradigm especially needs to emphasize that the researcher is engaged in the practice, because only by engaging in person can the researcher's reflexive thinking be stimulated, thus realizing the unity of the subject and object in the research process (Lindlof, 1995: 4). Moreover, for the media practice, more crucially, the personal participation of researchers is not only possible, but also more necessary with today's media empowerment. In a sense, this is a brand-new approach for media studies to probe into the media social power relationship. For example, American media anthropologist Michael Wesch (2009) adopted the method of personally making and uploading videos and interacting with other netizens in his research on YouTube video community practice. His first video about the background of his research, "An Anthropological Introduction to YouTube", was a huge success, with over two million views to date. 2 After that, he applied his personal experience and reflexive thinking of practice participation to his research on knowledge learning in the new media environment.

Of course, in reflexive participatory research, a research framework of objective narrative and analysis is also very important. Schatzki (1996), Halkier and Jensen (2011) all argue that interviewing can complement participatory observation. However, like the participatory observation method, the theory of practice also requires the researcher to intervene in the practice with the identity as both the subject and the object. Garfinkel (1991: 15) argues that social order exists only in the practitioner's "reflexive accountability", that is, the individual's subjective account is itself a component and process of constructing the duality of practice. Therefore, conversation analysis avoids the risk of subject-object separation during the interview process and completes the secondary construction of the duality of practice.

4. The Media Practice Paradigm: Values and Lessons

(1) The Values of the Media Practice Paradigm

The rise of the media practice research paradigm in the West is not only due to its "decentralization" perspective, which accurately reflects the multiple dimensions of media's entry and impact on social life in the current "mediatization" era, but also due to its ontological method of "duality" that comprehensively and dialectically reflects the interactive relationship between media action and social power.

In recent years, the positioning of media from "intermediation" to "mediation" has become the latest hotspot in media and communication research (Zhou Xiang and Li Jia, 2017; Dai Yuchen, 2016). The concept of "decentralization" advocated by the media practice paradigm provides an important research dimension and carrier for this media ontology turn. In essence, whether it is "intermediation" or "centralization", both use a functionalist perspective to locate the role of the media in social life. In the view of Couldry (2004: 123-125), the theory of practice is an important weapon to challenge media functionalism. He believes that media functionalism mistakenly places the media at the center of the entire social functional structure, and that the media and the overall social structure are not a mechanical "whole" and "part" relationship. In the era of mediatization, whether it is media text or media technology, they "no longer play the role of a neutral tool as in communication functionalism but have become a key node in the development of human society" (Dai Yuchen, 2016). Therefore, with the all-round penetration of media into social life and the all-round transformation of social systems, media practice has become an important "meso" carrier and "kink point", combining various social institution powers related to media and people's daily media use behaviors together (Couldry, 2012 / translated by He Daokuan, 2014: 7).

Therefore, from this perspective, the important value of the media practice paradigm is that it forms an important challenge to the media functionalism that has long restrained the development of communication studies. The formation of this challenge not only expands the topics of media studies in the mediatization age, but also allows us to re-examine many classic topics in traditional research paradigms from a practice perspective. For example, in the past research on the history of newspapers and magazines, newspapers were more regarded as tools from the perspective of media functionalism. Thus, "the history of newspapers and magazines is the history of the 'use and satisfaction' of newspapers and magazines, thus forming another double dualism: the dualism of the subjective and objective world, and the dualism of the agent and object" (Huang Dan, 2015: 13). Yet the introduction of the media practice paradigm provides a brand-new "way of talking about events", that is, a new concept of newspaper and magazine history with media as focal point and media practice as narrative path, while eliminating essentialism and teleology.

For another example, audience research in the context of functionalism either focuses on media effects or behavioral patterns, or emphasizes the cultural symbolism and implications of resistance of audience' media use. With the advent of the new media era, the focus of academic research has shifted from the previous passive audience to active participation and production behavior. In a sense, these studies "have not escaped the shackles of the outdated binary opposition between consumption and production: active/passive, powerful/non-powerful, confrontation/cooperation, etc." (Gu Jie, 2014: 4), thus ignoring the richness and complexity of today's audience in terms of behavior, roles, and even psychology. Yet the media practice paradigm provides a more comprehensive and open perspective for media research with the attribute of "practice", which is possessed by almost all social activities. For example, media use can be both conscious and rational, as well as unconscious behavior based on routinized daily life; media behavior can be driven by an individual's internal subjective will and can be simultaneously influenced by social structures and situations; media behavior can be both productive and participatory, but the many purely passive consumptions that still exist in abundance today cannot be ignored, such as users' "lurking" behavior in online communities (Crawford, 2009).

Of course, the emphasis on media should also avoid the "instrumental" implications of media mentioned by Huang Dan (2015: 14). That is to say, due to the emphasis on the power of media technology in reconstructing social order, the logic of decentralization and mediatization still risks falling back into technological determinism (Zhou Xiang and Li Jia, 2017: 14; Dai Yuchen, 2016). Therefore, the dualistic appeal and research approach of the second-generation practice theory provides a good opportunity for balancing technological determinism and social constructionism, because they never presume determinative elements of practice and power relations. Rather, actors and practice elements are "based on the practical logic of daily life experience to establish a symbiotic relationship and a holistic theoretical framework in the 'triadic dialectics' of 'media-human-society'" (Zhou Xiang and Li Jia, 2017: 149).

From the more macro level of social science, the relationship between media practice theory and media functionalism cannot be simply understood as one surpasses the other. In essence, both are macro-ontological frameworks that reflect the actions of subjects and social order.

If functionalism is understood from this level, according to Liu Hailong's point of view, research under the theoretical framework of functionalism can either accommodate empirical methods or be completed by the hermeneutics paradigm. More importantly, the explanation of social action in functionalist research focuses on the cause rather than the effect (i.e. function), "the reason is that the effect itself is too subjective and variable, and is not as inevitable and unique as the cause" (Liu Hailong, 2012: 11). This principle is exactly the same as the concept of practice theory that does not pay attention to the external form and purpose of practice but to the cause and process of practice. Therefore, in essence the practice paradigm has the potential and possibility of bridging the gap between the positivist and critical paradigms of communication. For example, from the perspective of research topics, the paradigm of media practice can not only describe media behavior patterns, but also dig deep into the power mechanism behind it; from the perspective of research methods, it can not only describe the details of actors' cognition and behavior through participant observation but can also find the interactive relationship between practice elements through in-depth interviews and other methods. Furthermore, when the media constantly begins to intersect with all aspects of social life, the renewal and reconstruction of media research paradigms not only needs to reorganize and adjust the relationship between existing paradigms, but also needs to strengthen the integration with the theories and methods of other disciplines. Because, "Only by re-understanding how communication and its technologies are embedded in people's lives, redefining human existence and the relationship between people, society, and objects, and discussing the meaning of communication and human existence, can there be truly unique theories of communication, then be connected with meta-theories of philosophy, and can we be qualified to dialogue with other disciplines, especially humanities and social sciences" (Hu Yiqing, 2016: 51).

2) References and Inspirations

The paradigm of media practice has injected fresh blood into media research with its new theoretical perspective and research object, so it has been paid more and more attention in the West in recent years. At the same time, this paradigm is also a theoretical paradigm involving the ontological level of society and actors and has the potential to span different social and cultural contexts. Therefore, it is necessary and possible for China's communication and media studies to learn from this paradigm. More importantly, this paradigm has also just started in Western academic circles. Although the practice theory itself has already a well-established foundation, it still faces many challenges in the process of grafting into the field of media research, and there are also many gaps in terms of specific research questions. To a certain extent, this means that the old-fashioned "localization" issue actually still boasts many opportunities for us.

Looking at the development of media practice research in the West, there are still no small gaps in the following two areas, which are also the research directions that we can give priority to when applying the media practice paradigm. First, the theory of practice emphasizes the coordination and interaction between a series of subjective and objective elements in complex social spaces. These elements include not only "spiritual" elements related to "people", but also some important "non-spiritual" elements, such as material equipment or practical skills. For example, the above-mentioned company hardware equipment or YouTube technologies play a decisive role in the differentiation of practice activities (Gu Jie, 2014; Hargreaves, 2011). For the emphasis on "object", scientific practice research has been one step ahead (Knorr-Cetina, 2001; Latour, 2005; Pickering, 1995). Knorr-Cetina (2001) even argues that in some human social practices, the mental and emotional states of actors are almost insignificant compared to materials. And Latour's Actor-Network Theory depicts an interdependent and closely related material network world for us. Therefore, from this perspective, increasingly advanced and sophisticated digital network technologies and devices play an increasingly important role for current media practices. Whether it is Internet access speed (Kwak et al., 2004) or the performance of social media software (Nardi, Schiano and Gumbrecht, 2004), they deserve further attention from a practice point of view.

Furthermore, another important "non-spiritual" practice element that deserves our attention is the practice skills of the actor. For example, sports practices such as tennis are very skill-demanding (Nobel and Watkins, 2003). The author believes that practice skills can be defined as "knowledge and ability that people need to master in a differentiated way for practice". Then, in future media practice research, this issue can also be cross-referenced and studied with media literacy research. That is to say, the focus should not just be on people's practical skills from a purely technical level, but also include considerations on dimensions of power, culture, social construction, and so on.

Second, although the paradigm of media practice advocates jumping out of the traditional "text-audience-effect" research framework, and today's media has increasingly developed from media texts to products with physical implications in daily life, the role of media texts still cannot be completely dismissed. In a sense, the existence of media texts is also the most unique feature of the media practice compared to other social practices. In practices such as search engines and YouTube mentioned by Couldry (2012 / translated by He Daokuan, 2014), text is undoubtedly an important component. However, there is no research in the existing media practice literature that has attempted to incorporate text as an important practice component into the operating mechanism and power relations of the entire practice. This path requires us not to simply pay attention to the so-called encoding and decoding practices, but to have a vision of connecting and linking semiotics, audience research, and even media political economy. Only in this way can we consider today's increasingly complicated and diffused media texts and the corresponding media practices.

While drawing on the research paradigm of media practice, it is also necessary to pay attention to combining the characteristics of China's own political, economic, and cultural environment, and to prevent the tendency of only repeatedly testing the theory and the unwillingness to recreate the theory based on the local situation in the process of theory introduction. Regarding this "localization" issue, the author agrees with the point of view put forward by Liu Hailong (2011) about the need to maintain the dual tension of application/theory and specificity/universality in the process of communication localization. This path choice is particularly important when the development of the media practice paradigm has not yet fully matured. That is to say, on the one hand, we must actively study and apply existing media practice theories to interpret the current media practice in China and provide a new "Chinese model" for the improvement of media practice theories. On the other hand, we must be good at constantly tapping into the unique resources of Chinese traditions and reality to back feed the theories, and then construct a media practice theory with unique explanatory power for the Chinese reality, or also with universal significance.

Starting from this line of thinking is the key to find the unique issues and variables of the current media practice in China. Viewing the research questions of the media practice paradigm listed in Table 1, studies on media and communication history may be the first topic for breakthroughs. Within the framework of the media practice paradigm, media and communication history should not be limited to the writing of the development history of media organizations such as newspapers and magazines, or television, but should pay more attention to the practice commonly promoted by users, media organizations, and technological development in the current new media technology environment, driven by various media technological forms. It is precisely because of the existence of multiple influencing factors that the development of such practices is often more variable. In fact, since the Internet entered China, we have continuously witnessed the rise and fall of many different media technologies or organizations. For example, since 2010, what power relations, such as technology, politics, and culture, have been behind the ups and downs of the Weibo practice? In essence, this issue can be discussed from the perspective of practice changes and routinization. In addition, from the perspective of operating norms of organizational practices, China's organizational media practice often has more political and cultural variables than that in Western contexts. For example, research on the Internet governance practice has increasingly paid attention to the uniqueness and importance of political and cultural variables in recent years (Feng, 2016; Jiang, 2016). Will the addition of these variables form a new normative system for media practice, thus bringing implications for guiding our media management policies and laws? This issue also touches on the uniqueness of China's media practice compared to that in Western context, thus adding more research materials to the exploration of the localization of the media practice paradigm.

Notes

1 The "rules" proposed by Schatzki and Giddens differ in their meanings. Schatzki's (2001:51) "rules" are clear rules for specific actions, such as recipes. And Giddens' "rules" are structural common understandings of practice.
2 See: https://www.youtube.com/watch?v=TPAO-lZ4_hU

References

Dai Yuchen (2016). Towards a Media-Centric Social Ontology? A Critical Examination of the European "Mediatization School". Journalism & Communication, (5), 47-57. 戴宇辰 (2016). 走向媒介中心的社会本体论?——对欧洲"媒介化学派"的一个批判性考察.《新闻与传播研究》

Gu Jie (2014). "YouTube Users' Agency: The Perspective of Media Practice". Beijing: China Radio and Television Press. 顾洁 (2014).《YouTube用户能动性: 媒介实践论的角度》. 北京:中国广播电视出版社.

何道宽译 (2014).《媒介、社会与世界: 社会理论与数字媒介实践》. 上海: 复旦大学出版社。Original book: Couldry, N. (2012) Media, Society, World: Social Theory and Digital Media Practice. London, UK: Polity Press.

Huang Dan (2015). New Newspaper and Magazine (Media) History Writing: Paradigm Change. Journalism & Communication, (12), 5-19. 黄旦 (2015). 新报刊(媒介)史书写:范式的变更.《新闻与传播研究》

Hu Yiqing (2016). Reshaping the Research Paradigm of Communication: What is Possible and What Can We Do. Modern Communication - Journal of Communication University of China, (1), 51-56. 重塑传播研究范式:何以可能与何以可为.《现代传播-中国传媒大学学报》

Liu Hailong (2011). Two Dimensions of Localization of Communication Studies. Modern Communication - Journal of Communication University of China, (9), 43-48. 刘海龙 (2011). 传播研究本土化的两个维度.《现代传播-中国传媒大学学报》

Liu Hailong (2012). Two Kinds of Functionalism in Chinese Communication Studies. Journalism Bimonthly, (2), 10-14. 刘海龙 (2012). 中国传播研究中的两种功能主义.《新闻大学》

Wang Bin (2011). From Techniques to Practices: The Spatial Course of Media Evolution and the Spatial Turn of Media Studies. Journalism & Communication, (3), 58-67. 王斌 (2011). 从技术逻辑到实践逻辑：媒介演化的空间历程与媒介研究的空间转向. 《新闻与传播研究》

Zhou Xiang, Li Jia (2017). "Mediatization" in the Network Society: Theories, Practices and Prospects. Chinese Journal of Journalism & Communication, (4), 137-154. 周翔，李镓 (2017). 网络社会中的"媒介化"问题：理论、实践与展望. 《国际新闻界》

Bannerman, S., & Haggart, B. (2015). Historical Institutionalism in Communication Studies. Communication Theory, 25(1), 1–22.

Berard, T. J. (2005). Rethinking Practices and Structures. Philosophy of the Social Sciences, 35(2), 196-230.

Bourdieu, P. (1977). Outline of a Theory of Practice. Cambridge, UK: Cambridge University Press.

Bourdieu, P. (1990). The Logic of Practice. Cambridge, UK: Polity Press.

Bourdieu, P. (1998). On Television and Journalism. London, UK: Pluto.

Bräuchler, B., & Postill, J. (Ed.). (2010). Theorising Media and Practice. New York, NY: Berghahn Books.

Couldry, N. (2004). Theorising Media as Practice. Social Semiotics, 14 (2), 115-132.

Crawford, K. 2009. Listening as Participation: Social Media and Metaphors of Hearing Online. Paper Read at COST Action 298: Participation in the Broadband Society, May 13-15, 2009, at Copenhagen, Denmark.

Feldman, M. S., & Orlikowski, W. J. (2011). Theorizing Practice and Practicing Theory. Organization Science, 22(5), 1240-1253.

Feng L (2016) Online Video Sharing: An Alternative Channel for Film Distribution? Copyright Enforcement, Censorship, and Chinese Independent Cinema. Chinese Journal of Communication DOI: 10.1080/17544750.2016.1247736.

Garfinkel, H. (1991). Respecification: Evidence for Locally Produced, Naturally Accountable Phenomena of Order, Logic, Reason, Meaning, Method, etc. In and as of the Essential Haecceity of Immortal Ordinary Society, (I) — An Announcement of Studies. In G. Button (Eds.), Ethnomethodology and the Human Sciences. New York, NY: Cambridge University Press.

Giddens, A. (1984). The Constitution of Society: Outline of the Theory of Structuration. Cambridge, UK: Polity.

Halkier, B., & Jensen, I. (2011). Methodological Challenges in Using Practice Theory in Consumption Research: Examples from a Study on Handling Nutritional Contestations of Food Consumption. Journal of Consumer Culture, 11(1), 101-123.

Hargreaves, T. 2011. Practice-ing Behaviour Change: Applying Social Practice Theory to Pro-Environmental Behaviour Change. Journal of Consumer Culture, 11 (1), 79-99.

Jiang, M. (2016) Managing the Micro-Self: The Governmentality of Real Name Registration Policy in Chinese Microblogosphere. Information, Communication & Society, 19(2), 203-220.

Kwak, N., M. M. Skoric, A. E. Williams, and N. D. Poor. 2004. To Broadband or Not to Broadband: The Relationship between High-Speed

Internet and Knowledge and Participation. Journal of Broadcasting & Electronic Media, 48 (1), 421-445.

King, A. (2000). Thinking with Bourdieu against Bourdieu: A 'Practical' Critique of the Habitus. Sociological Theory, 18 (3), 417-433.

Knorr-Cetina, K. 2001. Objectual Practice. In the Practice Turn in Contemporary Theory, Edited by T. R. Schatzki, K. D. Knorr-Cetina and E. v. Savigny. New York: Routledge.

Latour, B. (2005). Reassembling the Social: An Introduction to Actor-Network-Theory. Oxford, UK: Oxford University Press.

Lindlof, T. R. (1995). Qualitative Communication Research Methods. Thousand Oaks, CA: Sage.

Moores, S. (2005). Media/Theory. London, UK: Routledge.

Nardi, B. A., D. J. Schiano, and M. Gumbrecht. 2004. Blogging as Social Activity, or, Would You Let 900 Million People Read Your Diary? Paper Read at CSCW 2004, November 6-10, 2004, at Illinois, USA.

Nicolini, D. (2011). Practice as the Site of Knowing: Insights From the Field of Telemedicine. Organization Science, 22 (3), 602–620.

Noble, G., and M. Watkins. 2003. So, How did Bourdieu Learn to Play Tennis? Habitus, Consciousness and Habituation. Cultural Studies, 17 (3): 520-539.

Pickering, A. (1995). The Angle of Practice: Time, Agency, and Science. Chicago, IL: University of Chicago Press.

Postill, J. (2010). Introduction: Theorising Media and Practice. In B. Bräuchler & J. Postill (Eds.), Theorising Media and Practice (pp. 1-32). New York, NY: Berghahn Books.

Reckwitz, A. (2002). Toward a Theory of Social Practices: A Development in Culturalist Theorizing. European Journal of Social Theory, 5(2), 243-263.

Rivera, G., & Cox, A. M. (2016). A Practice-Based Approach to Understanding Participation in Online Communities. Journal of Computer-Mediated Communication, 21(1), 17-32.

Roig, A., Cornelio, G. S., & Ardèvol, E. (2009). Videogame as Media Practice. Convergence: The International Journal of Research into New Media Technologies, 15(1), 89-103.

Rouse, J. (2007). Practice theory. In S. P. Turner & M. W. Risjord (Eds.), Philosophy of Anthropology and Sociology (pp. 639-681). Amsterdam, Netherlands: Elsevier.

Schatzki, T. R. (1996). Social Practices: A Wittgensteinian Approach to Human Activity and the Social. Cambridge, UK: Cambridge University Press.

Schatzki, T. R. (2001). Practice Mind-ed Orders. In T. R. Schatzki, K. D. Knorr-Cetina & E. V. Savigny (Eds.), The practice turn in contemporary theory (pp. 42-55). New York, NY: Routledge.

Schatzki, T. R. (2001b). Introduction: Practice theory. In T. R. Schatzki, K. D. Knorr-Cetina & E. V. Savigny (Eds.), The Practice Turn in Contemporary Theory (pp. 1-14). New York, NY: Routledge.

Schatzki, T. R. (2005). Peripheral Vision: The Sites of Organizations. Organization Studies, 26(3), 465-484.

Shove, E., & Pantzar, M. (2007). Recruitment and Reproduction: The Careers and Carriers of Digital Photography and Floorball. Human Affairs, 17, 154-167.

Shove, E., Pantzar, M., & Watson, M. (2012). The Dynamics of Social Practice: Everyday Life and How It Changes. London, UK: Sage.

Silverstone, R. (1994). Television and Everyday Life. London, UK: Routledge.

Spaargaren, G. (2011). Theories of Practices: Agency, Technology, and Culture: Exploring the Relevance of Practice Theories for the Governance of Sustainable Consumption Practices in the New World-Order. Global Environmental Change, 21(3), 813-822.

Warde, A. (2005). Consumption and Theories of Practice. Journal of Consumer Culture, 5(2), 131-153.

Warde, A. (2014). After Taste: Culture, Consumption and Theories of Practice. Journal of Consumer Culture, 14(3), 279-303.

Werner, A. (2009). Girls Consuming Music at Home: Gender and the Exchange of Music through New Media. European Journal of Cultural Studies, 12(3), 269-284.

Wesch, M. (2009). YouTube and You: Experiences of Self-Awareness in the Context Collapse of the Recording Webcam. Explorations in Media Ecology, 8 (2), 19-34.

GLOBAL GOVERNANCE OF ONLINE CONTENT: CURRENT SITUATION, DISPUTES, AND PERSPECTIVES

Xu Peixi

Abstract: Social media platforms in the digital age have moved to the frontline of international communication. They gather billions of users and mobilize content from traditional news media. They empower grassroots and citizens and meanwhile become tools of competition of global powers. Against such a context, online content governance has increasingly become a central topic of global Internet governance. Nations as diverse as UK, Singapore, and China have adopted new content regulations. This article firstly reviews some national content regimes. Then it traces transnational content disputes in the era of traditional media, categorizing major disputes in the digital age. It finally proposes three perspectives to approach online content governance.

Keywords: Online Content, Global Governance, Current Situation, Disputes, Perspectives

Network information content governance is one of the most difficult topics in global governance of cyberspace, mainly involving national defense, publicity, cyber security and informatization, news, publishing, radio and television and other departments. Due to the different historical, cultural and security contexts of different countries, and the uneven economic and social development stages, people's views on freedom of speech and social responsibility, free circulation and privacy protection are very different. It is difficult for countries to reach a consensus on the governance of online information content. There is an urgent need to simplify the complexities, clarify the core disputes, and build a unified governance framework.

This paper studies the global governance of network information from four aspects. The first part introduces the current status of network information governance in some countries. The second part summarizes the reasons for the failure of the new international information order movement in the 1970s and 1980s. Non-Aligned Movement countries, Eastern countries, and Western countries were unable to reach a binding consensus text on the international governance of traditional media content. The third part sorts out the typical cases of cross-border content disputes in the digital age, and defines controversial topics such as race, religion, political stability, and pornography. The fourth part proposes three perspectives for contemplating the global governance of online information content.

1. Legislative Progress and Future Challenges of Various Countries

Looking at the situation of various countries, Singapore and China have preliminarily completed network information content legislation and reforms of regulatory agencies, continuously adjusting and implementing the governance rules in the digital age and have taken the lead in clarifying the responsibilities that platforms and users need to assume. In contrast, although the United States and the United Kingdom are currently undergoing content legislation and institutional reforms, they have not yet defined the responsibilities of online information content platforms in detail and are in the stage of exploration and transition.

U.K.

In April 2019, the United Kingdom issued the "Online Harms White Paper", announcing that the era of self-regulation of online information content has come to an end and a new era is coming.

The white paper recommends clarifying platform responsibilities and punishing companies that fail to perform their duties, including by fines, suspending network services, blocking websites or app access, handing over to judicial departments, and pursuing civil and criminal liabilities. The British government prepares for future legislation through a white paper, and after discussion by relevant groups, a bill will be formed and submitted to Parliament. Previously, the British government released the Communications White Paper in 2000, which laid the foundation for the Communications Act 2003 and instituted the Office of Communications. The 2019 Online Harms White Paper proposes the establishment of a new independent regulator to regulate cyberspace. Its main responsibilities will include implementing a new regulatory framework, formulating codes of practice, supervising Internet companies to enforce user agreements, and punishing companies that do not perform their duties.[1]

U.S.

Similar to the United Kingdom, the governance of Internet information content in the United States is in the exploratory stage, debating on legislation to enforce the duties of Internet information content platforms, with the main controversy being on the abolishment of article 230 of the Communications Decency Act (CDA). Section 230 of CDA, passed in 1996, exempts online information content platforms from responsibilities with regards to user-uploaded content. Two major crisis factors, internal and external, have led to the dispute over the preservation or abolition of Section 230. Externally, the 2016 U.S. presidential election caused panic on social media. The U.S. was worried about external forces interfering with U.S. political stability through social media, and the U.S. Congress and the executive branch strongly required social media platforms to review online information content more strictly. The U.S. Federal Trade Commission and Facebook finally reached a $5 billion settlement. Internally, in 2018, the Federal Bureau of Investigation, on suspicions of "assisting prostitution" and "money laundering", seized the Backpage

---

[1] Zhou Lina. New Movements of Internet Content Governance in the UK and International Trends [J], Journalism Review, 2019, 441(11): 81-89周丽娜.英国互联网内容治理新动向及国际趋势[J],《新闻记者》

website, arrested the core leadership of the website, and confiscated nearly $1 billion in property. After escorting such platforms for 20 years, Section 230 is unable to continue to provide legal asylum anymore.

Singapore

In May 2019, the Singapore Parliament passed the Protection from Online Falsehoods and Manipulation Bill (POFMA). The Bill aims to protect society from online disinformation and increase the transparency of online political advertising and related matters. The government has the right to require individuals or online content platforms to correct or take down false information that is directed for political purposes and harming public interests. Online platforms that refuse to comply can be fined up to S$1 million. Individuals who maliciously spread false information in an attempt to harm the public interest can be jailed for up to 10 years and fined up to S$100,000.

China

China's governance of online information content is extremely strict and unique. China's Tort Liability Law and Cybersecurity Law stipulate that both online information content platforms and users are responsible for the content. China restricts the ownership rights of online information content service providers, implements multi-departmental collaborative governance, holds the responsibilities for both for the two main entities - online information content service platforms and users, and restricts the flow of cross-border content mainly on the grounds of social stability and industrial development. Meanwhile, China advocates moral requirements such as "positive, healthy, uplifting, and virtuous", and even makes requirements for algorithms. In December 2019, the Cyberspace Administration of China issued the "Regulations on the Governance of Online Ecological Information Content", which listed specific acts such as "cyber violence, human flesh search, deep forgery, traffic forgery, and account manipulation" as illegal activities. However, with the continuous growth of its own strength and the gradual maturing of public mentality,

China's governance of online information content may become more open and transparent.

Although many countries are promulgating legislation or rules on online information, Internet giants such as Google, Facebook, Twitter, and Amazon are all concentrated in the United States. Users all over the world except China are using American platforms, and the debate is largely talks between governments around the world and American internet giants. On the one hand, hate speech, extremism, pornography, fake news flood the global network, and the status quo is untenable. On the other hand, until the dust settles on this negotiation, the First Amendment to the U.S. Constitution, Section 230 of the Communications Decency Act, and the user clauses of super American content platforms remain the main global rules.

There are two main challenges ahead. First, countries have clearly entered a legislative competition, and more incompatible rules will be introduced in the future. How to coordinate at the international level and establish relatively uniform standards has become a focus issue. Second, this increasingly tighter regulatory trend may cause substantial damages to freedom of speech and the prosperity of the digital economy, which needs to be balanced by establishing more innovative institutional design and regulatory mechanisms.

2. Cross-Border Content Disputes in the Age of Traditional Media

In the era of traditional media, cross-border information flow is the focus of international relations and news communication research. Kaarle Nordenstreng and Tapio Varis, professors at the University of Tampere in Finland, studied the international circulation of television programs in the 1960s and 1970s, and after surveying nearly 50 countries in the world, concluded that the international circulation of television programs was a one-way street, mainly from developed countries such as the United States, the United Kingdom, France, and West Germany to developing countries such as those in Eastern Europe, Asia, Africa and Latin America. This constitutes a key argument for the unbalanced international information flow and opens up a series of follow-up studies on "circulation" and "channel".[2]

In the late 1970s, the newly emerged political power, the Non-Aligned Movement, took this as evidence and launched the "New World Information Order" movement at the United Nations. At the same time, there was also the "New International Economic Order", which required changing the unfair international trade situation at that time. The Non-Aligned Movement sprang from the Asian-African Conference held in Bandung, Indonesia in 1955, and took the Five Principles of Peaceful Coexistence as the basis for cooperation between countries. In July 1976, the Non-Aligned Movement countries held a ministerial meeting in New Delhi. The New Delhi meeting's "Draft Declaration on the Decolonization of the Information Field" described the unbalanced, unjust, and undemocratic pattern of international communication at the time:

1) Present global information flows are marked by a serious inadequacy and imbalance. The means of communicating information are concentrated in a few countries. The great majority of countries are reduced to being passive recipients of information which is disseminated from a few centers.

2) This situation perpetuates the colonial era of dependence and domination. It confines judgements and decisions on what should be known, and how it should be made known, into the hands of a few.

3) The dissemination of information rests at present in the hands of a few agencies located in a few developed countries, and the rest of the peoples of the world are forced to see each other and even themselves, through the medium of these agencies.

4) Just as political and economic dependence are legacies of the era of colonialism, so is the case of dependence in the field of information which in turn retards the achievement of political and economic growth.

5) In a situation where the means of information are dominated and monopolized by a few, freedom of information really comes to mean the freedom of those few to propagate information in the

---

[2] Kaarle Nordenstreng, Tapio Varis. Television Traffic—A One-Way Street? UNESCO. 1974

manner of their choosing and the virtual denial to the rest of the right to inform and be informed objectively and accurately.

6) Non-aligned countries have, in particular, been the victims of this phenomenon. Their endeavors, individual or collective, for world peace, justice, and for the establishment of an equitable international economic order have been underplayed or misrepresented by international news media. Their unity has sought to be eroded. Their efforts to safeguard their political and economic independence and stability have been denigrated.[3]

Articles (1), (3), (5), and (6) indicated the three main demands of the Non-Aligned Movement countries in the New Order movement: the disparity in communication power among countries, the imbalance of international information flow, the prejudiced, distorted reporting on developing countries by Western media. Articles (2) and (4) explained the historical background of these three demands—colonialism. These six demands put forward by the Non-Aligned Movement countries directly dealt with the facts of international communication. Looking back even from the digital age, they still feel deafening. Nothing comparable to this has ever appeared in the text of national communication policies since.

Western countries such as the United States do not admit the allegations. However, in order to prevent developing countries from taking advantage of the majority of seats in the United Nations and its affiliated organizations to pass unfavorable resolutions, and in the midst of an economic crisis, they mainly adopted strategies of appeasement and dialogue in the late 1970s. However, in the 1980s, after Reagan of the U.S. and Thatcher of the U.K. came to power, the conservative forces represented by them unabashedly implemented unilateral foreign policies, taking advantage of Western commercial media dominance, and defining the New World Information Order as ideological conflicts between the United States and the Soviet Union, rather than the dispute over the flow of information between the global North and the South. Thus, they created domestic public opinions hostile to the New Order.

In 1984, the United States and the United Kingdom formally

---

[3] New Delhi, July 1976, Conference Abstracts, International Journalism Institute Materials, pp. 95-97

withdrew from the main forum of the New Order, UNESCO, marking the failure of the New World Information Order. After the drastic changes in the Soviet Union and Eastern Europe, the international community was even more silent on the sensitive term of balanced information flow. The globalization force of capital swept everything, and the principle of free flow of information returned strongly. The New World Information Order has left three important legacies: the Mass Media Declaration, the International Programme for the Development of Communication, and the MacBride report, but there has been no binding international treaty on media content. There are many reasons for the failure of the New Order: Developing countries only talking but doing little, blindly believing in multilateral organizations such as the United Nations, ignoring the future development trend of information communication technology, and failing to establish contact with the grass-roots forces, are all important reasons.

From the late 1970s to the early 1980s, contrary to most developing countries, China worked hard, pursued the basic national policy centered on economic construction, seized valuable development opportunities, and established a quasi-ally relationship with the United States, a major Western power. By the end of the 1990s and the beginning of the 21st century, when Chinese and foreign international communication scholars lamented and reflected on the New International Economic Order and the New World Information Order, they unexpectedly discovered that China has emerged from the camp of the third world, and had already achieved economic and other hard power levels standing on an equal footing with Western countries, having achieved almost all the goals that the New International Economic Order could dream of. But there is still a long way to go in terms of soft power, to fulfil the goals of the New World Information Order.

3. Cases of Cross-Border Content Disputes in the Digital Age

In the digital age, search engines such as Google, audio and video websites such as YouTube, and social media such as Facebook have rushed to the forefront of transnational information communication, serving as content dissemination platforms for all traditional media such as newspapers, magazines, radio and television, and attracting hundreds of millions of users, unleashing huge influence. While empowering the grassroots, they inevitably become tools amidst the game of great powers.

Some countries use intelligent technologies to mass-produce and spread fake news and reviews, locate users by analyzing large-scale databases, and use "bots" and algorithms to propagate information. The roles that these new methods play in influencing public opinion and current affairs cannot be underestimated.

The typical cross-border content disputes in the digital age mainly focus on race (such as the "Black Lives Matter" movement), religion (the Mohammed cartoon controversy), political stability (US-Russian social media controversy), pornography (the closure of the Backpage website), etc. Here are two cases involving political stability and religion.

(1) Content Related to Political Stability: Social Media Disputes between the United States and Russia

In December 2011, Russia held elections for the sixth State Duma. Former US Secretary of State Hillary Clinton interfered in the election in a high-profile manner. The U.S. government has publicly acknowledged to have spent $9 million to seek to deepen engagement with Russian civil society and organizations to promote universal values. The results of the Russian State Duma election that year were met with huge protest rallies. In the context of the spread of the "Jasmine Revolution" and "Facebook Revolution" in the Arab world, Russia truly felt the threat. Russia pursues the principle of "tit for tat", which is fundamentally different from the Chinese-style principle of "no conflict, no confrontation".

In January 2017, the U.S. intelligence agencies (CIA, NSA, FBI) jointly released the report "Assessing Russian Activities and Intentions in Recent Elections", arguing that Russian President Vladimir Putin had ordered operations against the 2016 U.S. election, indicating that Russia has used hidden capabilities such as hackers and mobilized various government departments, official media, and a social media water army. The U.S. elevated Russia's behavior to the level of information warfare, arguing that Russia's weaponization of the Internet has harmed U.S. foreign policy, national security, and economic prosperity. Russia naturally denied interfering in U.S. elections, believing that it was framed by the United States.

In November 2017, the U.S. Senate Intelligence Committee held a hearing on "Social Media Influence in the 2016 Elections", and the general counsels of Facebook, Twitter, and Google testified at the hearing. U.S. senators expressed strong dissatisfaction and disappointment with these technology companies at the hearing, accusing them of not distinguishing between friend and foe, focusing too much on global interests, and disregarding American interests. U.S. technology companies also realized that the hundreds of millions of users on their platforms not only had given them a competitive advantage, but can also create political risks for the platforms, making them the targets of public criticism.

In December 2017, Susan Wojcicki, CEO of Google's YouTube company, said that Google would significantly expand its content review team in 2018, likely to number 10,000 people. At the Halifax International Security Forum in Canada, Eric Schmidt, then executive chairman of Google's parent company Alphabet, said the company was studying how to use algorithms to lower the search ranking of content of Russian media such as Sputnik and Russia Today on Google.

The conflicts between the United States and Russia are also owed to European factors - European countries are concerned about Russian interference in European elections. In recent years, affected by unfavorable factors such as the immigration crisis, terrorism, and economic downturn, the European public mentality has become increasingly fragile, and right-wing populist xenophobic parties have risen. European countries worried about hacking, online rumors, and fake news interfering with the already delicate electoral ecology. The UK, the Netherlands, France, Germany, and others have all expressed similar concerns. Europe and the United States have made intensive responses at the institutional level. In April 2017, Europe and a number of NATO members signed a memorandum to establish the European Centre of Excellence for Countering Hybrid Threats in Helsinki, taking Russia as an imaginary enemy to study hybrid threats in terms of ideology, cyber-attacks, and cyber warfare.

(2) Religious Content: Denmark's Jyllands-Posten and France's Charlie Hebdo

Compared with the social media disputes between the United States and Russia, the differences between Europe, the United States and Islamic countries in cyberspace content are more extensive and difficult to reconcile. As countries around the world enter the digital age, these disputes are extremely easy to escalate.

In September 2005, the Danish newspaper "Jyllands-Posten" published 12 pictures of cartoon satirizing the Islamic prophet Muhammad, causing huge controversy, and sparking global violence. Jyllands-Posten invited 12 cartoonists to draw these cartoons that violated Islamic cultural taboos, depicting the prophet of the Islamic civilization as a terrorist and homosexual, in an attempt to test whether Muslims are integrated into the so-called "contemporary democratic society", whether they have embraced the so-called "modern secular society", whether they have accepted the concept of freedom of speech that tolerates "insults, laughter, and ridicule", and whether they have abandoned their religious sentiments.

This case hides a subtext: in real space, at first various ethnic groups were at peace with each other, but the media deliberately provoked and created this dispute, exaggerating it as a conflict between civilizations, and setting off a storm that swept the world. Yale University professor John Peters therefore criticized the Western-style concept of freedom of speech. He wrote, like the suppression of free speech, the promotion of free speech is itself also an act of provocation. He said that advocating for free speech is not just a statement about the world, it is an intervention.[4]

This "democratic test" launched in the name of freedom of speech was itself an act of provocation and attack. Peters criticized the Western liberal ideology behind this view of free speech. Peters said that liberals advertise themselves as the embodiment of all virtues, and if they do not reflect on themselves, then liberalism is very likely to become an ideological weapon in geopolitical struggles, plunging the 21st century into a period of warring states.

Following the same logic line, in January 2015, the French satirical

---

[4] John Peters, In Quest of Ever Better Heresies, Transnational Media Events, Eide, Kunelius, and Phillips (eds), NORDICOM, 2008, pp. 275.

magazine Charlie Hebdo was attacked by extremists for repeatedly publishing cartoons insulting the Prophet of Islam. The origin of this case is very similar to the Danish case, in which provocative gestures were repeatedly made in the name of testing. After the French incident, many Western media outlets reported on such cases from the dominant and popularized angle of "pencil and AK47" ("Liberty Vs. Terrorism"), portraying that pencils symbolize freedom of speech in the Western civilization, and AK47 symbolizes the violent evil of the Islamic civilization.

However, very few people went beyond the incident to criticize the foreign policy of the Sarkozy government of France, which had always kowtowed to the United States, and the huge damages caused by Western gunboats, missiles, and drones to the Middle East. From this macro background, the answer to the question of who the pencil is and who the AK47 is can be completely flipped.

The Internet has completely surpassed traditional media in terms of speed and breadth, posing more profound challenges. One of the reasons why the Danish and French incidents were able to have such a huge impact was the unlimited diffusion and magnification of these events by the Internet. In 2012, a 14-minute short film, "Innocence of Muslims", was uploaded to the American audio and video website YouTube and embedded in the ideological conflict (whether fake or real), causing controversy that continues to this day. Should the video site remove this video? Do search engines like Google Inc. treat search results the same way? These are all subjects of the current debate.

4. Three Perspectives of the Global Governance of Internet Information Content

When considering the global governance of online information content, the first perspective is from international law. The moral high ground of the debate is occupied by interpreting and citing the provisions of international law in a balanced way.

The field of international law already has some reserves of scattered knowledge and legal provisions. However, which treaty is quoted, which clause of a treaty is quoted, how to cite it in a balanced way, and how to implement it, are controversial. Article 19 of the Universal Declaration of Human Rights adopted by the United Nations General Assembly in 1948 states: "Everyone has the right to freedom of opinion and expression; this right includes freedom to hold opinions without interference and to seek, receive, and impart information and ideas through any media and regardless of frontiers."

Article 20, paragraph 2, of the 1966 United Nations International Covenant on Civil and Political Rights states: "Any advocacy of national, racial or religious hatred that constitutes incitement to discrimination, hostility, or violence shall be prohibited by law." The content of these international laws has never been implemented, and how to cite these provisions in a balanced way in the future has become a focus issue.

In controversies such as the cartoons involving the Islamic Prophet, the truth is actually quite simple. Both traditional and social media should avoid advocating ethnic and religious hatred, but when freedom of speech has evolved into an extremist ideology in the West and collided with another kind of extremism - religious extremism, it is extremely difficult to resolve.

The second is the academic perspective, this is, from an academic perspective, re-tracing and reflecting on western ideological roots on the governance of network information content.

The *Four Theories of the Press* published in 1956 is a typical academic work born in the context of US-Soviet confrontation. Authors including Wilbur Schramm slandered all non-Western media systems as totalitarian and authoritarian systems and glorified the Western model as the liberal theory and social responsibility theory.

As a best-selling textbook in Europe and the United States, *Four Theories of Newspapers* has influenced academia for nearly 30 years, until Herbert Altschull made a more objective and neutral classification. In 1984, Altschull stated in the book *Agents of Power* that newspapers, magazines, radio, and television are not independent actors, and that news media in all newspaper systems are agents for political and economic powers. There is no difference in the nature of the media system. There is no difference between good and bad media systems, only the developed and the developing. He described the functions of the media relatively objectively. *Last Rights: Revisiting Four Theories of the Press* published in

1995 and *Normative Theories of the Media* in 2009 more systematically expounded the fallacies of the *Four Theories of Newspapers*.

Nevertheless, the proposition of *Four Theories of Newspapers* still represents the mainstream opinion in the West. The West is good at describing the media system of other countries as a bad system and its own system as a good system. The same routine is also applied to the Internet model, describing its own model as a good model and the model of other countries as a bad model. This confrontational thinking mode is rooted in the West's view of the world. It is a mixture of centuries of colonial thinking, the Cold War thinking from the 1960s to the 1980s, and the notion of clash of civilizations that emerged in the 1990s. It is difficult to shake and constitutes the biggest challenge in global governance of internet information content.

The third is the community perspective. By interpreting the spirit of President Xi Jinping's vision of a cyberspace community with a shared future, the notion of community, the thought of Tianxia (world under heaven), and respect for civilizations are taken as the guiding ideology for China's participation in the global governance of online information content.

Since Xi Jinping was elected president in 2013, China has worked out a complete set of concepts and formed a relatively complete set of ideas for global governance, which are adequate for guiding China's participation in the global governance of online information content. On March 27, 2014, President Xi Jinping delivered a speech at the headquarters of UNESCO, and for the first time put forward the notion of "Respect for Civilizations" in an international occasion, expounding China's basic views on civilization, culture, and religion. Xi Jinping pointed out: "The exchange and mutual learning of civilizations should not be premised on lifting up one certain civilization or devaluing a certain civilization. To understand the true meanings of various civilizations, we must uphold an attitude of equality and humility. If you treat a civilization condescendingly, not only can the profoundness of this civilization not be understood, but you become hostile to it. History and reality show that pride and prejudice are the biggest obstacles to the exchange and mutual learning of civilizations."[5]

---

[5] Xi Jinping, Speech at UNESCO Headquarters, Paris, March 27, 2014. http://www.xinhuanet.com/world/2014-03/28/c_119982831.htm

Zhao Tingyang, a researcher at the Institute of Philosophy of the Chinese Academy of Social Sciences, analyzed the Western-style divisive and confrontational thinking pattern, and argues that it is difficult for the West to propose responsible rules for the world, believing that China's idea of Tianxia most fits this grave task. He wrote: "There must be 'enemies'. Enemies must be created if they don't exist. This deep sense of 'politics of division' can be seen in many phenomena, from the notion of pagans to racism, from the hot wars to the cold war, from colonialism to human rights interference, from economic and military hegemony to cultural hegemony, even in fantasies like Star Wars you can see the inexplicable urge to find the enemy. Pitting yourself against others, believers against pagans, the West against the East, the 'free world' against autocratic societies, and all things that are not opposite to each other against each other - such are the basic political ethos of the West. Such a political ethos has no heart for the world and is especially unable to shoulder responsibilities for the world."[6]

In a word, China believes that cyberspace is the most extensive channel for communication among civilizations, cultures and countries, and that in this new space it is necessary to avoid repeating the wrong paths taken by various countries in the traditional space and copying the traditional space's tendency to weaponize and the bipolar thinking of enemies and friends. We should uphold a kind of conciliatory thinking with regard to our world view, and achieve mutual respect and peaceful coexistence among civilizations, cultures and countries. This should become the basic guideline for China to handle cross-border content disputes.

(Xu Peixi, PhD, Professor, School of Television, Director of the Research Center for Global Governance of Cyberspace, Communication University of China. Xu's research fields mainly focus on international communication, Internet policy, cybersecurity, and grassroots media.)

---

[6] Zhao Tingyang, The Tianxia System: An Introduction to the Philosophy of World Institution, 2005, Jiangsu Education Press, p. 25 赵汀阳，《天下体系: 世界制度哲学导论》, 江苏教育出版社

TECHNOLOGY, SOCIETY, AND CIVILIZATION: THE INTERNET-INDUCED SHIFT IN MEDIA THEORY

Cui Lin and You Keke

Abstract: This article is based on the background that a series of media and social changes triggered by the Internet have been the focus of media research, however, the theoretical transformations aroused by the Internet has not been paid enough attention to by scholars. The authors propose that the transformations triggered by Internet have already gone beyond the vision and framework of conventional paradigms, causing shifts in media theories in technology, society, and civilization. On the level of technology, technical functionalism of media ecology has been unable to explain the relationship between technology and human beings in the digital revolution: people need to re-evaluate the value of information technology to human society from the macro perspective of information history. On the level of society, the theories in the information era based on futurism can hardly describe the structural role of the Internet in contemporary social development. They are replaced by the theory of "network society" which focuses on re-judging the basic social function of the Internet systematically. On the level of civilization, the changes between the contemporary civilization systems driven by the Internet have pushed research into the historical level. And the study on the relationship between media and civilization has also shifted from the prevailing state-centralism in the 19th century to the field of interactions of global civilizations. This paper tries to tease out and analyze media theoretical shifts driven by the Internet, so as to have a newer understanding of the influences of Internet on media theories on a general level.

Keywords: Theoretical Shift, Information History, Network Society, Interactions of Global Civilizations

Since the first successful experiment in 1969, the Internet has experienced more than 50 years of development, and its influence on human beings has gradually expanded and deepened. At the beginning of its development, the Internet was only a strategic research and development project of the U.S. military as a hedge against Soviet space technology in the context of the Cold War. As many scientific researchers used it as a tool, its civilian value gradually emerged. After the invention of the World Wide Web, the Internet finally became a virtual world accessible to all, and gradually developed into the main channel for all human beings to communicate. Just like a pebble thrown into the water, the impact on media technologies has also become the first wave that the Internet has affected the human society. Then, elements of social systems such as business and politics began to intervene, and the Internet rapidly expanded to become the basic platform for social development. Its social status also moved down from the superstructure level of traditional media and became the basic structure of various social systems that affect everything from the economic foundation to ideology. Information is no longer just a reflection of social entities, but a basic element of the development of contemporary human society. Therefore, the Internet has systematically rebuilt a new social structure, namely the cyber society. Later, when the effects of the Internet on different civilizational systems began to differ and differentiate, the influence of the Internet on human society began to enter the historical level. Historians realized that the Internet is very likely to trigger another revolution at the level of civilization, similar to the role the printing press played in the rise of the modern West.

As L. S. Stavrianos put it in *A Global History: From Prehistory to the 21st Century*, there is a time lag between technological change and the social change that makes it necessary.[1] In the course of its development on a macro level, the Internet's impact on human beings still follows the basic pattern: first on technology, then society, and then changing the path of civilization. Once the influence of the Internet on technology, society, civilization, and other aspects exceeds the scope, framework, and path of traditional media theories, the latter began to shift in its thinking. At the research level of media and technologies, with the development of network communication, the academic community's observation of media has gradually bid farewell to the early technocentric perspective, and the research framework has gradually shifted from the "media evolution theory" to a more macroscopic view of information history. On media and society, scholars have gradually jumped out of the "information age" framework based on futurism and turned to more basic, systematic, and structural network society theories. On media and civilization, with the wave of globalization driven by the flattening effect, the relationship between information and civilization has received unprecedented attention, and relevant theoretical studies have also turned to the perspective of interactions of global civilizations, having been dominated by the previous paradigm of "nation-state".

1. The Technical Level: from "Media Evolution" to the "Information History View"

Since the establishment of the Canadian communication school represented by Harold Innis and Marshall McLuhan, the relationship between media and society, information and civilization has received unprecedented attention from communication scholars. After the establishment of the media environment school represented by Neil Postman, the views of media as "environment" and "ecology" have been generally recognized. Against the background that digital technology has comprehensively changed forms of human communication and then affected forms of society, Paul Levinson put forward the media evolution

---

[1] Stavrianos, Leften Stavros. A Global History: From Prehistory to the 21st Century. Upper Saddle River, N.J: Prentice Hall, 1999. (Page 7 in the Chinese version) [美] 斯塔夫里阿诺斯：《全球通史：从史前史到21世纪》（第7版修订版）（上册），吴象婴、梁赤民、董书慧、王昶译，北京大学出版社

theory. However, entering the Internet era, theorists such as Kevin Kelly and Nicholas Negroponte studied the disruptive changes caused the by Internet technology from the perspective of information history, turning the technology- oriented media theories to a brand-new direction.

As a main founder of the media environment school, Marshall McLuhan explained the huge role of media technology on social change and human beings in his book *Understanding Media: The Extensions of Man*. At the beginning, he put forward the assertion that medium is the message,[2] that is, the truly meaningful information is not the information content provided to the audience in each era, but the medium itself. It can be said that the core of McLuhan's media view is that all technologies are media, and all media are the externalization and extension of ourselves.[3] In his view, media technology has a significant impact on the entire social complex, including the relationship between man and himself and between man and others.

Although Neil Postman, a student of McLuhan, who coined the notion of media environment, regarded media as a kind of environment, and focused on the influence of media on contemporary culture, nevertheless he claimed to be a disobedient student.[4] As a media technology optimist, McLuhan strongly criticized the mechanical, homogenous, disjointed "de-tribalization" age born out of phonetic writing and printing, but sang the praises of electronic media; while Postman showed obvious pessimism in media - he strongly advocates printing and criticizes electronic technology, believing that the printing culture embodies rationality and truth, but these have "surrendered" to technology. Postman was worried and pessimistic about the destruction of childhood by the television medium. He introduced it with Huxley's prophecy in *Amusing Ourselves to Death*, pointing out that the media define the real world with hidden but powerful

---

[2] McLuhan, Marshall. Understanding Media: The Extensions of Man. Corte Madera, CA: Gingko Press, 2003. (Page 33 in the Chinese version)【加】马歇尔•麦克卢汉：《理解媒介——论人的延伸》，何道宽译，商务印书馆

[3] Lum, Casey Man Kong. Perspectives on Culture, Technology, and Communication: The Media Ecology Tradition. Hampton Press Communication Series. Cresskill, NJ: Hampton Press, 2006. (Page 197 in the Chinese version)【美】林文刚：《媒介环境学：思想沿革与多维视野》，何道宽译，北京大学出版社

[4] Marchand, Philip. Marshall McLuhan: The Medium and the Messenger : a Biography. Cambridge: MIT Press, 1998. （Page7 in the Chinese version）【加】菲利普•马尔尚：《麦克卢汉传——媒介及信使》，何道宽译，中国人民大学出版社

hints,[5] and that human beings are quietly trending towards amusement. Although both McLuhan and Postman belong to "hard determinism", their theories on electronic media are diametrically opposed. Postman believes that electronic media not only amuses people to death, but also changes the relationship between information and actions, causing the gradual demise of people's abilities for social and political activities.

American media theorist Paul Levinson took the media theory in McLuhan's electric age, and creatively inherited and developed it in the digital age, which earned him the title "McLuhan in the digital age". Levinson's theoretical background is different from that of McLuhan and Postman. He rejected their "hard determinism" in favor of "soft determinism". He believes that there is no absolute relationship between people and technology, and people can make rational choices about technology. Under the nourishment of the evolution theory and media environment theory, Levinson creatively put forward the media evolution theory with theories such as humanization trend and compensatory media as the core. He believes that man is the master actively controlling the media,[6] and that man has the ability to control technology. Compared with McLuhan and Postman, Levinson has enhanced man's position as the main subject in the evolution of media.

However, Levinson's "soft determinism" is still an explanation path based on technical functionalism. For example, although his two books *The Soft Edge* and *New New Media* have also conducted historical investigations on the development and changes of media, his historical positioning of information on the theoretical level has not departed from the cognitive framework of evolutionary theory. In sharp contrast, researchers such as Kevin Kelly have provided a new research perspective - information history. In their view, information has not only become the basic environment for human existence, but also the basic element of the evolution of human history. As the material mask of science and technology is lifted, we can see that its core is also concepts and information. Both life and technology seem

[5] Postman, Neil. Amusing Ourselves to Death: Public Discourse in the Age of Show Business. New York: Viking, 1986. (Page 12 in the Chinese version)【美】尼尔·波兹曼：《娱乐至死》，章艳译，广西文学出版社

[6] Levinson, Paul. Digital McLuhan: A Guide to the Information Millennium. N.p.: Taylor & Francis, 2003. (Page 19 in the Chinese version) 【美】保罗·莱文森：《数字麦克卢汉》，何道宽译，社会科学文献出版社

to be based on immaterial information flow.[7] Since the writing of human history in the past was often marked by tools and energy, different historical stages were named the Stone Age, Bronze Age, Iron Age, Steam Age, and the age of electricity, so when Kevin Kelly and others regard information as the essence of natural life and technological systems created by human beings, the information history perspective becomes obviously different from the traditional tool history view and energy history view, and a new way for humankind to examine history. This new historical view transcends the technical functionalism described above at the cognitive and theoretical level, and redefines the role of information in human history, thus causing an unprecedented turn for technology-oriented media theories.

Kevin Kelly is devoted to the study of relationships between Internet technology, culture, media, humans, and technology. In his technical philosophy system, he not only has a broad research field of philosophy, sociology, economics, etc., but also maintains the basic viewpoints of system theory, information theory, and cybernetics. He introduced biology thinking into the interpretation of current technologies for the first time. Kevin Kelly believes that in the industrial age, the human body extension theory was about the thinking of animals extending their shells, which is closely related to genes; however, in the digital age, human beings have created things that have never been created before with their own thinking, so it can be said that technology is the extended body of concepts.[8] From the perspective of the relationship between humans and technology, Kevin Kelly neither believes that humans are enslaved by technology, nor that technology is completely controlled by humans. He believes that technology will co-evolve with humans, and this view of media goes beyond the pure optimism and pessimism of technology.

Nicholas Negroponte, known for his theory of *Being Digital*, pointed out that bits, as the "DNA" of information, are rapidly replacing atoms and become the basic elements of human society.[9] In his view, *Being Digital* has four powerful qualities that will bring it final victory: decentralization,

[7] Kelly, Kevin. What Technology Wants. New York: Penguin Publishing Group, 2011. (Page 11 in the Chinese version)【美】凯文·凯利：《科技想要什么》，熊祥译，中信出版社
[8] Ibid., (Page 46 in the Chinese version)
[9] Negroponte, Nicholas. Being digital. New York: Vintage Books, 1996. (Page 3 in the Chinese version)【美】尼古拉斯·尼葛洛庞帝：《数字化生存》，胡泳、范海燕译，海南出版社

globalization, pursuit of harmony, and empowerment.[10] On this basis, he claims that a post-information age has quietly arrived, an age that will remove geographical constraints; just as 'hypertext' has freed the constraints of printed space, digital life will become less and less dependent on specific time and place.[11] In his theoretical system, Negroponte showed the basic concepts, trend applications, and huge values of information technology, as well as the grand blueprint of the digital age. He also clarified the influence and values of information technology and the Internet on the times and people's lives.

Unlike Kevin Kelly and Negroponte who focused on the overall impact of Internet technology from a macro perspective, Zach Lynch focused on the significant impact that breakthroughs in neuroscience research will have on human society. He believes that in the fourth revolution, the target that can be precisely controlled by new tools that form new technologies is the most powerful factor in people's lives - thinking. He predicted that within 30 years, the neurosociety will be fully formed. In the neurosociety we are about to face, people will finally achieve sustained emotional stability, increased mental clarity, and the ability to extend their most needed sensory state into a dominant experience of reality. The most distinguishing feature of this neurosociety is that it provides humans with tools to survive in a highly interconnected urbanized world – tools that will not only be useful, but potentially miraculous."[12]

It can be said that Kevin Kelly's technology is an extension of human thinking, Negroponte's being digital and Zach Lynch's neural society are all subversive media theories based on the Internet era. The media theoretical turn they represent are inseparable from the development of the Internet. As people's research on the relationship between media and technology gradually gets rid of the cognitive framework of technical functionalism and evolutionary theory and examine the position of technology and information in human historical civilization from the macro perspective of information history, a clear turn has taken place for the theories of media technology in the Internet age.

---

[10] Ibid. (Page 269 in the Chinese version)
[11] Ibid. (Page 194 in the Chinese version)
[12] Laursen, Byron., Lynch, Zack. The Neuro Revolution: How Brain Science Is Changing Our World. United States: St. Martin's Press, 2009. (Page 265 in the Chinese version)【美】扎克•林奇：《第四次革命》，暴永宁、王慧译，科学出版社

2. On the Social Level: From Information Age to Network Society

In the late 1960s, developed countries such as the United States and Japan began to put forward the concept and theory of information age. Among them, Daniel Bell's Post-Industrial Society, Alvin Toffler's Third Wave, John Naisbitt's Information Society and others have become the fruit of information sociology research, causing great discussions in the society. Most of these information age theories are based on futuristic prediction paths, fully imagining the living conditions of human beings in the information age.

In the early 1990s, after the World Wide Web opened the door to the online world for everyone, the breadth and depth of the Internet's impact on society rapidly escalated, and its fundamental and structural influence began to attract the attention of sociologists, among whom the most representative is Manuel Castells. Looking at the actual information society and the network society, Castells systematically and deeply explored the structural transformation of society under the influence of the Internet and proposed the theoretical paradigm of network society in order to reveal the patterns of information technology and Internet in contemporary social changes. Compared with the traditional predictive information society theories, Castells' realistic network society theory is a major theoretical turn.

In a certain sense, the theory of network society is a further extension of the theory of information age, but it is obviously more basic, systematic, and structural. In the view of Daniel Bell, a representative of critical sociology in the United States, the information age (he calls it information society) has two boosting factors; one is the innovation and development of information technology, and the other is the rapid expansion of knowledge, that is, information and knowledge are at the heart of the information age. On this basis, Castells put forward informationalism, also known as post-industrialism. He pointed out that informationalism originated in the information age but is different from the concept of information age. He defines informationalism as a new form of society, oriented towards technology, that is, the pursuit of knowledge accumulation and a higher level of complexity in information processing.[13] He believes that our society is undergoing a revolution, and the core of the changes is not about knowledge and information, but how to apply these knowledge and information to knowledge production and information processing and communication. It can be said that Castells' informationalism is a systematic extension of the information age.

After completing the discussion of informationalism, Castells further pointed out that informationalism as a technological paradigm provides the basis for the architecture of the network society. In his book *The Rise of the Network Society*, Castells elaborates the structural role of informationalism in the rise of the network society, through more than 20 dimensions, including the global economy, network enterprises, cultural institutions, economic organizations, employment structures, virtual culture, fluid space, and eternal. He believes that the basic feature of social development since the advent of the information age is network society. It completely shakes the established form of all organizations or nation-states based on fixed domains with global economic power.[14] It can be said that the information technology revolution has given birth to a new social model, namely the network society, which not only has an impact on human beings in social life, but also produces great changes in the social structure.

After mobile communication technology further changed the relationship between the network and people, the network society theory also showed new development. Scholars such as Manuel Castells, Mireia Fernandez-Ardevol, Jack Linchuan Qiu, Araba Sey, and other scholars began to conduct further research on the social impact of wireless networks based on data collected from around the world. They point out that mobile communications have completed the most significant expansion similar to the network society based on personal computers and the Internet a decade ago and are becoming an integral part of people's daily activities.[15]

From the information age to network society, and then to mobile network society, research on media and society has been turning and progressing at the theoretical level, which means that people's understanding

[13] Castells, Manuel. The Rise of the Network Society. United States: Wiley, 2011. (Page 21 in the Chinese version)【美】曼纽尔·卡斯特尔:《网络社会的崛起》,夏铸九、王志弘等译,社会科学文献出版社
[14] Ibid. (Page 3 in the Chinese version)
[15] Ibid. (Page 65 in the Chinese version)

of information has entered a new level and an unprecedented judgment has been achieved. From now on, information is no longer just a reflection of social entities, but has gradually become the basic element of the development of contemporary human society; also, the media is no longer just a superstructure, but has gradually become the basic structure that affects various social systems.

Interestingly, among scholars who study the social impact of the Internet, Castells is not only representative of the network society theory he proposed, but his own changes in research objects are also deeply symbolic. Before focusing on the Internet, Castells' core research object was the city. The fact that he shifted from the founder of New Urban Sociology to the proponent of the theory of Network Society also symbolized that the Internet had replaced the city and became the infrastructure of contemporary society.

This turn of theoretical research and the shift of personal identity is not only related to Castells' educational experience, but also stems from his focus and thinking on issues of the reality. Castells' education and theoretical paradigms all originated from Europe. In the early 1970s, the world social movement flourished. Castells followed the critical theoretical thinking of Althusser, the founder of French structural Marxism, and ruthlessly criticized the epistemology of mainstream urban sociology in the United States represented by the Chicago School, as well as the empiricism and formalist epistemological methods popular in the field of sociology. He established the theoretical model of social criticism of material epistemology, and founded the neo-Marxist school of urban sociology, and the theoretical system of political economy of urban policy.

In the process of studying urban sociology, Castells' realist interpretation path and innovative social theory style led him to keenly grasp the reality in the new technological revolution and turn to information society research. In the early 1980s, the information technology revolution swept the world, impacting all areas of society, and cities bore the brunt of it. The informatization of the city and the shift of information towards urban society formed a development trend. The urban sociologist, who is based in reality and focuses on the future, immediately carried out his theoretical research on the information city and sociological research on information technology.

With the rapid development of information technology, information sociology topics spawned by informatization, networking, and globalization, as well as theoretical needs that transcend traditional sociological meanings, are increasing. Under such circumstances, Castells reconsidered information society from the perspective of technical rationality and began a wider and more difficult theoretical study of network society. In the mid-1990s, in the context of the rise of the globalized information network, Castells, with his rich accumulation in sociology and strong sociological imagination, combined global research data at that time, took information technology as the entry point, and created an Information Age trilogy - *The Rise of the Network Society*, *The Power of Identity*, and *End of Millennium*, in order to explain that the network society is "rising" as a new social form.

Since the shift of Castells' theoretical research, the new media represented by the Internet has received more and more attention from social theoretical research, with research perspectives continuously enriched and viewpoints gradually becoming more diverse. In the works of sociologists such as Castells and Clay Shirky, the positive effects of information technology on human social life are abundantly displayed. However, the frenetic enthusiasm for information technology in contemporary society has also led social theorists such as Sherry Turkle and Andrew Keen to begin to reflect on the negative effects of the Internet. Their theoretical research made people realize that the Internet not only brings people a sense of psychological loneliness, but also conducts data monitoring and snooping on people's lives.

Echoing Castells' theory, Clay Shirky argues that new technology not only has an impact on employment structure and social class, but it is also causing great changes in the economy. As for the social and economic impact of the Internet, Chris Anderson's research is more specific and profound. He points out that the rise of free economics is driven by technological progress in the digital age. He even believes that the most meaningful business model today is to use free things to make money.[16] Correspondingly, Sherry Turkle and Andrew Keen and others have calmly thought about and analyzed the drawbacks amid the prosperity of

---

[16] Anderson, Chris. Free: The Future of a Radical Price. United Kingdom: Hachette Books, 2009. (Page 42 in the Chinese version) 【美】克里斯·安德森:《免费: 商业的未来》, 蒋旭峰等译, 中信出版社

network technology against the background of the era's frenzy triggered by information technology. Turkle pointed out that while information technology brings great convenience, it also brings negative psychological effects to people; it weakens the relationship between people and makes people feel increasingly lonely - the "acting" on the Internet is tiring; they are tired of it and eager to get closer to reality. Young people are more and more nostalgic for the beautiful things that are fading away, and in their minds, the mobile phone and the online world are not another Walden from which they can escape. In "Netizen's Carnival: Reflections on the Disadvantages of the Internet", Andrew Keen expressed similar concerns, arguing that with the prosperity of the Internet, ignorance and low taste, individualism and totalitarianism also spring up.[17] In the book *Digital Vertigo* published later, Keen conducted a more in-depth reflection on the shortcomings of the Internet. He pointed out through Internet group events around the world that the misuse of scientific and technological progress will seriously affect human values, economy, and creativity. He also proposed how modern people can live a good life in the era of big exposure and big display.

3. On the Civilization Level: from State-Centrism to Global Civilization Interaction

After the Internet reconstructed the structure of contemporary society, the influence of the Internet began to enter the field of vision of historians, and the research on the Internet on the level of civilization gradually began to unfold and constantly deepen. Civilization is the oldest of all histories, it can endure constant economic or social changes and never decline.[18] What roles do media play in the development of civilizations? Lewis Mumford, Harold Innis, Elizabeth Eisenstein, Niall Ferguson, and

---

[17] Keen, Andrew. The Cult of the Amateur: How Blogs, MySpace, YouTube, and the Rest of Today's User-generated Media are Destroying Our Economy, Our Culture, and Our Values. United States: Doubleday, 2007. (Page 1 in the Chinese version)【美】安德鲁·基恩：《网民的狂欢》，丁德良译，南海出版公司

[18] Ferguson, Niall. Civilization: The West and the Rest. New York: Penguin Books, 2018. (Page XXXVI in the Chinese version)【英】尼尔·弗格森：《文明》，曾贤明、唐颖华译，中信出版社

others have continued to answer from different angles in the field of civilization. More importantly, the intervention of the digital revolution has not only shifted the theoretical perspectives of media scholars, but also has caused a major change in the way historians view civilizations. From Samuel Huntington's clash of civilizations to Jerry Harrell Bentley's global history, to the global information history of Kevin Kelly and Yuval Noah Harari, the digital revolution is eliminating the previous nation-state-centered perspective of civilization and turning to the position of global civilization interaction.

As early as 1934 in the book *Technics and Civilization*, Lewis Mumford first summed up the history of Western technological civilization for a thousand years. Mumford regarded technology and civilization as a one whole, arguing that it is a result of humankind's choices, intelligent activities, and struggles, deliberately or not.[19] Mumford divides machine systems and machine civilizations into three successive but overlapping and interpenetrating stages: eotechnic, paleotechnic, and neotechnic. He believed that the eotechnic age was a complex of water and wood, the paleotechnic age coal and iron, and the neotechnic age a complex of electricity and alloys. Through research, Mumford found that dynamic balance and nature protection are the characteristics of an open era. When a new technological level is reached in the neotechnic age, a balance will be approached between man and nature, between industry and agriculture, and between the birth rate and death rate of the population.

If Mumford has interpreted the impact of technology on human civilization from the perspective of machine civilization, then Harold Innis has shown the influence mechanism of media communication on the rise and fall of civilizations from the perspective of ancient civilization. The strengths of a new medium will lead to the emergence of a new civilization.[20] In 1951, Innis, in his book *The Bias of Communication*, directly linked the change of media with the change of civilization. The economist, who originally studied the history of Canadian economics,

---

[19] Mumford, Lewis. Technics and Civilization. United States: University of Chicago Press, 2010. (Page 6 in the Chinese version)【美】刘易斯·芒福德：《技术与文明》，陈允明等译，中国建设工业出版社

[20] Innis, Harold Adams. The Bias of Communication. Toronto; Buffalo, NY: University of Toronto Press, 2008. (Page 28 in the Chinese version)【加】哈罗德·伊尼斯，《传播的偏向》，何道宽译，中国人民大学出版社

turned his attention to the history of civilization and communication after the First World War, and is regarded as the founder and the most important early representative of the media technology school. In the process of research, Innis gradually discovered that the dissemination of information technology not only affects social economy, but also affects the entire civilization. On this basis, starting from the entire history of world civilization and communication, he proposed the famous communication bias theory. He divided communication and media each into two categories: the bias of oral communication and the bias of written communication, the bias of time and the bias of space. Time-biased media is manifested in its influence on cultural institutions, namely religious organization; space-oriented civilizations focus on geographic expansion and individualism, namely military politics. Starting from historical experience, he bluntly speaks of the contemporary crisis of Western civilization - paying too much attention to the expansion of space and territory, and achieving immediate goals through war, imposing cultural homogeneity on the people, and breaking the balance between time and space. This unbalanced civilization and communication structure will bring about a dangerous situation of political opportunism and public madness, the decline and collapse of the rich cultural traditions of various ethnic groups, and environmental pollution. Therefore, a stable society needs to maintain a certain balance between the concepts of time and space.

Corresponding and continuing the perspective of ancient civilization of Innis is Elizabeth Eisenstein's focus on modern Europe. She takes printing, a major technological invention of modern civilization, as the research object and re-examines the historical role of machine printing in the rise of modern Europe. Inspired by McLuhan's work on printing, *The Gutenberg Galaxy*, Eisenstein devoted 15 years to completing the book *The Printing Press as an Agent of Change*, a representative work that studies the relationship between printing and Western modern civilization. Eisenstein pointed out that printing changed the method of data collection, storage, and retrieval, and changed the communication network of European academic circles.[21] The resulting communication revolution had a profound impact on every

---

[21] Eisenstein, Elizabeth L.. The Printing Press as an Agent of Change. Cambridge: Cambridge University Press, 1980. (Page XV in the Chinese version)【美】伊丽莎白·爱森斯坦:《作为变革动因的印刷机: 早期近代欧洲的传播与文化变革》, 何道宽译, 北京大学出版社

aspect such as European humanism, the Renaissance, the Reformation, the Enlightenment, and the Scientific Revolution. Printing can be described as the agent of change for the great social transformation - the modernization of western society.[22] In addition, printing has also profoundly changed the historical concept of modern Western people - the establishment of the nation-state perspective is no longer just a political top-down behavior, it is also related to the civic consciousness of the entire members. Eisenstein demonstrated the enormous role that media played in the changes of modern civilization through her research on printing.

Since the influence of the Internet began to attract the attention of historians, Niall Ferguson, a British historian who approaches history with important economic activities such as finance, also began to pay attention to the influence of media on civilization. Ferguson is accustomed to discussing the development models of Eastern and Western civilizations from multiple dimensions such as military technology, scientific revolution, political systems, modern medicine, consumer society, and work ethics. Ferguson points out that for most of the past 300 years, barring a few sporadic temporary setbacks, the West has been the winner in the clash of the two civilizations. The main reason for this is the dominance of Western technology, which has not always existed.[23] He analyzes the decline of the Ottoman Empire from a historical perspective. On the one hand, it is due to its own long-standing arrogance. On the other hand, it is due to the military superiority built on the basis of science and technology in the West, and the rationality given to the government. In this process, Ferguson made a historical analysis of the role and influence of printing in the process of civilization change. He pointed out that the Reformation of 1517 and the subsequent schisms of Western Christianity were largely due to the revolutionary role played by the printing press, arguing that the printing machine is the most significant technological innovation before

---

[22] Cui Lin: "Agent of Change and Background Paradigms: A Comparison of the Social and Historical Influences of the Internet and Printing", Modern Communication, No. 5, 2014 崔林：《变革动因与背景范式———对互联网与印刷术社会作用与历史影响的比较》，《现代传播》

[23] Ferguson, Niall. Civilization: The West and the Rest. New York: Penguin Books, 2018. (Page 35 in the Chinese version) 【英】尼尔·弗格森：《文明》，曾贤明、唐颖华译，中信出版社

the Industrial Revolution.[24] However, this technological innovation failed to open a new door to modern civilization in China, the place where it originated. In Ferguson's view, China's national policy at that time was most likely to be blamed. However, in the era of Western Civilization 2.0, the balance of world power is tilting from west to east, and the rest of the 21st century will show us how this shift is going to be accomplished.[25]

The continuous promotion of globalization by the Internet has made historians begin to transcend the historical view centered on nation-state and gradually move towards a perspective that focuses on the interaction of global civilizations. Since the formation of the civilization theory in the 18th century, Western countries have gradually gone a long way along the lines of Eurocentrism, by whose influence the discipline on modern history has been based on nation-state since its birth.[26] This state-centric view of civilization looks at history from a divisive perspective, bluntly dividing the human civilization into various parts that do not interact with each other, and comparing them, with a strong sense of cultural hegemony in methodology. Since the nineteenth century, the theory of civilization based on nations began to prevail. Famous historians Oswald Spengler, Arnold J. Toynbee, Pitirim Sorokin and others proposed that there are clear boundaries between civilizations, and that civilization is a separate organism. By 1993, Samuel Huntington, in his book *The Clash of Civilizations*, pointed out that the post-Cold War world contained seven or eight major civilizations, and argued that the regional conflicts that are most likely to escalate into larger wars, are those between groups and nations of different civilizations. In other words, it is no longer ideology that triggers conflicts in the world, but the differences between cultures, also known as clash of civilizations.

However, with the deepening influence of globalization and the "global village", people have begun to realize that human history is a unified history. Some historians have begun to bid farewell to the past state-centrism thinking and move towards the perspective of global civilization interaction. In the view of historians who hold this view,

---

[24] Ibid., (Page 43 in the Chinese version)

[25] Ibid., (Cover page in the Chinese version)

[26] Duara, Prasenjit. Rescuing History from the Nation: Questioning Narratives of Modern China. United States: University of Chicago Press, 1996. (Cover 1 in the Chinese version) 【美】杜赞奇：《从民族国家拯救历史》，王宪明译，江苏人民出版社

Internet technology has strengthened the interaction and exchanges between countries, nations, and civilizations in the world, and the process of global integration has become the dominant trend in contemporary historical development. An inter-dependent community of a shared future is forming. In this context, historians have interpreted the concept of global civilization interaction from different perspectives. This historical concept gets rid of the prejudice of various regions, races, and national powers, and more emphasizes the interaction and communication between major civilizations. Although compared with the nation-state-centered view of civilization, the concept of interaction of global civilizations has not yet formed a complete system, and there have always been constant conflicts between civilizations, it provides historical view that is more in line with reality and future expectations.

The view of global history was put forward in 1963 by the famous historian and founder of global history research, William H. McNeill. In his book *The Rise of the West: A History of the Human Community*, McNeill argues that the development of world history is mainly promoted by exchanges and interactions among civilizations and cultures. This book created a precedent for the study of global history from the perspective of cross-cultural interaction, but due to the limitations of the times, McNeill did not completely get rid of Eurocentrism, especially in the last discussion, and even he himself realized this shortcoming. In 1990, in "'The Rise of the West' after Twenty-Five Years", he pointed out that his previous theories were no longer sufficient to explain the changes brought about by the development of globalization to global history. It was not until 2000 that Jerry H. Bentley, a professor of history at the University of Hawaii and a representative of new global history research, published the masterpiece *Traditions & Encounters: A Brief Global History*, that state-centrism began to be shaken.

Starting from the background of globalization, Bentley strives to explore the mechanism of cultural exchange and integration, takes cross-cultural exchange as the standard of historical staging, and proposes two themes - inheritance and communication. He pointed out that while people of various regions and ethnic groups in the world are constantly creating and developing their own political, economic, social, and cultural traditions, they are also constantly conducting and expanding exchanges and interactions with others. This historical view of the interaction of global civilizations has completely overturned the Eurocentric position and the narrow nation-state view, clarified the issues of unity and difference of human civilizations, and opened up a new research direction. One could argue that in this process, the development and popularization of the Internet has played an important role - it has enabled various regions and cultures in the world to break free from the shackles of state realms, and to conduct higher-frequency interactions; It has connected the world to make it an organic whole, and greatly promoted the formation of the global civilization view of history.

In fact, Kevin Kelly's re-examination of human history from the perspective of information history is the same as that of historians. As Kelly said, civilization is a public library full of thoughts and emotions of the past, one that may produce new ways of thinking and knowing, where a constant stream of real-time information flows, including the perceptions of what is happening.[27] It is in the macroscopic vision of the evolution of human civilization that Kevin Kelly re-examines the basic value of information for human history. He believes that the cores of natural life and the technological system created by human beings both lie in information, and information and the media it depends on have constituted the basic living environment for human beings and play a huge role in the entire human history and civilization. Therefore, the consensus on information society and information civilization should be based on an in-depth understanding of the long history.[28] He believes that information civilization, as a higher stage of the development of human civilization, is a higher-level one that is parallel to the entire traditional material energy civilization. Information civilization constitutes a higher-level whole of human civilization, and it provides a key to a deeper understanding of development.[29]

---

[27] Kevin Kelly: "The Technium", translated by Zhang Xingzhou, Yu Qian, etc., pp. 29-30, Publishing House of Electronics Industry, 2012. 【美】凯文·凯利：《技术元素》，张行舟、余倩等译，电子工业出版社

[28] Ibid., pp. XIV

[29] Tian'en, Wang. "A New Understanding of the Information Civilization 'Key' to 'Development.'" Social Sciences in China 40, no. 4 (October 2, 2019): 26. https://doi.org/10.1080/02529203.2019.1674033. 王天恩：《重新理解 "发展" 的信息文明 "钥匙"》，中国社会科学期刊杂志

Like the view of information history elaborated by Kevin Kelly, the Israeli historian Yuval Harari abandoned the single historical narrative and analyzed the impact of huge technological progress on humankind from the perspectives of the entire human history and science - earth-shaking changes in work, culture, education, leisure, health, political systems, etc. Harari's book *Sapiens: A Brief History of Humankind* clarifies the concept of global civilization interaction inherent in the changes of human history with a grand narrative. Through his observation of the development of human civilization and the interaction between civilizations, he classified human history into three major revolutions - cognitive revolution, agricultural revolution, and scientific revolution. He believes that, from the evolution of apes to homo sapiens, intelligence and production tools are the keys to the rise of human beings,[30] and human beings have formed a self-centered humanism and ascended to the altar with this kind of thinking and technology. Technology has solved the plagues, famines, and wars that human beings have suffred for a long time, and it is even possible to realize the ideal of immortality, happiness, and incarnation as gods. However, the development of information technology has broken this pattern, and artificial intelligence will replace everything created by homo sapiens. Harari uses this reverse perspective to warn human beings against future changes in technology and organization, and changes in human consciousness and identity. He pointed out that, artificial intelligence technology, as the most cutting-edge in the development of the Internet, is not only the most important scientific evolution in the 21st century and the most important scientific evolution in our human history, but also the most important change since the creation of life. People need to pay attention to issues in the technical aspects of artificial intelligence, and at the same time pay close attention to the possible impact of the development of artificial intelligence on society.[31] In the process of technological theories turning towards information history view, and historical concepts turning towards civilization interaction, the research at the technical level and the

---

[30] Harari, Yuval Noah. Homo Deus: A Brief History of Tomorrow. New York: HarperCollins, 2017. (Page 117 in the Chinese version)【以】尤瓦尔·赫拉利:《未来简史———从智人到智神》,林俊宏译,中信出版集团

[31] Yuval Harari: "Future Evolution under the Waves of Big Data and Artificial Intelligence", p. 26, "Interview with Media Technologists", 2017.【以】尤瓦尔·赫拉利:《大数据和人工智能浪潮下的未来进化》,《传媒科技人·专访》

discussions at the historical level finally formed a theoretical landscape of convergence.

To sum up, this paper aims to clarify the far-reaching influence of the Internet on media theory studies by sorting out the technological, social, and civilizational changes in media theories triggered by the Internet. Just as Eisenstein commented on printing - the transformative impact of printing on modern Western civilization is underestimated. In fact, our understanding and grasp of the impact of the Internet at all levels is also obviously insufficient. Especially at the level of civilization, it remains to be seen whether the Internet can have a revolutionary impact on modern Western civilization like the printing press and become the agent of change for a new round of development and rise of civilization. But obviously, such a research path has become increasingly important.

(Cui Lin, Professor, Doctoral Supervisor, School of Television, Communication University of China; You Keke, PhD student, Class Matriculating 2017, School of Television, Communication University of China)

ON THE LOGICAL FEATURES OF AI NEWS WRITING: A COMPARATIVE ANALYSIS OF DREAMWRITER REPORTS AND HUMAN REPORTS

Fu Xiaoguang and Wu Yutong

Abstract: This paper takes the writings of the news writing robot Dreamwriter and human reporters in 2020 as research objects and explores the patterns and characteristics of AI news, to clarify the stage AI writing is at and the role of human reporters. AI writing's logic programming is fixed, and its logic elements are limited. Its advantages lie in detailed basic data, preventing logical fallacies, rigorous logical reasoning, and its adapting to human logical habits. The disadvantage is that it lacks the abilities to establish connections with other events, including the abilities of analogy, deduction, and extension, as well as the abilities to judge and predict, including the use of judgment sentences, content selection, and topic selection. Human beings should play the leading role in human-machine collaboration, conduct flexible naturalization of logical structure in news production, interactively fit logical elements with the real environment, mobilize readers' "embodiment of thinking", and bring back the real meanings of news.

Keywords: Artificial Intelligence, Dreamwriter, Logic, News Production

In 1956, the field of artificial intelligence was born at the Dartmouth workshop in the United States. With exploration and industrialization, it gradually matured and became the core driving force for the development of various industries. In the first half of 2019, the global AI core industry market size exceeded US\$33.59 billion, and the market size of China's AI core industry exceeded US\$4.96 billion.[1] AI has been applied in the fields of domestic news production, automated news, virtual anchors, and intelligent production platforms.

"The 'robot' often mentioned in automated news is actually a software that automatically generates manuscripts. Through software applications, machines can replace manpower and improve the speed and quantity of manuscripts."[2] In 2006, the American company Thomson used AI to write financial news. In 2009, AI software "StatsMonkey" generated sports coverage on the Major League Baseball playoffs. Following this, Narrative Science, *Los Angeles Times*, the Associated Press, etc., have all set foot in this field. In China, in September 2015, Tencent launched "Dreamwriter"; in November of the same year, Xinhua News Agency's "Quick Pen Xiaoxin" was officially launched. In 2016, AI such as Yicai's "DT Draft King", Toutiao's "Xiao Ming", and The Cover's "Xiao Feng" were successively employed and applied in many fields such as sports events, financial broadcasts, weather forecasts, earthquake information, etc., shouldering part of the job of a human reporter.

1. Literature Review and Issue Explanation

By the end of 2020, there were 157 articles on CNKI with the themes of "robots" and "reporters", and 136 articles were highly related to this study. The existing research can be divided into three paths in terms of research paths. The first is describing the situation of a specific writing robot or a

---

[1] Xinhua News Agency. 2019 Research Report on "Media Transformation and Development in the Age of Artificial Intelligence" 新华社.2019年度 "人工智能时代媒体变革与发展" 研究报告[R/OL].(2019)[2020-07-20].http://www.xinhuanet.com/politics/download/2019ndrgznsdmtbgyfzyjbgqwjwjdcjg.pdf.

[2] Xu Xiangdong, Guo Mengmeng. News Production in the Age of Smart Media: Practice and Thinking of Automated Journalism Chinese Journal of Journalism & Communication. 2017,39(05):29-41. 许向东,郭萌萌.智媒时代的新闻生产:自动化新闻的实践与思考[J].国际新闻界

certain type of report and analyzing the advantages and disadvantages of AI writing. Wang Yue et al. "analyzed the works of machine news writing of sports events and pointed out the practical difficulties faced in semantic understanding, digital conflict, unstructured data, etc."[3] The second is the impact of the application of AI writing on the press and publishing industry. In terms of production process, Yu Guoming and others argued that "robots join news producers, speed up news production, increase news production content, improve news quality, and reduce writing costs",[4] Zhou Zhenghua and others argued "robots replace ordinary labor and enter the intelligence-intensive journalism industry. The editorial and publishing rights of news are gradually being transferred from flesh and blood individuals to algorithms."[5] In the field of news ethics, Yang Baojun and others argued that "the ethical risks of AI news are mainly manifested in the risks of inaccuracy, infringement, and abuse of algorithmic power."[6] The third is the thinking behind the relationship between technology and humanities. Ding Boquan pointed out that "Intellectual media are not omnipotent media. If media organizations and reporters rely too much on and blindly believe in communication technology, humanistic strengths that the media and news works should have will be weakened."[7]

Generally speaking, scholars have made more theoretical observations from the perspectives including philosophy of technology and cultural

[3] Wang Yue, Zhi Tingrong. The far-Reaching Influence of Robot Writing on Future News Production: Also Commenting on Xinhua News Agency's "Quick Pen Xiaoxin" [J]. News and Writing, 2016(02):12-14. 王悦, 支庭荣. 机器人写作对未来新闻生产的深远影响——兼评新华社的 "快笔小新" [J].新闻与写作

[4] Yu Guoming, Lan Meina, Li Wei. Intelligence: The Core Logic of Future Communication Model Innovation - Also on the Basic Operational Paradigm of "Artificial Intelligence + Media"[J]. News and Writing, 2017(03):41-45. 喻国明, 兰美娜, 李玮.智能化:未来传播模式创新的核心逻辑——兼论 "人工智能+媒体" 的基本运作范式[J]. 新闻与写作

[5] Zhou Zhenghua, Lian Ziyan. The Curtain Call and Rebirth of Journalism in the Era of Artificial Intelligence [J]. Journal of News Research, 2017,8(11):1-4. 周政华, 练紫嫣.人工智能时代新闻业的谢幕与重生[J]. 新闻研究导刊

[6] Yang Baojun, Du Hui. AI News: Ethical Risks, Ethical Subjects, and Ethical Principles [J]. Journal of Northwest Normal University (Social Science Edition), 2019,56(01):27-36. 杨保军,杜辉.智能新闻:伦理风险•伦理主体•伦理原则[J].西北师大学报(社会科学版)

[7] Ding Boquan. News Production and News Communication in the Era of Intelligent Media – Reflecting on the Relationship between Technology and Humanities [J]. Editorial Friend, 2019(05):6-12.丁柏铨.智媒时代的新闻生产和新闻传播——对技术与人文关系的思考[J].编辑之友

anthropology. Some scholars have proposed that, in response to the technical ethics debate in the relationship between man and machine, "adhering to a middle-of-the-way and mutually-beneficial view of news ecology will be an alternative choice"[8]. Based on Heidegger's philosophy of technology, we can "take mutual construction and mutual taming as the starting point to reflect on the new trend of the current relationship between human and technology"[9]. Research based on subjectivity proposed to "fully reflect the news ethics concept of 'people are the measure of the media'"[10]. Zhao Xin proposed that "artificial intelligence journalism is a kind of material culture created by humans to assist journalists...should each exert their strengths from emic and etic perspectives"[11].

The problem is that there are two very different assertions from existing research. Focusing on the present, some scholars hold technological optimism and propose that "in the field of journalism, which requires very high timeliness and accuracy, the role of robots obviously surpasses the work efficiency of human reporters."[12] While some scholars have pointed out that AI writing is still in the stage of weak artificial intelligence, "the application of intelligence in the field of journalism is still quite elementary...The professionalism of journalism, especially the power of human judgment and

---

[8] Xu Jiabiao, Wei Wenjuan, Gao Yanyang. An Ethical Examination of Robot News Production from the Perspective of Philosophy of Technology[J]. Contemporary Communication, 2019(01):89-91+99. 许加彪,韦文娟,高艳阳.技术哲学视角下机器人新闻生产的伦理审视[J].当代传播

[9] Jiang Xiaoli, Jia Ruiqi. On the Inter-construction and Mutual Taming of Technology and Humans in the Age of Artificial Intelligence: An Investigation Based on Heidegger's Philosophy of Technology [J]. Journal of Southwest Minzu University (Humanities and Social Sciences Edition), 2018,39(04): 130-135. 蒋晓丽,贾瑞琪.论人工智能时代技术与人的互构与互驯——基于海德格尔技术哲学观的考察[J].西南民族大学学报(人文社科版)

[10] Xue Baoqin. People are the Measure of the Media: A Study on the Subjectivity of News Ethics in the Age of Intelligence [J]. Modern Communication (Journal of Communication University of China), 2020,42(03):66-70.薛宝琴.人是媒介的尺度:智能时代的新闻伦理主体性研究[J].现代传播(中国传媒大学学报)

[11] Zhao Xin, Zhao Panchao. Rethinking the Production of Artificial Intelligence News Content from the Perspective of Cultural Anthropology [J]. China Publishing Journal, 2017(09):46-49. 赵鑫,赵盼超.文化人类学视野下人工智能新闻内容生产再思考[J].中国出版

[12] Shen Zhengfu. Construction of the Relationship between Technological Empowerment and Humanistic Spirit Inheritance in the Field of Information Communication in the Era of Intelligent Media [J]. Editorial Friend, 2019(05):20-26. 沈正赋.智媒时代信息传播领域技术赋能与人文精神传承的关系建构[J].编辑之友

value judgment, is still difficult for machine news to reach."[13] Regarding the future, some scholars believe that "there is no doubt about the trend of news writing in the future becoming comprehensively intelligent"[14], and "with the development of technology in the future, machine news will also have more warmth and texture."[15] Some scholars believe that "AI news writing cannot have human emotion and creativity...it will only be filled with modular clichés and lose the support of the audience."[16] This seems to be a return to the 20th century cycle of strong effect/limited effect research. This is related to the development stage of intelligent media, the position held by scholars, and research methods, but the adoption of grounds arguments is an important influencing factor. A large number of studies lack first-hand data and directly rely on media reports or developers' statements. For example, "Kristian Hammond, co-founder of the US company Narrative Science, predicted in an interview with Wired that by 2027, more than 90% of news in the United States will be done by robots"[17]; "McKinsey Global Institute's report predicts that by 2055, nearly half of existing jobs will be replaced by robots."[18] Such grounds of arguments can demonstrate vision but lack practical accuracy and credibility.

The depth of logic in news reports is an important factor in evaluating the validity and reliability of news delivery, and it is also one of the indicators to measure thinking abilities and subjectivity. Among the 136 papers, 50

[13] Chen Changfeng. Value Leadership, Making AI Journalism More Intelligent [J]. News and Writing, 2017(11): 1. 陈昌凤.价值引领,让AI新闻业有能更有智[J].新闻与写作

[14] Zhou Si. A Preliminary Probe into the Prospects of Intelligent News Writing - On the Screening and Integration of News Redundancy in the Age of AI Quantification [J]. View on Publishing, 2019(19):75-77. 周思.智能新闻写作前景初探——论AI量化时代对新闻冗余的筛选与整合[J].出版广角

[15] Yang Baojun, Du Hui. AI News: Ethical Risks, Ethical Subjects, and Ethical Principles [J]. Journal of Northwest Normal University (Social Science Edition), 2019,56(01):27-36. 杨保军,杜辉.智能新闻:伦理风险·伦理主体·伦理原则[J].西北师大学报(社会科学版)

[16] Wang Yuyan, Chen Dan. How can Reporters Integrate into "Intelligent Production" in the Era of Artificial Intelligence [J]. Media, 2020(03):39-41. 王雨妍,陈丹.人工智能时代记者如何融入"智能化生产"[J].传媒

[17] Li Zheng. The Value Positioning of Journalists in the Age of Artificial Intelligence [J]. View on Publishing, 2019(10):61-63.李政.人工智能时代新闻记者的价值定位[J].出版广角

[18] Mu Yi, Xia Kai, Ekaterina Novozhilova, Xu Kun. Information Processing and Attitude Cognition of AI Created Content: An Experimental Research Based on the Theory of Dual Information Processing [J]. Journalism Bimonthly, 2019(08):30-43+121 -122. 牟怡,夏凯, Ekaterina Novozhilova,许坤.人工智能创作内容的信息加工与态度认知——基于信息双重加工理论的实验研究[J].新闻大学

mentioned that the logical level of AI reports was different from that of humans but did not accurately define the stage of its logical development, and did not further explain the depth and specific differences of the logical level. Therefore, this paper adopts the content analysis method and selects AI reports and human reports on the same topic for comparative analysis, for their logical characteristics. On the one hand, this paper tries to locate the development of AI news and discover the advantages and disadvantages of AI's logical analysis abilities compared with human reporters at this stage. On the other hand, we re-examine issues such as how human journalists exert subjectivity in actual practice.

2. Research Path

Dreamwriter is the first writing robot in China that has been successfully applied to automated news. As early as September 2015, it released a financial news article titled "CPI Rose 2.0% in August, Hitting a New 12-Month High", with its volume of comments much higher than other reports in the same period. "Dreamwriter has developed from 1.0 to 5.0 in one year. Each version has added a complex piece of technology, and each technological iteration will bring changes to content production."[19] At the "2017 Tencent Media + Summit", Tencent Vice President Chen Juhong released the "2017 China New Media Trend Report", and Dreamwriter completed the abstract extraction, automatic image matching, and automatic editing on the spot within one second. "As of 2019, Dreamwriter has written about 500,000 articles a year, with a total of 80 million characters. The average daily output in a certain month is two to three thousand articles in finance and sports."[20] It has written on fields such as weather, traffic, real estate, auto shows, 4S store maintenance data, and sales information.

---

[19] Chen Zhonghao, Cui Can, Wang Ruilu, Zhang Yan. Tencent Dreamwriter: The Sixth Media Research Report on the Development of Automated News [R/OL].(2017)[2020-07-20].https://mp.weixin.qq .com/s/fF9v9YRkJsPzgA2HtlnSfQ. 陈钟昊, 崔灿, 王睿路, 张研. 腾讯Dreamwriter: 自动化新闻发展之路媒体调研报告之六

[20] Liu Kang. How Artificial Intelligence Can Help Media Production and Operation [J]. Journalism Review, 2019(03): 8-9. 刘康.人工智能如何助力媒体生产和运营[J].新闻记者

1. Sampling

The authors searched Baidu with the keywords "This article is written by Tencent Robot Dreamwriter"(本文由腾讯机器人Dreamwriter撰写), and grabbed all the reports from January 1 to July 20, 2020. After manual screening and data cleaning, duplicate manuscripts and manuscripts of non-news genres, such as car quotes were eliminated, we got reports on three types of topics: sports news published on "Tencent Sports", from January 1 to March 12, 2020; financial news published on "Tencent Finance", from May 14 to July 9, 2020; weather news published on "Watch Point Express"(看点快报), from May 9 to July 14, 2020. Thirty samples were selected for each type of report. Using the systematic sampling method, the first report is selected every other day. A total of 90 valid samples were selected.

In order to form an effective comparison with AI news, human reports most similar to the types of AI reports were selected as research objects. They are the NBA game reports of Tencent Sports from January 1 to March 12, and weather forecast by Tencent News from May 9 to July 18. for the day. Since AI financial reports were all fund net worth information, and there was no such human report besides ones by Dreamwriter in 2020, the period between February 1 and April 30 was chosen, which spanned the same amount time but did not overlap with Dreamwriter's reporting period. In this period, a search was made for reports published on Tencent Finance that contained the keyword "fund"(基金) to evaluate the overall situation of fund-related content before fund net worth reports appeared. Thirty samples were selected for each type of reports. Using the systematic sampling method, the first report is selected every other day. A total of 90 valid samples were selected.

2. Category Construction

According *to Elementary Lesson in Logic*, the constituent units in ordinary logic include concepts, judgments, and reasoning. Concepts include conceptual connotation and extension, and judgments are divided into simple judgments, compound judgments, inevitable judgments, and possible judgments. Logic is divided into non-modal reasoning and modal reasoning. Non-modal reasoning includes deductive reasoning, inductive reasoning, and analogical reasoning.[21] According to Hu Huatao's *Pragmatic Logic Research on News Reasoning and Argumentation*, "News reasoning and argumentation are by no means deductions in the form of pure thinking in a closed state, but thinking expression activities in daily specific news contexts, including journalists' experience as they directly perceive people and things, etc., on the spot, constituting the starting point of logical cognition".[22] Accordingly, based on the careful observation of the samples, this paper adds two categories of extended content and detailed description on the basis of basic logic elements, and establishes the final measurement index.

A total of 12 variables in two dimensions, logical level and extension situation of the report content, were coded and measured. The logical level includes 10 dichotomous variables including (1/0) conceptual connotation, conceptual extension, simple judgment, compound judgment, inevitable judgment, possible judgment, deductive reasoning, inductive reasoning, analogical reasoning, and modal reasoning. The extension situation includes whether to include (1/0) detailed description and extended content.

Category	Index Explanation
Conceptual connotation	Introduction of basic information or essential attributes of teams, companies, solar terms, and other objects. Qualitative description, with sentences such as "...is..." "...that is..." "so-called... means..."("......是......""......即......""所谓......是指......")
Conceptual extension	The scope of the team, company business, weather conditions, and other concepts, e.g., who are the team members. Description of the quantity, with sentences such as "...includes...", "...has...", "...can be divided into..." ("......包括......""......有......""......可分为......")

---

[21] Department of Logic, Department of Philosophy, Nankai University. Elementary Lesson in Logic (Second Edition) [M]. Tianjin: Nankai University Press, 2008: 33-58. 南开大学哲学系逻辑学教研室.逻辑学基础教程（第二版）[M].天津: 南开大学出版社

[22] Hu Huatao. Pragmatic Logic Research on News Reasoning and Argumentation[J]. Chinese Journal of Journalism & Communication, 2012,34(02):58-63.胡华涛.新闻推理与论证的语用逻辑研究[J].国际新闻界

Simple judgment	In general, declarative sentences express judgments, and simple judgments are judgments that do not contain other judgments, including single-sentence descriptions of scores, temperatures, fund net worth, etc.
Compound judgment	Contains "and", "if", "although..." ("并且""如果""虽然......但是......"), etc., which are formed by connecting several judgments with logical connectives
Inevitable judgment	Contains words such as "certainly", "necessarily", "absolutely" ("一定""必然""绝对")
Possible judgment	Contains words such as "may", "maybe", "perhaps" ("可能""或许""也许")
Deductive reasoning	Draw universal propositions and general conclusions from individual judgments
Inductive reasoning	Draw individual conclusions from general premises
Analogical reasoning	Deducting that other attributes are the same because some attributes are the same, including metaphors for players
Modal reasoning	The premise and conclusion are both modal judgments, and the conclusion is drawn according to the relationship between the two.
Detailed description	Description of event development details and process
Extended content	References to background information, past history, other similar events

Table 1 Research Category Index System for
Logic Analysis on AI Writings

The content analysis of 180 samples was carried out, and the proportion data of each variable in the 30 samples was obtained. Through the vertical comparison between the three types of AI news and the horizontal comparison with human-generated news, the advantages, disadvantages, and characteristics of AI reports, and the unique value of human writing were obtained.

3. Analysis of the Characteristics of AI Writings

The overall data shows that AI writing has two characteristics.

First, the logic pattern of AI writings is fixed: the percentages in each news types are polarized between 0 and 100%, indicating that the language templates of similar reports are highly similar and contain consistent logical elements. The differences between different reports lie in the replacement of concepts and data.

Category	Reporter	Conceptual connotation	Conceptual extension	Simple judgment	Compound judgment	Inevitable judgment	Possible judgment	Deductive reasoning	Inductive reasoning	Analogical reasoning	Modal reasoning	Detailed description	Extended content
Sports	AI	0	100%	100%	76.67%	0	0	100%	0	0	0	100%	3.33%
	Human	23.33%	96.67%	100%	96.67%	16.67%	6.67%	100%	10%	40%	0	100%	56.67%
Finance	AI	100%	0	100%	0	0	0	0	0	0	0	0	0
	Human	40%	36.67%	100%	93.33%	10%	50%	86.67%	60%	16.67%	6.67%	86.67%	63.33%
Weather	AI	0	0	100%	20%	3.33%	0	100%	6.67%	0	0	0	0
	Human	10%	0	100%	80%	13.33%	30%	80%	23.33%	0	3.33%	40%	43.33%

Table 2 Comparison between Dreamwriter Reports and Human Reports

The premise of a consistent logic pattern is in a same content structure. The sports samples are all NBA game reports, which consist of four parts: game results, player technical statistics, game review, and both teams' lineups. Most of them are simple judgments, such as "The Heat has a huge advantage in the low post. In this quarter, they grabbed 16 rebounds, including 7 offensive rebounds. Among them, Adebayo contributed 5 rebounds and scored 3 points with his advantage under the basket to help the team lead by three points." Multiple "rebounding" judgments formed inductive reasoning, leading to the judgment of "huge advantage", which is put in the beginning according to the inverted pyramid structure of news. Such inductive words appear frequently in the texts, as shown in Table 3.

Keyword	Frequency	Keyword	Frequency
Smooth coordination 流畅配合	48	Crazy attack 疯狂进攻	21

Feels pretty good 手感颇佳	32	Build a wall of copper and iron筑起铜墙铁壁	14
Frequent three-pointers频飙三分	32	Falling into the error trap 掉进失误陷阱	13
Three-pointers like rain 三分如雨	28	No in the zone 状态欠佳	13
Huge advantage 优势巨大	27	Strengthen defense 加强防守	10

Table 3 Frequency of Inductive Words in Sports
Reports Written by Dreamwriter

The other two types of reports are also generated from fixed writing templates. The 30 samples of the weather forecast are all composed of five parts: time, place, weather, clothing suggestions, and warm reminders. The weather is a simple judgment of whether it is sunny, overcast, partly cloudy, or windy. Based on this, clothing suggestions and physical comfort levels are inferred. Financial reports write about fund net values, upward or downward trends, and introductions of funds, and there is no reasoning involved.

Second, there are limited logical elements in AI writing, with few kinds of judgment and reasoning in each type of report. Reasoning is a new judgment derived from known judgments, which has the functions of expanding knowledge, identifying information, and rational reasoning. AI Sports reports only have four kinds: concept extension (both teams' lineups), simple judgment, compound judgment, and inductive reasoning, while human reports contain nine kinds; AI financial reports have only two kinds: conceptual connotation and simple judgment, while human reports involve ten kinds; AI weather reports involve five kinds including conceptual connotation and inductive reasoning, while human reports contain ten kinds. This is related to the fact that "robots are good at writing structured manuscripts involving a large amount of data, simple logical connections, and high data accuracy"[23], and the lack of template types resulted in fewer logical elements.

Starting from the above two characteristics, AI reporting has the following advantages.

First, basic data is detailed, blocking the source of logical fallacies. A concept is a definition of a symbol and is mainly used for disambiguation. The ambiguity and uncertainty of concepts are the source of logical fallacies in reporting, often stemming from reporters' misunderstanding of the connotation and extension of concepts. For AI news, the database guarantees the correctness of concepts. "Starting from the 2015-16 season, Tencent bought out the NBA's exclusive broadcasting rights in the new media market in mainland China for five years, and at the same time purchased a full set of NBA data."[24] Liu Kang, head of Dreamwriter, said, "Official data is authoritative by default. They will have a weight rating when they use it, and if it's not always authoritative, they will downgrade the weight rating...and verify against their own backup database"[25]. With the mass amount of information, as long as machine learning and programming logic are correct, through normalization and model processing, concepts can be retrieved accurately and without errors, and data omission and misuse are less likely to occur. In the samples surveyed for this paper, each sports report is accompanied by member composition information at the end of the article, and each financial report is accompanied by a company introduction and performance report. The information is detailed and accurate under the premise of accurate concepts.

Second, logical reasoning is rigorous and efficient. A correct reasoning process is the solid foundation for drawing reliable conclusions. The reasoning process of AI is completed under the control of the program. "First buy or create a database yourself; then let Dreamwriter learn the

[23] Xie Xuefang, Zhang Jiaqi. AI Empowerment: Artificial Intelligence and Reconstruction of the Media Industry Chain [J]. View on Publishing, 2020(11):26-29. 解学芳,张佳琪.AI 赋能:人工智能与媒体产业链重构[J].出版广角

[24] Chen Zhonghao, Cui Can, Wang Ruilu, Zhang Yan. Tencent Dreamwriter: The Sixth Media Research Report on the Development of Automated News [R/OL].(2017)[2020-07-20].https://mp.weixin.qq.com/s/fF9v9YRkJsPzgA2HtlnSfQ. 陈钟昊,崔灿,王睿路,张研.腾讯Dreamwriter: 自动化新闻发展之路媒体调研报告之六

[25] Ibid.

data in the database and generate corresponding writing styles"[26]. The whole process of writing is controlled by algorithms, discarding redundant information, selecting relevant information, and completing the report in a fixed template. The prescriptiveness of the templates determines the controllability of reasoning. Human reporting, on the other hand, is affected by personal factors such as the reporter's knowledge background, value judgment, and subjective emotions. And fallacies can fall under disguise, easily appearing in a seemingly correct argumentation process, making it difficult to ensure the correctness of logical reasoning. Taking stock market reports as an example, most of them are short briefs, but they are labor-intensive and difficult to see the whole picture. "We need to monitor the changes of more than 2,400 listed companies in Shanghai and Shenzhen exchanges in real time...One person on average usually monitors around 100 stocks. A full monitoring of the Shanghai and Shenzhen stock markets requires a team of more than 20 people to comprehensively handle it".[27] AI can free human reporters from the complicated repetitive work. On July 9, 2020 alone, Dreamwriter published 380 reports on fund net worth on Tencent Finance. "For the generation and publication...of formula news information, the time is generally not more than 30 seconds, and the error rate is much lower than that of human writing."[28]

The third is that AI writing adapts to human logic habits. With regards to sentences, this advantage is reflected in the application of AI to compound judgments. Compound judgments are usually composed of branch judgments and logical connectives, such as "although..."(虽然…但是…), "if...then..."(如果…那么…), "not only...but also..."(不仅…而且…), etc., which represent the logical properties of compound judgments, indicating the relationships between branch judgments – common ways of expression in people's daily life. Compared with simple judgments,

[26] Xu Xiangdong, Guo Mengmeng. News Production in the Age of Smart Media: Practice and Thinking of Automated Journalism Chinese Journal of Journalism & Communication. 2017,39(05):29-41. 许向东,郭萌萌.智媒时代的新闻生产:自动化新闻的实践与思考[J].国际新闻界

[27] He Fangming. The Influence and Application Prospects of Manuscript Writing Robots on News Production [J]. Youth Journalist, 2018(33):77-79. 何芳明.写稿机器人对新闻生产的影响及应用前景[J].青年记者

[28] Yu Guoming. The Development of Artificial Intelligence and the Pattern of Changes in the Media Landscape [J]. News and Writing, 2016(02):1. 喻国明.人工智能的发展与传媒格局变化的逻辑[J].新闻与写作

complex judgments have a deeper logic level, which can reflect relational information in addition to factual information. The data shows that in sports news 76.67% of AI reports contain compound judgments, vis-à-vis 96.67% of human reports. The difference between the two is not dramatic, indicating that the grammatical structure of AI reports has a certain degree of matching with human logic habits, and there is no unbreakable technical barriers. In terms of corpus, "the connection between phrases and paragraphs is made through human-like colloquial expressions...so that different expressions can be formed with different competitions and different scores"[29]. In the AI reports, there were 28 occurrences of "three-pointers like rain", 21 occurrences of "crazy attacks", 14 occurrences of "build a wall of copper and iron", and 13 occurrences of "fall into the error trap". Such expressions reflect the behavioral trajectory of the athletes and discourse habits of the judges. On January 17, 2020, the AI report of the Jazz against the Pelicans game mentioned, "Favors scored 7 points in this quarter, and also blocked the layup of the Jazz in the last minute trying to turn the situation and made a 'perfect revenge on his old team'". "Perfect revenge" is the use of words with specific meanings. This shows human-like logical extension.

The disadvantage of AI reporting is its weaker ability to make connections to other events. First of all, this is reflected in analogical reasoning, which uses past experience to predict the future and is often used to draw daily inferences. Vivid expressions are used to create vivid imagery, assisting the audience to understand unfamiliar texts, and embodying the inclination of reporting in analogy objects. AI writing is lacking in this aspect. Among the human reports, 40% of sports reports and 16.67% of financial reports contain analogical reasoning, such as comparing players and movements to "robots", "tanks", "snakes out of their holes", and "going through empty roads in the early morning", as well as analogies of a company and the situation as "Lehman Brothers", "suffering a cold" and so on. The corresponding AI reports do not contain such analogical reasoning. But it is undeniable that analogy is logically necessary, and the premise does not act on the conclusion with certainty. Human reports should try to avoid the misuse of analogy.

[29] Liu Kang. AI Can Provide Personal Customization in the Future [J]. News Tribune, 2017(04): 22-23. 刘康. 未来AI可以提供个人定制[J].新闻论坛

Number	Analogy Text	Time of Report
1	Leonard showed his key abilities and robot-like stability at this point 莱昂纳德此时展现出自己的关键能力和机器人般的稳定性	Jan.1, 2020
2	He attacks the low post like going through empty roads in the morning 他杀内线就像过清晨无人的马路	Jan. 11, 2020
3	At that moment, the big Lopez guarded the basket like Buddha. 那一刻的大洛佩兹就如同如来佛祖一般镇守在篮下	Jan. 17, 2020
4	Destroys the opponent's defenses with his kaleidoscope of attacks 用自己万花筒般的进攻摧毁对手的防线	Jan. 23, 2020
5	Kemba Walker is like a snake out of a hole in one offense 肯巴-沃克在一次进攻中犹如灵蛇出洞	Jan. 29, 2020
6	Temple is like being helped by God 坦普尔有如神助	Feb. 2, 2020
7	The ball draws a high arc like a rainbow 球划出一道高高的弧线，就像一道彩虹一般	Feb. 15, 2020
8	James comes back full of energy after the All-Star weekend break fully-charged 詹姆斯经过全明星周末的休整，就像进行了一次充电，回来后活力十足	Feb. 22, 2020
9	Facing his old master with thick eyebrows, he was like a low post high-rise pillar, sending out 3 blocks successively 浓眉面对旧主，就像内线擎天一柱，先后送出3次封盖	Feb. 26, 2020
10	The Warriors are cthe underdog among the underdogs 勇士完全是弱旅中的弱旅	Feb. 28, 2020
11	After the benched Lakers got into the game, they were like a group of tigers and wolves 湖人替补阵容上场后，更像一群虎狼之师	Feb. 28, 2020
12	After James got the ball, facing Brooks' defense, he pushed Brooks to the basket like a tank 詹姆斯拿到皮球后，面对布鲁克斯的防守，像坦克一样推着布鲁克斯到篮下	March 9, 2020

13	There are indeed some similarities between the current market environment and 2013 当前市场环境和2013年确实有一部分相似性	Feb 29, 2020
14	There are also opportunities in the Hong Kong market 香港市场也存在机会	March 13, 2020
15	Some people compare Bridgewater to the then Lehman Brothers 有人将桥水与当年的雷曼兄弟相提并论	March 18, 2020
16	He used a joke as an analogy: Many people originally thought they had a cold, but later you told me that they had advanced cancer and could not be saved at all. 他用一个段子作为比喻：很多人就原本以为得了一个感冒，后来你告诉我到了癌症晚期了，根本就救不活。	March 20, 2020
17	If we take the year 2020 where we are now as an example, it is actually asking a person living in 1720 to predict today in increments of 300 years 如果以我们现在所在的2020年为例，它其实是在要求一个生活在1720年的人，以300年的增量，来预测今天	April 25, 2020

Table 4 Analogy Texts in Human Reports

The second disadvantage of AI writing is its lack of deductive reasoning and extension. Deductive reasoning is to derive individual knowledge on the premise of general knowledge. The validity of a deductive conclusion depends on whether the premises are provable. In the content generation process, this means to call on other information besides the main information, including background material. For example: "International oil prices have plummeted unprecedentedly, and the net values of oil and gas funds have also hit a record low", "the matchup between the Lakers and the Bucks is regarded as a preview of the finals, and it is also regarded as the MVP battle between James and Antetokounmpo", and "Henan ushered in large-scale heavy rainfall. Most of the province was covered by heavy rain, and there were also big areas of heavy rainstorms in the central part", etc. 60% of human financial reports contain deductive reasoning, while AI reports do not. Respectively in sports, finance, and weather, 56.67%, 63.33%, and 43.33% of human reports contain extensions, while there is only one AI report that does. Compared with the simple judgment frequently used by AI news, deductive reasoning and extended materials imply causality, which helps readers to grasp the key theme of the report and improve the credibility of the news. The inadequacy of AI in this regard leads to a lack of depth in its reports.

The disadvantage of AI reporting is also reflected in its weaker abilities to judge and predict. At the micro level, this is reflected in the fact that there are very few possible and inevitable judgments. In human reports, samples with inevitable judgments are 16.67% in sports, 10% in finance and 13.33% in weather; while samples with possible judgments are 6.67% in sports, 50% in finance and 30% in weather. As for AI reports, only one weather forecasts contains inevitable judgments, and the rest contains zero.

The presentation of news by journalists is a process of structured composition and conceptual refinement, including forecasting of event trends.[30] Possible and inevitable judgments in financial reporting increase newsworthiness. "For investors who want to buy this new fund, they must subscribe with the thinking of 'proportional allotment' for most of the rest of the day", "these funds may be further increasing their positions" and other judgment words are instructive, but "for more news reports that require detailed descriptions, rational judgments, and attribution explanations...It is often difficult to design a universal writing module, and the writing robot is powerless"[31]. These tasks can only be completed by human assistance.

At the meso level, AI reporting cannot make detailed choices. In weather forecast, 40% of the human reports describe features of solar terms, airflow movements, etc. in detail, but there is no such content in AI reports. Taking two stories from July 16, 2020, as an example, the full text written by Dreamwriter is as follows:

[30] Zeng Qingxiang, Lu Jiayi. News Production in the Context of New Media: Subject Network and Intersubjectivity [J]. Journalism Review, 2018(04):75-85. 曾庆香,陆佳怡.新媒体语境下的新闻生产:主体网络与主体间性[J].新闻记者
[31] He Fangming. The Influence and Application Prospects of Manuscript Writing Robots on News Production [J]. Youth Journalist, 2018(33):77-79. 何芳明.写稿机器人对新闻生产的影响及应用前景[J].青年记者

Xiqing, Tianjin Weather Forecast on July 16

Time: July 16

Location: Xiqing, Tianjin

Weather: Overcast, with a minimum temperature of 24°C, a maximum temperature of 34°C, and a southwesterly wind of level 3.

Dressing suggestion: Due to hot weather, cool summer clothes such as short shirts, short skirts, shorts, and thin T-shirts are recommended.

Warm reminders: The weather is mainly partly cloudy to overcast during the day. Although the sun is not strong, it will still make you feel a bit hot and not very comfortable.

The manual reports contain such statements:

Today started the beginning of the hottest part of summer (Rufu). As the saying goes, 'Hot is in Sanfu, cold in Sanjiu'. Sanfu days (dog days) usually appear between Xiaoshu and Chushu. Sanfu (three Fu) is the collective name for the first, middle and last days of Fu, and it is the hottest time of the year. The climate is characterized by high temperatures, low air pressure, high humidity and low wind speed. Why is Sanfu hot? It is because of long sun exposure, and a lot of ground radiation accumulation...

Human journalists, cultured in humanities, can judge the importance of things with their social experience, and selectively narrate certain content. If AI News does not adjust in this regard, it will be too cookie-cutter and lack human touch.

At the macro level, AI's topic selection process is not completely automated. Xu Xiangdong believes that "in determining news value, refining report topics...artificial intelligence will provide some constructive creative opinions...This process may require human assistance"[32]. Therefore, although AI news has the advantages such as blocking logical fallacies, rigorous logical reasoning, and adapting to human logic habits, its abilities to analogize, deduce, extend, predict, and judge are weak, with logical elements scattered in the reports, on scores, temperatures, and other details. It failed to, through a coherent logical chain, layer by layer, generate opinions, refine key themes, and apply them to the overall report.

4. Attribution Analysis of the Limited Logic Abilities of Robot Writing

With regards to logical deduction, AI is driven by algorithms and programs, while humans rely on consciousness. This is the fundamental difference between the two information generation mechanisms. Whether the logical level of AI can approach humans depends mainly on the degree of development of the intelligent system. At present, AI at home and abroad is mainly based on writing according to templates and automatic summarization, while the self-generation mode has not yet been popularized. Writing according to templates is a mode of manuscript generation that populates data in a fixed structure. Firstly, the narrative frame and expression method are determined according to the subject matter and length, so as to customize a variety of templates; secondly, template retrieval and judgment are carried out according to the data category, and the target template is selected; finally, the data in the news site or database is imported to generate news text. This mode is mostly used for news reports with a complete database and a reproducible format, such as earthquakes, ball games, and financial briefs. Quakebot of the Associated Press, Heliograf of *The Washington Post*, Dreamwriter, Quick Pen Xiaoxin, DT Draft King, etc. in China all use this generation mechanism.

Automatic summarization is to extract key information based on the given text. The formation process of Baidu's automatic summary is as

---

[32] Xu Xiangdong, Guo Mengmeng. News Production in the Age of Smart Media: Practice and Thinking of Automated Journalism Chinese Journal of Journalism & Communication. 2017,39(05):29-41. 许向东,郭萌萌.智媒时代的新闻生产:自动化新闻的实践与思考[J].国际新闻界

follows. Firstly, all the texts obtained from the search are processed by word segmentation and sentence segmentation to obtain a set of words and sentences. Secondly, the importance of each sentence is sorted through an algorithm. Key information is extracted, similarity is calculated, and redundant information is removed. And the novelty of sentences is evaluated by a penalty factor. Finally, sentences are combined in order of relevance to form summaries.[33] "As of 2018, Microsoft XiaoIce has automatically generated summaries of announcements of 26 types of listed companies in Shanghai and Shenzhen, and 90% of traders in Chinese financial institutions are using the summaries generated by XiaoIce"[34]. Self-generation is through deep learning, "allowing artificial intelligence programs to learn and imitate human writing in an all-round way. From news gathering, information processing, data analysis to final text writing, all is done by artificial intelligence programs"[35]. But this mode has not yet been widely used. Most of the deep learning techniques currently used are the Seq2Seq model combined with the Attention strategy. Seq2Seq includes two stages: encoding and decoding, which are respectively composed of two recurrent neural networks (RNNs). "Encoding is to compress the input sequence into a fixed-length semantic vector, and the RNN neural network in the decoding stage will decode character by character...The output of the previous decoding is used as the input of the next decoding."[36] The Attention mechanism is used to ensure semantic accuracy, lock keywords, and avoid overfitting. The essence of Seq2Seq+Attention is machine translation, which generates new text based on existing text, not original.

[33] Shentu Xiaoming, Gan Tian. Technical Principles and Realization Methods of Robot Manuscript Writing [J].Media Review,2017(09):15-19. 申屠晓明,甘恬. 机器人写稿的技术原理及实现方法[J].传媒评论

[34] Jin Song. The Sixth Generation of Microsoft XiaoIce is Released in China: Largest Comprehensive Upgrade in History [EB/OL]. (2018-07-28)[2020-07-23]. http://news.cri.cn/20180728/ cb8049ca-1b9b-bdb0-3bb3-82e4938ef7d3.html. 靳松.史上最大规模全面升级 微软小冰第六代在华发布

[35] Guo Qi."AI+Reporter": Limitations and Possibilities of Human-Machine Collaborative Writing Mode in the Age of Intelligent Media [J]. View on Publishing, 2019(24):67-69.郭琪."AI+记者":智媒时代人机协同写作模式的局限性与可能性[J].出版广角

[36] Shentu Xiaoming, Gan Tian. Technical Principles and Realization Methods of Robot Manuscript Writing [J].Media Review,2017(09):15-19. 申屠晓明,甘恬. 机器人写稿的技术原理及实现方法[J].传媒评论

The core principles of the above three drafting modes are natural language processing, which is divided into natural language understanding and natural language generation. The reason why AI writing cannot reach the logical depth of human beings is because of the limited ability of machine learning. Writing according to template only requires the machine to understand the data and templates, while autonomous generation is about processing characters. The second is because writing templates are limited. When the types of judgment and reasoning correspond to each template style, AI reporting can realize inductive reasoning. It is because its technical pattern is based on information points to generate judgments. Liu Kang, head of Dreamwriter, said: "Reporting the Olympic diving competition...Each athlete has a set of professional scores, including board walking, aerial posture, splash effect, etc. During Dreamwriter's learning process, it breaks down the scores of each step, and combines and grabs them in the database at will. At the same time, it integrates the rules of the competition itself, and finally restore these scores into a set of expressions."[37] Scholars' innovations in automatic writing methods are also based on the idea of "induction". "For NBA games, we first construct a score difference function based on the score difference between the two teams and propose a data slicing algorithm and data synthesis algorithm based on the nature of the score difference function."[38] According to the characteristics of the combined data, different conclusions are written and templates are generated. The achievement of deduction, analogy, modal reasoning, etc., however, require developers to continuously enrich algorithms, but "it is difficult to find enough models to develop targeted robot writing"[39]. Third, the application fields of deep learning are limited.

[37] Chen Zhonghao, Cui Can, Wang Ruilu, Zhang Yan. Tencent Dreamwriter: The Sixth Media Research Report on the Development of Automated News [R/OL].(2017)[2020-07-20].https://mp.weixin.qq.com/s/fF9v9YRkJsPzgA2HtlnSfQ. 陈钟昊, 崔灿, 王睿路, 张研.腾讯Dreamwriter: 自动化新闻发展之路媒体调研报告之六

[38] Chen Yujing, Lyu Xueqiang, Zhou Jianshe, Li Ning. Research on Automatic Writing of NBA Sports News [J]. Acta Scientiarum Naturalium Universitatis Pekinensis, 2017, 53(02):211-218. 陈玉敬, 吕学强, 周建设, 李宁.NBA赛事新闻的自动写作研究[J].北京大学学报(自然科学版)

[39] Ouyang Hongyu. Liu Kang, Director of Tencent AI Project: Media Industry Forced by Robotic Writing to Raise Entry Threshold [EB/OL].(2018-05-05)[2020-07-23].https://baijiahao.baidu .com/s?id=1599605471852132642&wfr=spider&for=pc. 欧阳宏宇.腾讯网AI项目总监刘康:机器人写作倒逼媒体从业准入门槛提高

Microsoft XiaoIce already has the ability to generate metaphors. Song Ruihua, chief scientist of Microsoft XiaoIce, said that the general principles of metaphors are constructed through three elements: tenor, vehicle, and explanation. "The tenor is generally abstract, such as love, while metaphor is concrete. The connection between these two concepts is expressed by Word Embedding, which transforms the former to a vector. And after dimensionality reduction, it is projected on this two-dimensional space. They are combined through natural language connectives to form a metaphor."[40] But the metaphor skills have not yet been applied in news writing. Furthermore, human language expressions often imply causality, omitting modal reasoning or commonsense content. Microsoft XiaoIce team has developed the association capacity of AI, trying to make it have the ability to capture information other than text, but they stopped at cross-modal understanding. They realized scene simulation by retreating images according to words but did not realize same-modal background information retrieval, deductive reasoning, analogical reasoning, etc. in news writing.

5. Re-discussing the Subjectivity of Human Beings in News Production

A scholar argued that "artificial intelligence robots pose the need for legislation for being 'not a thing'. This type of robot is not an ordinary thing. It has thinking and is a special subject with partial subjectivity."[41] "The essential attribute of a subject is that it has independent consciousness."[42] Based on the feature analysis and attribution analysis of AI writing, it can be seen that there are still technical limitations in the development of AI

---

[40] IT Home. Microsoft XiaoIce's Big World: Conversing, Singing, Metaphors, and Imagination[EB/OL].(2019-11-24)[2020-07-24].https://tech.ifeng. com/c/7rsDIaYIQ2a. IT 之家.微软小冰的星辰大海: 会对话, 唱歌, 比喻, 还有想象

[41] Ge Xuyue. Analysis on the Subject Status of Writing Robots as "Authors" [J]. Exploration and Free Views, 2019(08):192-196+200. 葛许越.写作机器人"作者"主体地位辨析[J].探索与争鸣

[42] Xue Baoqin. People are the Measure of the Media: A Study on the Subjectivity of News Ethics in the Age of Intelligence [J]. Modern Communication (Journal of Communication University of China), 2020,42(03):66-70.薛宝琴.人是媒介的尺度:智能时代的新闻伦理主体性研究[J].现代传播(中国传媒大学学报)

logic capabilities at this stage, and it is difficult for AI to achieve thinking highly similar to that of humans. In current news production, human beings should give full play to their subjectivity by virtue of their unique value in human-machine collaboration.

"Subjectivity is the subject attribute in the 'subject-object' relationship, that is, the essential attribute of the subject of cognitive activities and practical activities. It is mainly reflected in autonomy."[43] From the era of oral communication to the present, human beings have been involved in news production, during which humans' subject status has not changed. What has changed is the form of media interaction and the makeup of the subject roles. In AI writing, humans have not transferred the rights of creation to machine. From machine learning to information generation, AI always reflects the attributes of things, and its subject-like role is actually the role of things that have been domesticated by humans. "It is a theory, method, technology, and application system that uses digital computers or machines controlled by digital computers to simulate, extend and expand human intelligence, perceive the environment, acquire knowledge and use knowledge to obtain the best results"[44]. For now, AI does not have subjectivity or intersubjectivity.

In the process of human-machine collaboration, human beings should maintain subjectivity in thinking. The first is the flexible naturalization of logical structure in news production. The essence of AI reporting is repetition, processing information on the same topic with a unified template, and the language form is rigid, resulting in productization of news. And "the most obvious feature of news reasoning is its eclectic form... essentially practical reasoning, it is not necessary to be shackled by the form of logical language."[45] The subjectivity of human beings is reflected in the degree of differentiation of news products. Journalists develop new

[43] Cui Ziduo. The Scientific Implications of Subjectivity and the Principle of Subjectivity [J]. The Journal of Humanities, 1993(01):19-20. 崔自铎.主体性与主体性原则的科学涵义[J].人文杂志

[44] China Electronics Standardization Institute. Artificial Intelligence Standardization White Paper (2018), [R/OL].(2018)[2020-12-17].http://www.cesi.cn/images/editor/20180124/20180124135528742. pdf中国电子技术标准化研究院.人工智能标准化白皮书（2018）

[45] Hu Huatao. Pragmatic Logic Research on News Reasoning and Argumentation[J]. Chinese Journal of Journalism & Communication, 2012,34(02):58-63.胡华涛.新闻推理与论证的语用逻辑研究[J].国际新闻界

ideas within the norms, avoid mechanical duplication, increase or decrease reasoning types according to content characteristics, and use omission, substitution, and other ways to innovate logic patterns.

The second is the interactive fitting of logical elements and the real environment. "The most essential feature of news reasoning is reasoning in a specific news situation."[46] The reasoning process is difficult to predict, and the conclusion is formed in the constantly changing thinking, so it is necessary to reserve a variety of logical elements. At present, limited by technical conditions, the logical elements of AI are relatively limited. The underlying logic of "program" is "preset", and "reasoning" is a known patterned process, which is contrary to the essence of news reasoning. Human reporters, on the other hand, have a strong ability to establish connections with other events, and can use a variety of logical elements to complete deductions, such as utilizing information with a high degree of relevance to the reporting object for analogical reasoning, and utilizing background information for explanation and deductive reasoning, etc. Humans can also connect multiple pieces of reasoning to form a coherent logical chain, with a strong control over news facts, displaying pronounced subjectivity.

The deep implication of human control of subjectivity is to mobilize the reader's "embodiment of thinking". The significance of news is not only to inform and dialogue, but also in "social consciousness", "a kind of awareness and sense of security, which can build people's confidence in perceiving any important and interesting things"[47]. The logical structure of news prompts the audience to go deeper in the reading, layer by layer, to integrate with the news situation, deconstruct discourse in the same frequency resonance of logic, and participate in realizing social construction, and at the same time it also promotes the improvement of the public's logical thinking abilities. "The logical method of news is generated from the daily thinking of journalists. Journalists, through reflection on experience, abstract and generalize the non-daily thinking structure with universal significance, and then internalize this into the daily thinking of

---

[46] Ibd.

[47] Stephens, Mitchell. A History of News. New ed. Fort Worth, TX: Harcourt Brace College Publishers, 1997. (Page 10-11 in the Chinese version) [美]米切尔·斯蒂芬斯. 新闻的历史[M]. 陈继静, 译. 北京: 北京大学出版社

the broad audience, becoming a necessary means to enhance the wisdom of the public."[48] Such a return of the meaning of news cannot be achieved by AI writing that relies on program frameworks.

With the development of AI, the term "human-computer gaming"(人机博弈) is frequently mentioned, and voices have gradually emerged that AI will fit human thinking and complete writing independently. Even discussions were triggered of "whether AI will replace human reporters". According to the research results and the current situation of the industry, the news production capacity of AI has been exaggerated to a certain extent. Li Guojie argued in "Three Paradoxes of Artificial Intelligence": "The operation of a computer can be attributed to the formal transformation of existing symbols, and the conclusion is already contained in the premise. It does not generate new knowledge in essence and will not enhance human understanding of the objective world"[49]. At this stage, the role of AI is to assist human labor and simplify processes. Engineers and journalists play a decisive role. In addition, although AI is involved in emotion, association, prediction, etc., the technology is either immature or specialized, and it has not yet become a general technology in different scenarios. Facing the waves of AI, human beings need to maintain a rational and clear understanding of their own subjectivity.

(Fu Xiaoguang, Professor, Doctoral Supervisor, School of Television, Communication University of China; Wu Yutong, Master's student of Internet Information, Class Matriculating 2019, School of Television, Communication University of China)

* This article is a research milestone of the key project "Research on the Construction of China's Media Talent System" of the Key Research Base of Humanities and Social Sciences of the Ministry of Education of China, project number: 19JJD860001

[48] Hu Huatao. Pragmatic Logic Research on News Reasoning and Argumentation[J]. Chinese Journal of Journalism & Communication, 2012,34(02):58-63.胡华涛. 新闻推理与论证的语用逻辑研究[J].国际新闻界

[49] Li Guojie. Three Paradoxes of Artificial Intelligence [J/OL]. Communications of the CCF, 2017(11). 李国杰. 人工智能的三大悖论[J/OL]. 中国计算机学会通讯

BLOCKCHAIN NEWS: TECHNOLOGIES, SCENARIOS, VALUES, AND LIMITATIONS

Tu Lingbo

Abstract: The application of blockchain technology in the field of news communication needs to be carefully observed. Mainly used at the application level, blockchain news can be specifically used in content production and distribution, fact checking, copyright protection, benefit distribution mechanisms, and others. By analyzing the technical, business, and public patterns of blockchain news, this paper believes that its potential value lies in the transparency of news, the reconstruction of a consensus trust mechanism, the realization of commercial value and social value. However, we should also see the romanticization and technical limitations of blockchain news and be wary of hypes of the concept and business traps.

Keywords: Blockchain, News, Media Technology, News Transparency, Content Industry

In the evolution of journalism from digital to intelligent, blockchain technology, as a distributed ledger-based storage consensus technology and decentralized network architecture, its potential in media technology is increasingly being paid attention to by the journalism industry which is in transition. And "blockchain + journalism" has also become a major research hotspot. Although the blockchain technology is not yet fully mature, it has gradually expanded from an underlying technology to broader application scenarios such as financial services, business applications, Internet of Things, smart cities, and social governance. In a new round of global technology and industry waves, blockchain technology is considered an important change, the infrastructure that constitutes Web 3.0 and the key force for promoting the information industry.

On the one hand, we should prudently keep observing the relevance of blockchain technology to journalism, and on the other hand, we should get rid of the technology-centric myth and think about the fundamental problems faced by journalism through the phenomenon of media technology. As some scholars have pointed out, neither artificial intelligence nor blockchain should be blindly touted as a decisive force to change human society.[1] In general, the development of the Internet has exacerbated the narrative discourse of "crisis-transformation" in the journalism industry, reflecting the industry's anxieties about the uncertainties of its own development and its imagination of future transformation. Because of this, blockchain technology, based on decentralized network, distributed ledgers and consensus trust mechanism has a certain degree of isomorphism with the social function and value of journalism, and is regarded as an eligible path to rebuilding sustainable journalism models and a response to the crisis of journalism. This paper is devoted to surveying the main applications of blockchain technology in journalism and related research at this stage, trying to explain the concept and characteristics of "blockchain news", and analyzing the imagination and worries surrounding blockchain technology, further examining the challenges and opportunities for journalism.

1. From an Underlying Technology to Application Scenarios: Re-Analysis of the Blockchain News Concept

(1) The Concept and Connotation of Blockchain News

From a social point of view, blockchain is a new type of social trust mechanism, that is, a secure value transfer system maintained by smart

---

[1] Shi Anbin, Wang Peinan. New Trends of Global News Communication in 2019 - Global Interviews Based on Five Hot Topics [J]. Journalism Review, 2019, 000(004):37-45. 史安斌, 王沛楠. 2019全球新闻传播新趋势——基于五大热点话题的全球访谈[J]. 新闻记者

contracts, which can reach information consensus without a central node. Some researchers have pointed out that the blockchain can build a trust foundation in a low-cost way in the scenario of multi-stakeholder participation, aiming to reshape the social credit system.[2] In short, in principle blockchain technology can greatly reduce the cost of forming social trust, so the application of this technology in the economic and social fields becomes very important.

Blockchain news refers to a news communication form of journalism as an application of blockchain technology, rather than the Internet media that mainly report on blockchain technology and industry development. Some scholars believe that blockchain news refers to a distributed network-based, cryptocurrency-driven news content production media, and it also refers to a new form of digital news with technical characteristics such as decentralization, anonymity, and common maintenance.[3] According to the "Regulations on the Administration of Blockchain Information Services" issued by the Cyberspace Administration of China, the term blockchain information services refers to using websites, software applications and other forms, which are based on blockchain technology or systems, to provide the public with information services.[4] It can be seen that blockchain news is a part of the application of blockchain information services, and is a general term for the production, communication, use, and platform of news information based on blockchain technology.

The connotation of blockchain news is on shaping a new trust mechanism. From the perspective of journalism, blockchain news will build a trust mechanism based on consensus technology, immutability, and decentralization, which will challenge the centralized trust mechanism of authoritative media (platforms) to a certain extent. This of course also offers the possibilities of "saving" journalism from a crisis of confidence,

---

[2] Zeng Shiqin, Huo Ru, Huang Tao, et al. Review of Blockchain Technology Research: Principles, Progress and Applications [J]. Journal of Communications, 2020(01):134-151. 曾诗钦,霍如,黄韬,等. 区块链技术研究综述:原理、进展与应用[J]. 通信学报

[3] Zhao Yunze, Zhao Guoning. The Concept, Principles and Value of Blockchain News [J]. Contemporary Communication, 2019(03):47-50. 赵云泽,赵国宁.区块链新闻的概念、原理和价值[J].当代传播

[4] Cyberspace Administration of China. Regulations on the Administration of Blockchain Information Services. [EB/OL]. http://www.cac.gov.cn/2019-01/10/c_1123971164.htm [2019-01-10]. 国家网信办. 区块链信息服务管理规定

increasing its transparency and reshaping its social responsibility.[5] Fundamentally, there can be no benign news communication without trust mechanisms and consensus. The application of blockchain in journalism will not change the essence and core of journalism, but it provides new possibilities for journalism to change: the news industry uses blockchain technology as the underlying structure to establish a consensus mechanism based on technology, while the public coordinates the organizational structure of the news platform through self-organization and explores diversified news production and communication models.

(2) Specific Applications of Blockchain Technology in Journalism

At present, the applications of blockchain technology in journalism are mainly reflected in four aspects: content production and distribution, fact checking, copyright protection, and benefit distribution mechanism.

First, content production and distribution. Blockchain technology enables collaborative content production and decentralized content distribution, with editors, users, and the community acting as "content curators" together. Users can participate in community governance. For example, when users believe that there is a behavior that violates the community consensus, they can initiate suits. If the majority votes in favor, the corresponding content communication behavior will be punished.

Second, fact-checking. Some news aggregators, such as TheWorldNews. net, are based on blockchain technology and neural networks to provide users with verified news by region and time stream. Civil also puts fact-checking at the heart of the entire news business process,[6] by issuing CVL tokens. Users can directly sponsor newsrooms, and journalists can also collaborate on content, creating a direct connection between professional news producers and the audience.

Third, copyright protection and digital advertising. Po.et is committed to solving the problems of ownership, usage rights and historical tracking

---

[5] Wang Jiahang. How "Blockchain+" Reconstructs the Ecology of the Content Industry [J]. News and Writing, 2020(01):12-16. 王佳航. "区块链+"如何重构内容产业生态[J].新闻与写作

[6] Tan Xiaohe. Journalism Based on Blockchain: Modes, Influences and Constraints - Investigations Centered on Civil [J]. Contemporary Communication, 2018(04):91-96. 谭小荷.基于区块链的新闻业:模式、影响与制约——以Civil为中心的考察[J].当代传播

of digital assets. Po.et means proof of existence. The creator uploads and records metadata such as the title, author, and timestamp onto the Po.et blockchain, and uses smart contracts to retain proof and track the flow, creating a healthy communication ecology among content producers, media organizations and audiences, which helps to establish source accountability. In addition, the Po.et community operates based on the consensus of content creators, and authors can participate in activities such as contributing content, authorization, and delegation. Truth Media launched the Truth Data Cloud project in 2016, aiming to apply blockchain technology to build a more transparent digital advertising ecosystem, establishing direct connections between advertisers and consumers, and users can benefit from sharing their own data. However, this ICO project failed to raise the minimum amount and ended in November 2018.

Fourth, a decentralized benefit distribution mechanism. For example, on the Tron Weekly Journal (TWJ) platform, content creators not only have full ownership of their works, they can sell them to users and websites at self-determined prices, and they can also carry out marketing activities and introduce advertisements independently. Thirty percent of the platform's annual net profit will be distributed to token holders. As for Steemit, it mimicked the structure of the news community Reddit. Different from Reddit, Steemit will issue a bonus on the website every day and give users a certain token reward according to the proportion of the number of likes on their articles.

2. Imagination and Expectations: How is Blockchain News Different?

If we say blockchain technology has very significant advantages in data tracking, false information verification, copyright protection, and reconstruction of income distribution mechanisms, etc., and can promote the diversification of specific application scenarios and functions of this technology in journalism, then, behind these expectations for this technology there are the basic principles and potential values of blockchain news.

(1) Three Principles of Blockchain News

The first is the rules of blockchain news in its underlying technology, namely decentralization, transparency, and consensus trust. Blockchain is decentralized, and every user has access to a public ledger. These fully decentralized, verifiable proofs-of-work facilitate the formations of specific consensus mechanisms.[7] That is, through two-way encryption activities, the blockchain can realize the full record of content and metadata and can guarantee a certain degree of anonymity and security for all parties involved in the transaction. The addition of blocks needs to be based on the consensus of nodes, and the tampered historical blocks will be considered invalid. Blockchain provides a trust creation mechanism based on digital algorithms. Different from traditional transactions relying on authoritative institutions, blockchain solves the problem of ownership confirmation based on mathematical principles, the problem of security trust in the transaction process based on technical advantages, and the problem of trust execution based on smart contracts.[8] The above is the media technology availability of blockchain news.

The second principle is on business, which is self-sustainability and fair distribution. Currently, the development of blockchain news in business operations focuses on peer-to-peer payments, digital ad tracking and protection of digital assets. Many studies have pointed out that blockchain technology can accurately track the flow of content, protect content copyright, and use virtual currency to obtain new crowdfunding business models.[9] Content publishers can pay small rewards to node users to store content, which will improve the content distribution model, optimize the distribution mechanism, and explore the establishment of a self-sustainable business model. In the age of algorithms, a major drawback of the traditional attention economy is that traffic is increasingly "monopolized" by super

---

[7] Buterin, V. (2013). Bitcoin Network Shaken by Blockchain Fork. Bitcoin Magazine, 13 March. Retrieved from https://bitcoinmagazine.com/3668/bitcoin-network-shaken-by- blockchain-fork/

[8] Tang Wenjian, Lyu Wen. How will Blockchain Redefine the World [M]. China Machine Press, 2016. 唐文剑，吕雯. 区块链将如何重新定义世界[M]. 机械工业出版社

[9] Deng Jianguo. News = truth? Blockchain Technology and the Future of Journalism [J]. Journalism Review, 2018(05):83-90.邓建国.新闻=真相?区块链技术与新闻业的未来[J]. 新闻记者

platforms, and monetization of the content industry is dominated by "head" accounts. The business model of journalism has faced greater challenges, and there are few successful cases of paid news. With blockchain news, the data of news reports is linked to the blockchain to realize the proof and tracking of content ownership; smart contracts make it possible to transfer value over long distances without third-party support, which significantly reduces the cost and risk of transactions, allowing authors to receive direct compensation, and providing possibilities for a fair distribution of income in the news industry.

(2) The Potential Value of Blockchain News

In the field of news communication, there are two kinds of expectations on the macro level for the blockchain technology: one is to hope that it can repair the current problems in the journalism industry and promote the close connection between the industry and the public; the second is that blockchain technology can subvert the existing communication ecology and create a shared, open, mobile, and public news collaborative production mechanism. In fact, the news industry's expectations of the potential value of blockchain technology are related to the multiple tensions between the industry and technology, business, and the public, for a long time.

1. *The Immutability Technology of Blockchain May Realize the Transparency of News*

In 1997, Bill Kovach and Tom Rosenstiel first clearly put forward the principle of transparency, which advocates that news gathering, organization and communication are open to the public, and that both people within and outside of newsrooms have opportunities to monitor, inspect, criticize, and even get involved in the news production process.[10] In recent years, the principle of transparency has been further explained as four aspects: transparency of news media and producers' identities,

---

[10] Kovach, Bill, and Tom Rosenstiel. The Elements of Journalism: What Newspeople Should Know and the Public Should Expect. 1ˢᵗ rev. ed., Completely updated and Rev. New York: Three Rivers Press, 2007. [美]比尔·科瓦齐, 汤姆·罗森斯蒂尔, 刘海龙译. 新闻的十大基本原则[M]. 北京大学出版社

transparency of the news production process, transparency of news texts, and transparency of audience comments.[11]

Although the principle of transparency has gradually been accepted by the news industry, it is still a self-disciplinary behavior of the industry itself. The news production process and technology especially lack effective guarantees in this regard. Blockchain technology has the potential to provide a breakthrough solution to journalism transparency by enforcing transparency through technological means. Most of the current forms of news transparency are symbolically "point-types" of transparency; With the help of blockchain technology, decentralized "chain-types" of transparency can be achieved.[12] With regards to news producers, blockchain technology can theoretically delineate behavioral subjects based on users rather than accounts. With regards to the news production process, a shared, immutable ledger helps to track the news production process, and through an open source blockchain platform, the fairness of the algorithm can be maintained, with the help of distributed peer-to-peer auditing and user communities. With regard to the news text, blockchain technology can verify, track, and control content, as well as incentivize users to conduct fact-checking.

2. *The Consensus Trust Mechanism of Blockchain May Reshape Public Discussions and Dialogues*

Consensus is the basis of news communication activities. Consensus is the agreement on information systems between communication subjects and the sharing of symbols and meanings. If communication lacks consensus, its effectiveness will be greatly reduced. It is based on the consensus mechanism established by professional news communication activities that public discussions and dialogues through mass media can be realized. In this sense, the mass media is considered a medium for public

---

[11] Lu Jiayi, Qiu Yunqian, Gao Hongmei. Zero Control and Mirror Spectacle: A Study on Transparency in Citizen Journalism [J]. Chinese Journal of Journalism & Communication, 2019,41(05):39-59. 陆佳怡,仇筠茜,高红梅.零度控制与镜像场景:公民新闻的透明性叙事[J].国际新闻界

[12] Yuan Fan, Yan Sanjiu. From "Point Types" to "Chain Types": the Further Advancement of News Transparency by Blockchain Technology [J]. Chinese Editors Journal, 2019(03):14-19. 袁帆,严三九.从"点式"到"链式":区块链技术对新闻透明的再推进[J].中国编辑

discussions and dialogues - it is a public sphere. However, in recent years, concerns about the decline of the public feature of mass media and the scarcity of public dialogues have been many. A major reason is that the agreement on professional journalism has crippled. While news activities are decentralized, the consensus mechanism established by it has encountered great difficulties. If at the social level, the formation of consensus mainly depends on members of the community to repeatedly discuss and reach agreements within a certain institutional framework, then at the technological level, the potential of blockchain news lies in nodes reaching agreements on the final data and form consensus on the algorithmic level. At present, the consensus algorithms used by blockchain news platforms mainly include three types: Proof of Work (PoW), Proof of Stake (PoS), and Delegated Proof of Stake (DPoS). PoW is the current mainstream blockchain consensus mechanism. It emphasizes decentralization and public features at the same time, which of course, has also caused a large consumption of resources. In theory, all these consensus mechanisms can identify and evaluate the reliability of information publishers without the need for endorsement by a third-party organization. Because the consensus mechanism of the blockchain is guaranteed by the consensus protocol and is both fault-tolerant and effective at the technological level, the system trust of the blockchain information can be achieved between nodes, providing a platform for common dialogues and discussions among the public through the connections of nodes. However, although blockchain technology provides such possibilities, in practice, it may be influenced by various social factors, which may lead to various application forms.

3. *Realizing Both the Social and Commercial Values of Journalism*

With the content payment system driven by traffic, the value of content is no longer determined by media organizations but by users. However, due to the super platforms' "monopoly" of traffic channels, the "head" effect of central nodes, and the "bias" of algorithms, etc., good content may not be able to cash in their real value. For example, for news content such as those that are serious, in-depth, and high-quality, it is difficult to obtain fair commercial returns from the Internet traffic system. Viewing the operational pattern of modern journalism, if without sufficient economic support, the sustainability of professional journalism will face enormous challenges, and its social function and value will be greatly reduced. Blockchain technology has the potential to realize the transformation from "Internet of Traffic" to "Internet of Value". The value system established on blockchain technology may break through the current social media-centric sorting algorithms, weakening the value of channels and making it easier for the professional value of the content itself to stand out, leading to content directly bringing returns. From the perspective of the entire journalism industry, blockchain technology provides an alternative solution for the attention economy and makes it possible to establish an alternative public information infrastructure, and even form a value network of information sharing. In the "walled garden" of social media, the disruption of information flow increases the costs of data storage, services, and transactions. The minimization of trust promised by blockchain technology helps to construct an environment of low transaction cost.

3. The Romanticization of Blockchain News and its Limitations

Today, among the various assumptions about the development of blockchain news, there is still a huge gap between the potential value of blockchain technology and its practical applications. The iteration from old to new media technologies is often accompanied by the optimism of "technocentrism", while ignoring the utopian imaginations carried by these technologies. These imaginations are usually derived from the enduring values of journalism and the passion for urgent solutions for the crises that the current news industry faces.

(1) Blockchain Technology is Not the Only "Key"

Blockchain technology brings new possibilities for reconstructing the production relationship of news and the structure of the news industry. But while its technical advantages are emphasized, it also brings about concealment, as well as a schism regarding existing media technology. On the one hand, the elements that restrict the transparency, authenticity, and publicness of journalism are not only technology, but are most importantly people, who are the subject of the news industry. On the other hand, some of the blueprints for journalism depicted by blockchain technology can already be realized under existing technical conditions, such as cloud ledger databases, which are cheaper and easier to operate than blockchain technology. It remains to be seen whether blockchain technology can be embedded in daily news production and be integrated with news production on the technological level.

It cannot be ignored that blockchain technology itself has many problems. Blockchain technology has a "trilemma" of security, scalability, and decentralization, which requires trade-offs around specific needs.[13] The blockchain news media that can juggle all aspects of performance well only exists in technical imaginations. For example, the security of a private chain is strong, however, the recording authority is monitored by the decision-making center, the reading authority is open or restricted, and true decentralization is difficult to achieve; The public chain has a higher degree of decentralization, but the IPFS (InterPlanetary File System) does not have outstanding advantages in specific issues such as data storage, but consumes a large amount of resources and is difficult to apply to specific news communication situations. From an external point of view, it is still difficult for blockchain news media to provide a truly differentiated experience and compete with mature platforms; from an internal point of view, decentralization increases the difficulty of platform management, and assimilation and differentiation within the community have also become thorny issues common to many platforms. Decentralization is the trend of blockchain technology development, but it also increases the difficulty of management and fault tolerance.

(2) Beware of Concept Hypes and Discourse Traps of Blockchain

When an academic hotspot receives a lot of attention and is widely discussed, it also points to the wrestling between various powers. Any

---

[13] Zeng Shiqin, Huo Ru, Huang Tao, et al. Review of Blockchain Technology Research: Principles, Progress and Applications [J]. Journal of Communications, 2020(01):134-151. 曾诗钦,霍如,黄韬,等. 区块链技术研究综述:原理、进展与应用[J]. 通信学报

academic trend labelled "new" may contain the inherent discursive pattern of self-replication and reproduction of the power structure.[14] For a new technology such as blockchain, we must be very vigilant against all kinds of swindles or business speculation under the guise of this technology. So, we need to remain calm and sober at the academic level and avoid rashly drawing some irresponsible conclusions.

Behind the new technology lies the issue of redistribution of benefits. For example, behind the adjustment of different weights in the algorithm, the platform changes the distribution of benefits and powers. Mumford revealed the internal relationship between technology and capitalism: the advancement of technology serves the interests of the ruling class, while the improvement of machines has become the common purpose of the whole society in the name of concepts such as "progress" and "liberation". Blockchain technology may not be developing in a direction of increasing technicalization, but in a direction that is becoming more and more beneficial to a certain group of people.

(3) Potential Risks of Using Blockchain Technology in Journalism

The application of blockchain technology also has potential risks and drawbacks, which may bring new exclusivity and injustice in practical applications. Blockchain conforms to the inherent patterns of technological evolution. It can significantly reduce transaction costs and promote the flow of information, but it also increases the difficulty of management. How to govern and guide the development of blockchain has become a top priority. Some scholars in the legal field have pointed out that it is necessary to change from "supervision" to "governance", to guide the healthy development of the blockchain. For example, the "co-vote" mechanism is a concept and regulatory tool for blockchain governance.[15]

The decentralization, transparency, consensus trust, etc. of blockchain

---

[14] Pan Zhongdang, Liu Yusi. What is "New"? The Power Trap in the Discourse of "New Media" and the Researcher's Theoretical Introspection: An Interview with Professor Pan Zhongdang [J]. Journalism and Communication Review, 2017(01): 2-19. 潘忠党, 刘于思. 以何为"新"? "新媒体"话语中的权力陷阱与研究者的理论自省——潘忠党教授访谈录[J]. 新闻与传播评论

[15] Yang Dong. "Co-Vote": A New Dimension of Blockchain Governance [J]. Oriental Law, 2019, 69(03):58-65. 杨东."共票": 区块链治理新维度[J]. 东方法学

news are realized by the technology mandatorily. From the perspective of professional journalism, it means that the relationship between news communication subjects is facing towards the trust on the blockchain technology system. On the one hand, the power of journalists is further transferred, but on the other hand, the possibility of the collapse of any technical system means news communication subjects risk losing control in journalism. From a social point of view, the indiscriminate chain record of information on the blockchain may also erase the diversity of information and build a unitary settlement system and meaning system, which poses challenges to issues like the diversity of people's lives in the Internet society (including the right to forget information, etc.). One scholar argues that the mandatory pursuit of transparency will destroy the vitality of public space.[16] The communication of information and the information society should be more transparent, but mandatory transparency does not necessarily lead to a better digital life.

4. Behind Blockchain News: Discourse on Journalism Crisis

To discuss the applications and development prospects of blockchain technology in journalism, it is also necessary to analyze the widespread anxiety and crisis discourse in the current news industry. Since the rise of the Internet, especially in the era of social media, "crisis-transition" has gradually become the mainstream narrative in the industry. The word "crisis" has a strong emotional touch, implying the urgency of reality and the panic for the future. Wang Chenyao believes that at a time when dangers and opportunities coexist, journalism must respond to this uncertainty through innovation.[17] The journalism industry urgently needs to rethink and reposition its own value and role. The blockchain technology emerging in this context has naturally become a discourse resource that the news

---

[16] Han, Byung-Chul. Transparenzgesellschaft. Dritte Auflage. Berlin: Matthes & Seitz, 2013. [德]韩炳哲. 透明社会[M]. 中信出版社

[17] Wang Chenyao. News Innovation: Uncertain Redemption [N]. Chinese Social Sciences Today, 2016-05-05(003). 王辰瑶. 新闻创新: 不确定的救赎[N]. 中国社会科学报

industry can invoke and is embedded in the discourse network of the "news paradigm" shift.

(1) Uncertainties in the News Industry and the Frenetic Pursuit of New Technologies

Looking at the history of news, every new media technology has brought great shocks, but the changes brought by the Internet media may be different from all others. Upon entering the Internet era, centralized mass media organizations lost their status as information monopolies and faced huge uncertainties. The news industry's crisis first manifested as "newspaper industry crisis", and then spread to traditional media represented by newspapers. In the face of fierce competition from technology companies, the pursuit of cutting-edge technologies has become the norm for news organizations. Described by Oxford University's Reuters Institute for the Study of Journalism as the "Shiny Things Syndrome", media organizations often start a frenzied pursuit of new technologies without investigations and a clear plan.[18] Sometimes, the blind pursuit of new technologies can hurt the news industry even more than technological stagnation.

In this sense, the imagination of blockchain news is actually a continuation of technical optimism, with the purpose to rely on newer media technologies to solve the crisis that the traditional news industry is declining. However, research has found that the overall abundance of information, as well as the degree of political polarization, both influence the trustworthiness of journalism.[19] The crisis faced by the news industry has a more complex socio-political context, and it is not only affected by the impact of media technologies, nor can it be solved by integrating newer media technologies.

---

[18] Anger J. Time to Step Away from the 'Bright, Shiny Things'? Towards a Sustainable Model of Journalism Innovation in an Era of Perpetual Change[J]. 2018.

[19] Columbia Journalism Review. The Fall, Rise, and Fall of Media Trust. https://www.cjr.org/special_report/the-fall-rise-and-fall-of-media-trust.php

(2) The Business Dilemma and Data Labor
Problems Faced by the News Industry

In the news industry crisis, the immediate problem faced by news media is the profit dilemma: advertising revenue has fallen sharply, and social media and news aggregation sites have taken away a large amount of market and user share without taking corresponding public responsibilities. The traditional news model is gradually being marginalized. In the midst of uncertainties, news outlets have tried to fix past business models through digital transformation, but with little success. For example, surveys show that only major media outlets such as *The Wall Street Journal* and *The New York Times* have benefited from digital subscriptions. Blockchain technology can significantly reduce transaction costs, allowing media to benefit from micropayments, which seems to provide a solution for media organizations to solve the profit dilemma. Can blockchain technology really bring about a fair and balanced distribution of benefits? Some scholars have proposed to replace "Data is Capital (DaC)" with "Data is Labor (DaL)"[20]. The blockchain-based content ecosystem based on proof of contribution is worth looking forward to for the data labor practice. However, there are also academics who are cautiously skeptical about blockchain's potential to empower digital labor, arguing that "decentralization" is a much older issue, an eternal struggle to shift power from the few to the masses.[21]

Behind the business crisis is the issue of data ownership. The business model of social media is to monetize the data and traffic generated by users. Users do not directly pay for the value they obtain from news, and the platforms do not pay for the data contributed by users and news producers. As data increasingly becomes the core of business models, the drawbacks of this free economy - its inefficiency and imbalance are also increasingly apparent. In addition, the massive, centralized storage of user

---

[20] Arrieta Ibarra, Imanol and Goff, Leonard and Jiménez Hernández, Diego and Lanier, Jaron and Weyl, Eric Glen, Should We Treat Data as Labor? Moving Beyond 'Free' (December 27, 2017). American Economic Association Papers & Proceedings, Vol. 1, No. 1, Forthcoming. Available at SSRN: https://ssrn.com/abstract=3093683

[21] Kaminska, I. (2015). A New Raison D'être for Cryptocurrency, but an Age-Old Problem. FT Alphaville. The Blog, News and Commentary. 20 October. Retrieved from http://ftalphaville.ft.com/2014/10/20/2012052/a-new-raison- detre-for-cryptocurrency-but-an-age-old-problem/?

data in tech companies brings digital surveillance and information security concerns.

(3) The Crisis of Confidence in News Industry and the "Decline" of its Publicness

More important than the business crisis, the global news media may be facing a systemic crisis of trust. In this context, the potential of blockchain technology to reconstruct trust mechanisms has attracted the attention of the news industry. In the Western context, professional journalism is of great value in maintaining the functioning of a democratic society, which is also seen as a source of legitimacy for journalism. Journalists should aim to tell their audience what is true and important.[22] On social media, however, fake news and filter bubbles have made opinions increasingly stratified. Beliefs and emotions have replaced facts and logic as the criteria for decision-making, which directly challenges the very meaning for the existence of professional journalism. The penetration and manipulation of political power and the erosion by commercial interests have jointly exacerbated the crisis of confidence in journalism.

To some extent, the current crisis facing journalism is the result of the failure to reconcile commercial and public values. There is a paradox between the news model and the business model, and the two belong to different logic and discourse systems.[23] The imagination and expectations of the journalism industry for blockchain news also point to the urgent need to rebuild public trust. Jarrod Dicker, CEO of Po.et, believes that the news production model of blockchain technology will eventually make news or media companies lose their intermediary status. However, if you go beyond the career-centric orientation, you will find that blockchain technology will liberate more content value.[24] Blockchain technology

---

[22] Kovach, Bill, and Tom Rosenstiel. The Elements of Journalism: What Newspeople Should Know and the Public Should Expect. 1st rev. ed., Completely updated and Rev. New York: Three Rivers Press, 2007. (Page 41-58 in the Chinese version) [美]比尔·科瓦齐，汤姆·罗森斯蒂尔，刘海龙译．新闻的十大基本原则[M]．北京大学出版社

[23] Peng Zengjun. The Redemption of Journalism [M]. China Renmin University Press. 2018. 彭增军．新闻业的救赎[M]．中国人民大学出版社

[24] Columbia Journalism Review. Jarrod Dicker on What the Blockchain Can Do for News. [EB/OL]. [2018-03-02]. https://www.cjr.org/innovations/blockchain-poet.php

provides the possibility for the kind of social news activities with weak boundaries and high integration. Not only do professional journalism activities integrate with non-professional ones, but journalism activities as a whole also integrate gradually with other social activities. Journalism returns and becomes embedded in daily life, becoming an important means of living and backdrop of life.[25] In fact, in addition to the technical potential and imagination of blockchain, news practitioners also need to break through the discourse of "crisis - salvation" and broaden their imagination of news itself.

5. Conclusion and Discussion

The application of blockchain technology in journalism and its technical potential and room for imagination make it a frontier research topic in the current news industry. The emergence of blockchain news at this juncture deserves serious analysis and reflection. Some distinctive features of blockchain news, such as decentralization, immutability, emphasis on rewards and income distribution, user participation in community governance, etc., have brought new possibilities for the pursuit of transparency in journalism, the rebuilding of consensus trust mechanisms and public discussions, the realization of business and social values, and other aspects.

Of course, it is obviously not enough to only analyze these aspects of blockchain technology in journalism. It is also necessary to reflect on the crisis currently faced by the news industry and the innovative potential of the new technology that the industry hopes to rely on. The application and imagination of the blockchain technology by the industry are mostly rooted in the need brought about by the real crisis. In the imagined application of this technology, not only the underlying technology is given affordance, but a new news eco-system was imagined: one that is driven by market incentives and self-transactions, assumes social responsibilities, and realizes the value of the content. However, we also need to criticize the

---

[25] Li Hongjiang, Yang Baojun. The Travel of the "Liquid" Theory and its Inspiration to Journalism Research [J]. Social Science Front, 2019(09):254-261. 李泓江, 杨保军. "液态" 理论的旅行及其对新闻学研究的启示[J].社会科学战线

romanticization and limitations of blockchain news and be more cautious about the technology's prospects in journalism. When applying the blockchain technology, the news industry needs to avoid discourse traps and potential risks and promote the integrated innovation of "technology-society". To find the answer for the crisis of journalism, one needs to go back to the social context. Only then can the development of blockchain news return to the essence of technology and be truly beneficial to public interest and the construction of a health news industry.

(Tu Lingbo, Professor, School of Television, Faculty of Journalism and Communication, Communication University of China)

Printed in the United States
by Baker & Taylor Publisher Services